The FOUNDATIONS
of WESTERN
MONASTICISM

Saint Antony of the Desert

Nihil Obstat
E. Thomas Bergh, O.S.B.
Censor Deputatus

Imprimatur
Edm. Can. Surmont
Vicar General
Westminster
January 28, 1924

The FOUNDATIONS of WESTERN MONASTICISM

Edited by

William Edmund Fahey, Ph.D.

SAINT ANTONY OF THE DESERT

By Saint Athanasius

THE HOLY RULE OF SAINT BENEDICT

Edited by William Edmund Fahey, Ph.D.

THE TWELVE DEGREES OF HUMILITY AND PRIDE

By Saint Bernard of Clairvaux

TAN·CLASSICS

TAN·CLASSICS

The editor dedicates this volume
with gratitude and affection to those communities
within the family of Saint Benedict, which
have shown him such generosity over the years:

The Monastery of the Holy Spirit (Conyers, Georgia)

Pluscarden Abbey (Elgin, Scotland)

Our Lady of the Assumption Monastery (Clear Creek, Oklahoma)

Saint Benedict Abbey (Still River, Massachusetts)

Hospes fui, et suscepistis me.

CONTENTS

PREFACE TO THE FOUNDATIONS
OF WESTERN MONASTICISM

ASCENDING THE HEIGHTS—
AN INTRODUCTION TO
CHRISTIAN MONASTICISM

By William Edmund Fahey, Ph.D.

———————— • ————————

THE heart of the White Mountains lies in the Franconia Notch, near the center of New Hampshire—location of the fabled "Old Man" of the Granite State. Three connected mountains offer the best views of the region: Little Haystack, Mount Lincoln, and Mount Lafayette. Each summit near or above 5,000 feet affords a distinct but related vantage point for observing the fundamental character of the Appalachian chain as it moves dramatically through New England. Which of the three mountains presents the best view is difficult to say, and although there are higher peaks and more dramatic scenery else-where, as an introduction to the White Mountains and the region, the three taken together remain unsurpassed.

This volume is not unlike a simple handbook introducing hikers to the Franconia region: its pages concentrate on three superlative heights, which will provide novices with an essential first viewing of Christian monasticism. St. Antony of the Desert, St. Benedict of Nursia, and St. Bernard of Clairvaux rise above other figures of Catholic history. To travel with them and to seek a view upon the heights of their personal holiness and wisdom is to secure passage into the rich and complex world of monasticism. Like an introduction to the Franconia region that focuses solely on Haystack, Lincoln, and Lafayette, and therefore *not* on the Pemigewasset River, the Flume George, or Boise Rock, this introduction to Christian monasticism is selective. Despite all the appeal of other features, it will remain selective so as to provide a focused exploration.

By nature, all introductions must be selective and provide a succinct guide to the key features of a subject. Again, this book provides an introduction to *Christian* monasticism. It speaks nothing of Hindu Sannyasa or Buddhist Sangha. It does not offer a response to the question of why Muslim culture discourages monasticism. It does not unearth the roots of monasticism in Ancient Israel—whether through the Nazirites, Essenes, or Theraputae. St. Pachomius is not allowed a place amongst the founders discussed here, nor St. Basil or St. Augustine. The exotic practices of Stylites and Dendrites, the traditions of the Copts and the ancient Irish, and much else is kept for other guides.

This guide introduces its readers to three men and three works. *The Life of St. Antony*, the *Rule of St. Benedict*, and the *Twelve Degrees of Humility and Pride* are offered as a simple and short path to the essence of Christian monasticism. St. Antony is presented as monasticism's foremost founder, St. Benedict as its greatest law-giver, and St. Bernard as its greatest mystic. Taken together, these men and these writings will allow the reader to ascend the heights of Christian monasticism and arrive at certain vantage points which may suggest later forays, but should suffice in themselves. The words of the editor are designed merely to provide assistance in the reading of the primary text and encouragement for future journeys.

Our words "monk" and "monasticism" are derived from a very old set of Greek words: *monachos anachoretes*—a person who stepped aside from the rest of society. In the Hellenistic world, the concept originally applied to those who would not participate with the political system, pay taxes, or bow to social pressure. In time, the Greek expression was applied to a specific spiritual concept in the Aramaic language: *ihidaya*. *Ihidaya* described someone dedicated to spiritual perfection who elected to seek this perfection by the voluntary rejection of the common human inclinations and social customs related to the desire for wealth, power, and bodily pleasure. To be a "monk," of its very nature, was and remains about both social withdrawal and spiritual perfection. Yet it is gravely mistaken to believe that the essence of monasticism was or is withdrawal or separatism. This confusion reverses the ends and the means of monasticism and contributes to the mistaken notion (held by believers, critics, and seekers) that monasticism is a rejection of the world, a scorning of life, or a sign of social and psychological vulnerability. Monasticism, as the literature will indicate, is one of the most demanding states of life in which a human can place himself, and it is a way of being whose attention and activity is ordered *towards*, not *away from*.

The silence and solitude depicted in monastic biographies and rules made a theatre for contemplation and action, not a hideaway from conflict or responsibility. If anything, responsibility and conflict came to the fore in the monastic life. It was for true freedom that monks clapped on the iron practices of obedience and restraint. The intellect and the will came under rigorous self-discipline, not because the monk rejected the world or his fellow man, but because he sought out a superlative opportunity for uniting his thoughts, words, affections, and actions to the divine will and mind of God and he sought to do so freely and with love. This required some specialized knowledge and, more importantly, considerable mental resolve, fitness and stamina, regular training, and constant struggle. It should not, therefore, come as a surprise that the language of monasticism is so richly analogous to military or athletic language. The vigor of monastic concepts and words is akin to that found in the Old Testament Prophets or the writings of St. Paul. Only a virile and heroic language could begin to approach the interior world experienced by the monks. Only an elaborate, but also agonistic, imagery could sustain the ideas monastic writers were trying to express. The literature of monasticism is at once muscular and poetic, rhetorical and systematic.

Again, the common images and attitudes towards monasticism in our era should not distract us. It is true that the monk stands alone at times; the monk does embrace solitude, but the student of monasticism must ask with sympathy, "why?" The answer can be heard clearly in the rallying cry of that first monastic age: because the good life means preferring nothing to Christ, seeking nothing but His pleasure, His worship, His Justice, and His companionship. This quest was made possible by the monk's unshakeable confidence in His mercy. Yet as readers of these texts will see, this solitary focus on Christ did not mean that the monk sought to be a lonely individual or that loneliness was essential to monastic life. It is potentially misleading to see in monasticism the birth of some value such as individualism—or the birth of western culture itself for that matter. Such things may be *derived from* the monastic endeavor; they were not, however, its *aim*. Finally, monks do not view creation, society, or mankind as evils. The monk simply loves what is highest and best. All creation is understood in light of the one great desire: union with God. For Christian monks, this did not and does not demand a rejection of creation, only an ordering of love, desire, thought, and action. An attentive reader will see that the texts contained in this volume demonstrate that the ordering of these things often freed the monk for a greater service to others. As Pope Benedict XVI states at the conclusion of his encyclical *Deus Caritas Est,* "Those who draw near to God do not withdraw from men, but rather become truly close to them." What is more, they show to all a path to the very heights of wisdom and peace. For that reason, they remain for all a subject for admiration and imitation.

Further Reading

The literature available on western monasticism is voluminous. The following recommendations are offered so that readers may deepen their interest in and love for the subject. It is the editor's opinion that primary sources are usually best (hence this volume as a starting point), but often readers seek a more systematic presentation of monastic spirituality or a unified narrative of monasticism over time.

General Introductions and Histories (works specific to the authors and orders discussed in this volume follow in the subsequent chapters):

Charles-Forbes-René, Comte de Montalembert, *The Monks of the West*, 2 vols. (Boston: Thomas B. Noonan & Co, 1860). Montalembert's book is widely ignored due to its strong tinge of Romanticism. Yet this monumental work, written over the course of several decades, bears witness to how a worldly man could return to the Christian heart of European culture and find personal consolation. The work is detailed, thoroughly documented, and exquisitely written.

C. H. Lawrence, *Medieval Monasticism: Forms of Religious Life in Western Europe in the Middle Ages* (London: Longman, 1984). In this volume, Lawrence provides an excellent scholarly narrative history of monasticism.

Jean Leclercq, O.S.B., *Alone with God*, trans. E. McCabe (New York: Farrar, Strauss & Giroux, 1961). Dom Leclercq turns his attention in this work to the emermetical side of monasticism, that is, a systematic introduction to the spirituality and life of the hermit.

Thomas Merton, O.S.C.O, *The Silent Life* (London: Burns, Oates & Washbourne, 1957). One of the most influential Cistercian writers of the modern period offers a succinct work that goes to the center of the monastic experience and monastic spirituality, while providing a historical survey of the entire monastic movement in the West. The prologue and epilogue deliver a profound challenge to the anti-spiritual assumptions of the modern world.

M. Raymond, O.S.C.O., *The Silent Spires Speak* (Milwaukee: The Bruce Publishing, 1966). Fr. Raymond was a contemporary of Thomas Merton, but today is little-known. This volume is a dialogue between a jaded College student and a Trappist monk, suggesting that monasticism offers to the world an essential clarity on the place of contemplation in everyone's life.

Hubert Van Zeller, O.S.B., *Approach to Monasticism* (New York: Sheed and Ward, 1960). Zeller presents what remains one of the most sober assessments of what monasticism as practiced really demands and what sort of person it will not tolerate.

Benedict XVI, *Church Fathers*, 2 vols. (San Francisco: Ignatius Press, 2008 & 2010). In these volumes, one will find addresses on the individuals at the center of this anthology: St. Athanasius, St. Benedict, St. Gregory the Great, and St. Bernard.

The literature on *Lectio Divina*—the slow and contemplative reading and enacting of Sacred Scripture—is overwhelming. Three books must suffice:

Michael Casey, O.S.C.O., *Sacred Reading—The Ancient Art of Lectio Divina* (Liguori, MO: Liguori Publications, 1995).

Tim Gray, *Praying Scripture for a Change: An Introduction to Lectio Divina* (Boulder, CO: Ascension Press, 2009).

Mario Masini, *Lectio Divina* (New York: St. Pauls/Alba House, 1988).

An important aspect of monasticism has always been its influence on art and culture. Readers of monastic works could receive a false impression that monks are so "otherworldly" that they have no interest in architecture or art or the material world. The following three books are fine correctives to such a view. Monks have long provided Christians with an example of how to appreciate and act upon the priority of the spiritual above the material, while still recognizing the goodness of creation and the human (and more than human) capacity for creativity found amongst all men:

Sacheverell Sitwill, *Monks, Nuns, and Monasteries* (New York: Holt, Rinehard & Winston, 1965).

Peter Fergusson, *Architecture of Solitude* (Princeton: Princeton University Press, 1984).

Terryl N. Kinder, *Cistercian Europe: Architecture of Contemplation* (Kalamazoo, MI: Cistercian Publications, 2002).

SAINT ANTONY
OF THE DESERT

By Saint Athanasius

PREFACE TO THE LIFE
OF SAINT ANTONY

LIGHT IN THE DESERT —
PREFERRING NOTHING
TO CHRIST

By William Edmund Fahey, Ph.D.

———— • ————

A CROSS the southern desert of Egypt in the Red Sea Mountains sits Der Mar Antonios, the monastery established in honor of St. Antony the Great shortly after his death in A.D. 356. Even today it is a remote spot, away from the thriving cities of the Nile, hidden amidst the arid highlands. Was it here that St. Athanasius received the sheepskin cloak of Antony the Great, one of the fathers of monasticism? In his last days, St. Antony had specified that the bishop of Alexandria should be one of the few recipients of one of the few existing personal belongings of Antony. To bestow a cloak, we know from Elijah, was long considered a blessing, as well as a symbol of succession and the transferral of authority. In that year St. Athanasius had been on the run, a hunted man now in his third exile. The Roman imperial government, dominated by heretical Arian leadership, sought to crush the resistance of those who clung to the Nicene belief that Christ was fully God as well as fully man. Pope Liberius had already been arrested and the small minority of priests and bishops willing to voice their views on

3

the divine and co-equal nature of God's Son were once again fugitives, if not incarcerated. As the most outspoken defender of Nicene orthodoxy, Athanasius was a marked man.

For six years St. Athanasius remained in exile, sometimes hiding in the desert, sometimes moving secretly about the cities in northern Egypt. Athanasius wrote many of his finest works during this period, among them the *Life of St. Antony*. For many years the two men had been in communication—although Athanasius was Antony's junior by some four decades—and it is fair to say that while Athanasius's work was not written by a close friend in the natural sense, the spiritual bond between the two was intense. Athanasius composed the text in Greek, having interviewed Coptic-speaking monks who knew St. Antony. Within a few years of its completion Bishop Evagrius of Antioch translated the *Life* from Greek into Latin. Why the work was rendered into Latin, we cannot say for sure. It would seem that Evagrius was a friend or associate of St. Jerome, who then lived in Palestine and whose network of friends were arduously studying and promoting monasticism. In any case, it was Evagrius's translation that entered into the Western Mediterranean in the 370s. It was this text that was discovered a decade later in the humble cottage of some monks which the friends of St. Augustine came upon while walking one afternoon in the countryside just beyond the walls of Trèves along the Moselle in Germany. In the account of St. Augustine, the *Life of Antony* and the example of this Egyptian saint became the spark for numerous ascetical quests of men and women, who left behind the ordinary concerns of the world to become wholly at the service of God.

St. Antony's profound humility compelled him to discourage his own veneration, as readers of his life will discover. St. Antony tried so very hard not to leave any trace of his remains behind and his monks succeeded in a secret burial. Nevertheless, the *Life of St. Antony* was designed as a pattern of life for widespread veneration and imitation. This is ironic, but profoundly beneficial for the development of Christian spirituality.

The suggested readings at the end of this introduction will guide readers who wish to continue studying Antony the Great. To Antony are attributed many letters, which survive in Greek, Latin, Syriac, Coptic, and Arabic. A rich body of modern literature now exists for the study of early Christian monasticism and the monasticism of Egypt, but the work that launched all future studies, whether spiritual or historical, was Athanasius's *Life of Antony*. A few features of that *Life* are worth consideration.

Athanasius presents Antony's spiritual program for readers in its authentic simplicity. The young Antony responded to hearing the Word of God. He came from a comfortable family background, but shortly after the death of his parents he heard the words which would forever change his life, and the life of western civilization: "If thou wilt be perfect, go sell all that thou hast and give to the poor, and come follow me and thou shalt have treasure in heaven." (*Matt.* 19:21) Unlike the young man in Scripture and so many others through the ages, Antony responded immediately. Looking forward, such obedience—the word literally means "attentive listening"—would become central to the organization of western monasticism and the spirituality of the monk (e.g., *The Rule of St. Benedict*, chapter 5).

St. Antony developed his program in four locations, always in response to grace and the circumstances around him. The first was his hometown, Herakleopolis, and one of its nearby villages. Antony placed himself under the tutelage of wise Christian men and learned Scripture by ear, while working with his hands. He renounced the possessions and the ease into which he was born. Then followed many years of honing his monastic excellence: some years in the Nitrian Desert; some sixty miles west of the ancient cosmopolitan center of Alexandria; some on Mt. Pispir (Der el Memum) in an abandoned Roman fort. Careful readers will observe that though removed from centers of population, St. Antony was never so remote as to be completely free from human exchange. Indeed, during the height of persecution, Antony spent time in Alexandria and elsewhere giving courage to the martyrs and ministering to their needs. Finally, Antony departed to the "inner wilderness" far to the south and east of Cairo, on Mount Galala, where eventually his followers would establish the community of Der Mar Antonios.

When one reads over the events of his life or considers his advice to others, one can discern that his spiritual program has two essential parts: the discipline of the body, and what we may call the spirituality of the present moment. The discipline of the body can, of course, be found amongst pagans and Jews in antiquity. One thinks of the program of Pythagoras, which had great influence over Plato's thought, or the Stoics. Indeed, the virtue of temperance had many champions in antiquity. Only when the body and its cravings were brought under control could the soul be properly and rationally governed. In his meditation on St. Paul's maxim from *2 Cor.* 12:10, "When I am weak, then am I strong," Antony understood it in a manner that would have been very attractive to a host of ancient observers: "when the enjoyments of the body are weak, then is the power of the soul strong."

Yet the second part of Antony's program reveals how the motives for bodily discipline and the self-governance of the soul differed from that of Greco-Roman philosophical movements. Athanasius describes what he calls St. Antony's "strange-seeming principle":

> He held that not by length of time is the way of virtue measured and our progress therein, but by desire and by strong resolve. . . . Each day, as though beginning his religious life, he made greater effort to advance . . . as though always beginning, he was earnest each day to present himself such as one ought to appear before God: clean of heart and ready to obey His will and none other.

Antony has set the stage for subsequent development in Christian spirituality. The age in which the second coming of Christ was thought increasingly imminent had passed. So too, during Antony's life was passing the sense that persecutions would usher in some glorious End

Time. Antony transforms that simple eschatology into a deeper sense that God is already present, just as Jesus had said. The kingdom is at hand now, and so each day one must simply renew a resolve to be present to the God who is present, not to prepare for some future. Thus, St. Antony's governance of his soul, his austerity in thought, speech, and way of life, was not an end in itself. For all his emphasis on the will, the goal was not simply the will to power, but rather to live a life that would allow Antony each day to say with confidence: "nothing shall separate me from the love of Christ." Everything that readers tend to thrill over when encountering the life of Antony—his instant renunciation of wealth, his effective Scripture-based education, his combat with demons, the miracles, his extra-ordinary mortifications of mind, desire, and body, his combating of heresy, his shunning of schism, his good counsel, his ability to defeat pagan philosophers by their own dialectical sparring, his good death—all these were undertaken day after day to maintain loving union with Christ.

It is only appropriate to make a brief cautionary statement regarding the depiction of St. Antony which follows. It is the life of Antony, but it is the Life of Antony written by St. Athanasius. We know from the extant letters of Antony that he had a learned, even scholarly side that Athanasius does not draw out. He knew some Greek and was engaged in reconciling aspects of Greek philosophy with Christian revelation; he was linked to a vast network of both scholars and ascetics; and he seems to have been less pre-occupied with the defeat of heresy and paganism than Athanasius. No biography can fully reveal the complexity of any human, especially a saint. Athanasius distills for us the essence of Antony: his confidence (which would explain his lesser concern with pagans and dealing directly with heretics), his self control, and his Christocentric way of being.

St. Antony in this biography and in other early sources consistently appears to readers as an exemplar of how the Christian holy man could subvert the sensual and power-based lifestyle of paganism. He demonstrates that the only true freedom comes from renouncing the will, the only true power comes from governing one's soul. And contrary to later notions of monasticism as a haven for the weak and disengaged, Antony demonstrated the heroic and virile nature of monasticism. In sum, Antony set out the simple monastic program, at once scriptural and natural: to seek God—to overcome all obstacles, especially those internal obstacles of will and always to prefer nothing to Christ.

Further Reading

For those who simply wish to read more early Christian writings from the world of Egyptian Christianity—by St. Antony and others—the following works may prove stimulating:

> Samuel Rubenson, *The Letters of St. Antony: Monasticism and the Making of a Saint* (Fortress: Minneapolis, 1995).
>
> *The Lives of the Desert Fathers*, trans. Norman Russell (Cistercian Publications: Spencer, MA, 1980).
>
> *The Desert Fathers*, trans. Helen Waddell (Vintage: New York, 1998).
>
> *The Desert Fathers: Sayings of the Early Christian Monks*, trans. Benedicta Ward (Penguin: London, 2003).

Thoughtful Catholic reflections on both Antony and Athanasius can be found in the following nineteenth century works:

> Bl. John Henry Newman, *The Church of the Fathers* (University of Notre Dame Press: Notre Dame, 2002).
>
> Roger Bede Vaughn, O.S.B., *The Life and Labours of St. Thomas of Aquin*, vol. 2 (Longmans & Co.: London, 1872).

Amongst modern scholarship, serious readers should consider starting with the following:

> Derwas Chitty, *The Desert a City: An Introduction to the Study of Egyptian and Palestian Monasticism Under the Christian Empire* (St. Vladimir's Press: Yonkers, 1977).

John Chryssavgis, *In the Heart of the Desert: The Spirituality of the Desert Fathers and Mothers* (World Wisdom: Bloomington, IN, 2003).

Douglas Burton Christie, *The Word in the Desert: Scripture and the Quest for Holiness in Early Christian Monasticism* (Oxford University Press: Oxford, 1993).

William Harmless, *Desert Christians: An Introduction to the Literature of Early Monasticism* (Oxford University Press: Oxford, 2004).

INTRODUCTION

From St. Augustine's *Confessions*, Bk. 8, Ch. 6.

WHEN, therefore, I had declared to him [Pontitianus, a fellow Christian] that I bestowed myself much in the reading of those Scriptures, he took occasion in the course of his speech to discourse unto us of Antony, the Egyptian monk, whose name was excellently famous amongst Thy servants; but, as for us, we had never heard of him until that hour.

But he, so soon as he perceived this, insisted the longer in speaking of him, insinuating the knowledge of so great a man to us, who were wholly ignorant, and wondering withal at that same ignorance of ours. We, on the other hand, were amazed to hear that so lately, and almost in our own days, such wonderful things had been wrought by Thee, in the True Faith and the Catholic Church; so that all of us wondered, we at the hearing of things so strange, and he that we had never heard of them before.

From this he went on to speak of the teeming monasteries, and of them who are a sweet savor unto Thee, and of the fruitful bosom of the barren desert, whereof also we had heard nothing. Nay, more, there was a monastery at Milan, full of holy brethren, close without the walls of the city, under the fostering care of Ambrose, and yet we knew nothing of it. So did he proceed in his discourse, and we held our peace, listening intently. Whereupon he went on to tell us further how once at Treves, he himself, with three companions, while the Emperor was detained at the afternoon games in the circus, went out to walk in some gardens near the city walls; thus it chanced that they became separated into two parties, one of the three keeping with him and the other two walking together. These latter two, as they wandered up and down, came at length upon a poor cottage, inhabited by divers servants of Thine, *poor in spirit, of whom is the Kingdom of Heaven,* and there they found a book wherein was written the life of Antony.

One of them began to read the same, to wonder at it and to be inflamed by it, and even whilst he was reading to resolve upon leading such a life as that, leaving the service of the world, to become wholly Thine.

SAINT ATHANASIUS'
PREFACE

————————●————————

I T IS A good rivalry that you have entered on with the monks in
Egypt, trying to equal them or surpass them in your practice of
virtue. For with you also there are now monasteries, and the name of
monk is in repute. This purpose deserves praise, and may God fulfill it
according to your prayers.

And since, too, you have inquired of me about the blessed Antony's
way of life, wishing to learn how he began his religious life and what
he was before it, and what the end of his life was like and whether the
things that are said about him are true, in order to bring yourselves to
imitate him; with the greatest willingness I do your bidding. For I, too,
gain much help from merely remembering Antony; and I know that
you also when you hear, besides admiring the man, will wish to imitate
his purpose. For the life of Antony is to monks a sufficient guide to
religious life. Do not, then, disbelieve what you have heard about him
from those who have told you; rather believe that you have heard but
little from them. For indeed it would be very hard for them to relate all,
seeing that even I, whatever I may write by letter at your urging, shall
yet give you but little account of him. Do you therefore cease not to
question those who sail your way, and then perhaps as each tells what
he knows, the story may become somewhat more worthy of the man.

Now when I received your letter, I wanted to send for some of
the monks who used to be most constantly with him, so that I might
learn more and send you a fuller account. But as the sailing season was

13

ending and the letter carrier pressed me, I have hastened to write to your goodness what I myself know (for I saw him often), and what I was able to learn from himself; for I was his assistant for no little time and poured water on his hands. Throughout I have been most careful to give the facts, so that no one need doubt when he hears more; and, on the other hand, that no one may think little of the man through not learning enough about him.

BOOK ONE

How Antony Trained Himself

---●---

CHAPTER ONE
The Call of God

A NTONY was of Egyptian race, his parents of good birth and good
means—Christians too, so that he also was brought up in
Christian wise. As a child he lived with his parents, knowing nothing
but them and his home; and when he grew to be a boy and was advancing in age, he refused to learn letters, desiring to be away from the
company of children. All his wish was, as is written of Jacob, to dwell
unspoiled at home. (Cf. *Gen.* 25:27).

With his parents he frequented the church, not with a child's inat-
tention, nor with the contempt of later years, but obeying his parents
and listening to the lessons that were read and carefully keeping the
fruits of them in his own life. Nor again, though he found himself in a
fairly rich home, did he worry his parents for rich and varied food nor
care for the enjoyment of it; he was satisfied with what was there and
asked no more.

After his parents' death he was left alone with one very young sister.
He was eighteen or twenty years old and had charge of the home and
of his sister. Less than six months after the death of his parents he was

15

going out to church as usual, and collecting his thoughts, he pondered as he went how the Apostles, leaving all things, followed the Saviour; and the people in the *Acts* who sold their possessions and brought the price and laid it at the feet of the Apostles for distribution among the needy—what good and great hope was laid up in Heaven for these. With these thoughts in his mind, he entered the church; and it so fell that the Gospel was being read then, and he heard the Lord saying to the rich man, *If thou wilt be perfect, go sell all that thou hast and give to the poor, and come follow me and thou shalt have treasure in heaven.* (Cf. *Matt.* 19:21). Then, as though it was from God that his thoughts of the Saints had come and this reading had been for his sake, as soon as he went out of the church he gave to the villagers the property he had from his parents (it was 300 acres of land, fertile and very beautiful) that they might not interfere with him and his sister. And all else that they had in personal property he sold, and raised a fair sum of money, which he gave to the poor, keeping a little because of his sister.

But when, again entering the church, he heard the Lord saying in the Gospel, *Be not solicitous for the morrow* (cf. *Matt.* 6:34), he could not bear to wait longer, but went out and distributed this also to the poor. His sister he commended to known and trusty virgins, and put her with a Sisterhood to be brought up; and then he gave himself for the future to the religious life, minding himself and living a life of hardship, in front of his own house. For as yet monasteries were not so universal in Egypt, and no monk yet knew the great desert; but each who wished to attend to his soul exercised himself alone not far from his own village.

Now there was at the time in the neighboring village an old man who had practiced the solitary life from youth. Antony, seeing him, was eager to imitate him, so he too at first began to stay in the places near the village. From there, if he heard anywhere of an earnest soul, he went forth like a wise bee and sought him out; nor would he return to his own place till he had seen him and got from him what would help him on his way to virtue; then he went back. There, then, he made his first steps, steadying his mind not to turn back to his inheritance nor to think of his kindred, but to give all its desire and all its energy to keeping up the religious life. He worked with his hands, having heard, *if any man will not work, neither let him eat* (cf. *2 Thess.* 3:10), spending the money partly on bread, partly on the poor. He prayed constantly, having learned that in private we must pray without ceasing. (Cf. *Luke* 18:1). For he so listened to the reading that nothing of what is written escaped him, but he retained everything, and for the future his memory served him instead of books.

Living this manner of life, Antony was beloved by all. He made himself really subject to the devout men whom he visited and learned for himself the special religious virtues of each of them: the graciousness of one, the continual prayer of another; he observed the meekness of one, the charity of another; studied one in his long watchings, another in his love of reading; admired one for his steadfastness, another for his fasting and sleeping on the ground; watched one's mildness, another's patience; while in all alike he remarked the same reverence for Christ and the same love for each other. Having thus gathered his fill, he returned to his own place of discipline and thereafter pondered with himself what he had learned from each and strove to show in himself the virtues of all. He had no contentions with those of his own age, save only that he would not be found second to them in the better things; and this he did in such manner that none was grieved, but they too were glad on his account. Seeing him such, then, all the village people and the devout with whom he had intercourse called him a man of God and loved him as a son or as a brother.

CHAPTER TWO
First Temptations

B UT the devil, the hater and envier of good, could not bear to
see such resolution in a young man, but attempted to use against
him the means in which he is skilled. First he tried to draw him back
from the religious life by reminding him of his property, of the care of
his sister, his intimacy with his kindred, the love of money, the love
of fame, the manifold pleasures of the table and the other relaxations
of life—and lastly the hardness of virtue and how great is the labor
thereof, suggesting that the body is weak and time is long. So he raised
in his mind a great dust cloud of arguments to drive him aside from
his straight purpose. But when the enemy saw himself powerless in face
of Antony's resolution and that rather he was himself overthrown by
his firmness and routed by his faith and beaten by Antony's constant
prayer, then placing his trust in "the weapons that hang at his waist"
(cf. *Job* 40:11) and glorying in these (for these are his first snare against
the young), he advanced against the young man, disturbing him by
night and so besetting him by day that even onlookers could see the
struggle that was going on between the two. He suggested evil thoughts,
and the other turned them away by his prayers. He roused feelings, and
Antony, ashamed, defended himself by faith and prayers and fastings.
The wretched fiend even stooped to masquerade as a woman by night,
simply to deceive Antony; and he quenched the fire of that temptation
by thinking of Christ and of the nobility we have through Him, and of
the dignity of the soul. (Cf. *1 Cor.* 6:15). Again the enemy suggested
the delight of pleasure; but he, angered and grieved, thought over the
threat of the fire and the torment of the worm. (Cf. *Mark* 9:43). These
he opposed to his temptations and so came through them unhurt. So
all these things turned to the confusion of the adversary, for he who
thought to be like to God was now mocked by a youth, and he who
gloried over flesh and blood was now defeated by a man clad in the
flesh. For with him wrought the Lord, who for us took flesh and gave

to the body the victory over the devil, so that those who truly strive can each say, "*Not I, but the grace of God with me.*" (*1 Cor.* 15:10).

As neither by this means could the serpent conquer Antony, but saw himself thrust out of his heart, at length, gnashing his teeth as it is written (cf. *Ps.* 111:10), like one in a frenzy, he showed himself in appearance as he is in mind, coming to Antony in the shape of a black boy and as it were flattering him. He no longer assailed him with thoughts, for the deceiver had been cast out, but using now a human voice, he said, "Many have I deceived, and very many have I overthrown; yet now, when I attacked you and your works as I have attacked others, I was not strong enough?' Antony asked, "Who are you that say such things to me?" Then at once he answered in piteous tones, "I am the lover of uncleanness; I take charge of the ensnaring and the tempting of the young; and I am called the spirit of fornication. How many have I deceived who meant to be careful! How many that were chaste have I drawn away with temptations. I am he through whom the prophet reproaches the fallen, saying: You were deceived by a spirit of fornication, for it was through me that they were tripped up. I am he that so often beset you and as often was defeated by you." Then Antony thanked God, and taking courage against him, said to him, "Then you are much to be despised, for your mind is black and your strength as a child's. I have not one anxiety left on your account, for '*the Lord is my helper, and I will despise my enemies.*'" (Cf. *Ps.* 117:7). Hearing this, the black spirit instantly fled, cowering at his words and fearing even to approach the man.

This was Antony's first victory over the devil; or rather, this was the triumph in Antony of the Saviour, *who condemned sin in the flesh, that the justice of the law may be fulfilled in us, who walk not according to the flesh, but according to the spirit.* (Cf. *Rom.* 8:3, 4).

But thereafter Antony did not grow careless and neglect himself, as though the devil were beaten; neither did the enemy cease his wiles, as having failed. For he wandered round again like a lion seeking some chance against him. And Antony, having learned from the Scriptures that the craftinesses of the enemy are many (cf. *Luke* 10:19), gave himself earnestly to the religious life, deeming that, though the foe had not been able to beguile his heart with bodily pleasures, he would surely try to ensnare him by other means—for the devil is a lover of sin. More and more, therefore, did he repress the body and bring it into subjection, lest after winning at one point, he should be dragged down at another. He decided, therefore, to accustom himself to harder ways. And many wondered, but he easily bore the hardship, for the eagerness of the spirit, long abiding with him, wrought in him a good habit; so that a small occasion given by others led him to a great exercise of zeal. For such was his watching that often he passed the whole night unsleeping; and this not once, but it was seen with wonder that he did it most frequently. He ate once in the day, after sunset, and at times he broke his fast only after two days—and often even after four days. His food was bread and salt, his drink only water. Of meat and wine it is needless to speak, for nothing of this sort was to be found among the other monks either. For sleep a rush mat sufficed him; as a rule he simply lay on the ground. The oiling of the skin he refused, saying that it were better for young men to prefer exercise and not seek for things that make the body soft—rather to accustom it to hardships, mindful of the Apostle's words: *When I am weak, then am I strong.* (Cf. *2 Cor.* 12:10). For he said that when the enjoyments of the body are weak, then is the power of the soul strong.

He had also this strange-seeming principle: he held that not by length of time is the way of virtue measured and our progress therein, but by desire and by strong resolve. Accordingly, he himself gave no thought to the bygone time, but each day, as though then beginning his religious life, he made greater effort to advance, constantly repeating to himself St. Paul's saying: *Forgetting the things that are behind, and reaching out to the things that are before* (cf. *Phil.* 3:13); keeping in mind, too, the voice of Elias the Prophet saying, *The Lord liveth, before whose sight I stand this day.* (Cf. *3 Kings* 17:1). For he observed that in saying *this day*, he did not count the bygone time; but as though always making a beginning, he was earnest each day to present himself such as one ought to appear before God: clean of heart and ready to obey His will and none other. And he used to say within himself that from the way of life of the great Elias a religious man must always study his own way of life, as in a mirror.

CHAPTER THREE
His Life in the Tombs

HAVING thus mastered himself, Antony departed to the tombs that lay far from the village, having asked one of his acquaintance to bring him bread from time to time. He entered one of the tombs, his friend closed the door of it on him, and he remained alone within. This the enemy would not endure, for he feared lest by degrees Antony should fill the desert too with monks. Coming one night with a throng of demons, he so scourged him that he lay on the ground speechless from the pain. For, he declared, the pain was so severe that blows from men could not have caused such agony. By God's providence (for the Lord does not overlook those who hope in Him), his friend came the next day bringing him bread, and when he opened the door and saw him lying on the ground, as dead, he lifted him and took him to the village church and laid him on the ground. Many of his kin and the village people watched beside Antony as for one dead. But towards midnight Antony came to himself and awoke, and seeing all asleep and only his friend waking, he signed to him to come near and asked him to lift him again and carry him back to the tombs without waking anyone.

So he was carried back by the man, and the door was closed as before, and he was again alone within. He could not stand because of the blows, but he prayed lying down. And after his prayer, he shouted out, "Here am I, Antony; I do not run away from your blows. For though you should give me yet more, *nothing shall separate me from the love of Christ."* (Cf. *Rom.* 8:35). Then he sang the Psalm, *If armies in camp should stand together against me, my heart shall not fear.* (Cf. *Ps.* 26:3).

The monk, then, thought and spoke thus. But the enemy of all good, marveling that even after the blows he had courage to go back, called together his hounds and burst out in fury, "Do you see that we have not stopped this man, either by the spirit of fornication or by blows, but he challenges us; let us attack him another way." For plans of ill are easy to the devil.

Thereupon in the night they made such a crashing that it seemed the whole place was shaken by an earthquake; and as if they had broken through the four walls of the building, the demons seemed to rush in through them in the guise of beasts and creeping things, and the place was at once filled with the forms of lions, bears, leopards, bulls, serpents, asps, scorpions and wolves. And each moved according to its own likeness. The lion roared, ready to spring, the bull seemed thrusting with its horns, the serpent crept yet reached him not, the wolf held itself as if ready to strike. And the noise of all the visions was terrible, and their fury cruel.

Antony, beaten and goaded by them, felt keener bodily pain. Nevertheless he lay fearless and more alert in spirit. He groaned with the soreness of his body, but in mind he was cool and said jestingly, "If you had any power in you, it would have been enough that just one of you should come; but the Lord has taken your strength away, and that is why you try to frighten me, if possible, by your numbers. It is a sign of your helplessness that you have taken the shapes of brutes!" Again he said cheerily, "If you can, and if you have received power over me, do not wait, but lay on. But if you cannot, why are you chafing yourselves for nothing? For our trust in the Lord is like a seal to us, and like a wall of safety!"

So, after making many attempts, they gnashed their teeth at him because they were befooling themselves and not him.

And the Lord in this also forgot not Antony's wrestling, but came to his defense. For looking up, Antony saw as it were the roof opening and a beam of light coming down to him. And the demons suddenly disappeared, and the soreness of his body ceased at once, and the building was again sound.

Antony, seeing that help was come, breathed more freely, being eased of his pains. And he asked the vision, "Where wert Thou? Why didst Thou not show Thyself from the beginning, to end my suffering?" And a voice came to him: "I was here, Antony, but I waited to see thy resistance. Therefore since thou hast endured and not yielded, I will always be thy Helper, and I will make thee renowned everywhere." Hearing this Antony arose and prayed, and he was so strengthened that he perceived that he had more power in his body than formerly. He was at this time about thirty-five years old.

CHAPTER FOUR
Alone in the Desert
(At Pispir, now Der el Memun)

THE next day, going out with still greater zeal for the service of God, Antony met the old man before mentioned and asked him to live in the desert with him. He refused because of his age and because this was not as yet usual, but Antony at once set out for the mountain. Yet once more the enemy, seeing his zeal and wishing to check it, threw in his way the form of a large disc of silver. Antony, understanding the deceit of the Evil One, stood and looked at the disc and confuted the demon in it, saying, "Whence a disc in the desert? This is not a trodden road, and there is no track of any faring this way. And it could not have fallen unnoticed, being of huge size. And even if it had been lost, the loser would certainly have found it had he turned back to look, because the place is desert. This is a trick of the devil. You will not hinder my purpose by this, Satan; let this thing perish with thee." And as Antony said this, it disappeared like smoke before the face of the fire.

Now as he went on, he again saw, not this time a phantom, but real gold lying in the way. Whether it was the enemy that pointed it out or whether it was a higher power, training the disciple and proving to the devil that he cared nothing even for real riches, he himself did not say, and we do not know—only that it was gold that he saw. Antony marveled at the quantity, but avoided it like fire and passed on without looking back, running swiftly on till he lost sight of the place and knew not where it was.

So with firmer and firmer resolution, he went to the mountain, and finding beyond the river a fort, long deserted and now full of reptiles, he betook himself there and dwelt in it. The reptiles fled at once as though chased by someone; and he, closing up the entrance and laying in bread for six months (the Thebans do this, and often it keeps unspoiled for a whole year), and having water in the fort, went down into the inner rooms and abode there alone, not going out himself and not seeing any who came to visit him. For a long time he continued this life of asceticism, only receiving his loaves twice in the year from the house above.

His acquaintances who came to see him often spent days and nights outside, since he would not let them enter. They seemed to hear a tumultuous crowd inside, making noises, uttering piteous cries, shrieking, "Stand off from our domain! What have you to do with the desert? You cannot stand against our contrivings." At first those outside thought there were men fighting with Antony, who had got in to him by a ladder, but when they bent down through a hole and saw no one, then they thought it was demons and feared for themselves and called to Antony. He listened to them, though he gave no thought to the demons; and going near to the door, he urged the people to go home and fear not, saying that the demons made these displays against the timid. "Do you therefore sign yourselves and go away bravely and leave them to make fools of themselves." So they went away, protecting themselves with the Sign of the Cross, and he remained and was nowise hurt by them. Nor did he weary of the struggle. For the aid of the visions that came to him from on high and the weakness of his enemies brought him much ease from his labors and prepared him for greater earnestness. His friends used to come constantly, expecting to find him dead; but they heard him singing: *Let God arise, and let his enemies be scattered: and let them that hate him flee from before his face. As smoke vanisheth, so let them vanish away: as wax melteth before the fire, so let the wicked perish at the presence of God.* (*Ps.* 67:2–3). And again: *All the nations surrounded me, and by the name of the Lord I drove them off.* (Cf. *Ps.* 117:10).

He spent nearly twenty years in this solitary religious life, neither going out nor being seen regularly by any. After that, many longed and sought to copy his holy life, and some of his friends came and forcibly broke down the door and removed it; and Antony came forth as from a holy of holies, filled with heavenly secrets and possessed by the Spirit of God. This was the first time he showed himself from the fort to those who came to him. When they saw him they marveled to see that his body kept its former state, being neither grown heavy for want of exercise, nor shrunken with fastings and strivings against demons. For he was such as they had known him before his retirement. The light of his soul, too, was absolutely pure. It was not shrunk with grieving nor dissipated by pleasure; it had no touch of levity nor of gloom. He was not bashful at seeing the crowd nor elated at being welcomed by such numbers, but was unvaryingly tranquil, a man ruled by reason, whose whole character had grown firm-set in the way that nature had meant it to grow.

Through him the Lord healed many of those present who were suffering from bodily ills and freed others from evil spirits. And the Lord gave Antony grace in speech, so that he comforted many in sorrow; others who were at strife he made friends; charging all not to prefer anything in the world to the love of Christ. And when he spoke and exhorted them to be mindful of the good things to come and of the love of God for us, who *spared not his own Son, but delivered him up for us all* (cf. *Rom.* 8:32), he induced many to take up the solitary life.

And so from that time there were monasteries in the mountains, and the desert was peopled with monks who went forth from their own and became citizens of the kingdom of Heaven.

BOOK TWO

Antony's Teachings

———•———

CHAPTER FIVE
What a Monk's Vocation Is

WHEN he had need to cross the canal of Arsenoe (the need was his visitation of the brethren), the canal was full of crocodiles. And simply praying, he entered it with all his companions, and they passed through unhurt.

He returned to the monastery and continued the same holy and generous labors. He preached constantly, increasing the zeal of those who were already monks and stirring many others to the love of the religious life; and soon, as the word drew men, the number of monasteries became very great; and to all he was a guide and a father.

One day, when he had gone out and all the monks came to him asking to hear a discourse, he spoke to them as follows in the Egyptian tongue:

The Scriptures are enough for our instruction. Yet it is well that we should encourage each other in the Faith and stimulate each other with words. Do you, therefore, bring what you know and tell it like children to your father; while I, as your elder, share with you what I know and have experienced. First of all, let one same zeal be common to all, not to give up what we have begun, not to be faint-hearted in our labors, not to say we have lived long in this service, but rather as beginners to have greater zeal each day. For the whole life of a man is very short, measured beside the ages to come, so that all our time is nothing compared to eternal life. And in the world, every merchandise is sold at its worth, and men barter like value for like. But the promise of eternal life is bought for a trifle. For it is written: *The days of our years . . . are threescore and ten years. But if in the strong they be fourscore years: and what is more of them is labour and sorrow.* (Cf. *Ps.* 89:10). If, then, we spend the whole eighty years in the religious life, or even a hundred, we shall not reign for the like space of a hundred years, but in return for the hundred, we shall reign through ages of ages. And if our striving is on earth, our inheritance shall not be on earth, but in Heaven is our promised reward. Our body, too, we give up corruptible; we receive it back incorruptible.

Therefore, children, let us not faint, nor weary, nor think we are doing much: For the sufferings of this present time are not worthy to be compared to the glory that shall be revealed to us. (Cf. *Rom.* 8:18). Neither let us look back to the world, thinking that we have renounced much. For the whole earth is but a narrow thing compared to all Heaven. If, then, we were lords of the whole earth, and renounced the whole earth, that, too, would be worth nothing beside the kingdom of Heaven. As though a man should make light of one bronze coin to gain a hundred pieces of gold, so he that owns all the earth, and renounces it, gives up but little and receives a hundredfold. If, then, the whole earth is no price for Heaven, surely he who has given up a few acres must not boast nor grow careless, for what he forsakes is as nothing, even if he leave a home and much wealth.

There is another thing to consider: if we do not forsake these things for virtue's sake, still we leave them later on when we die—and often, as *Ecclesiastes* reminds us, to those whom we would not. (Cf. *Eccles.* 2:18). Then why not leave them for virtue's sake and to inherit a kingdom?

Therefore let none of us have even the wish to possess. For what profit is it to possess these things which yet we cannot take with us? Why not rather possess those things which we can take away with us— prudence, justice, temperance, fortitude, understanding, charity, love of the poor, gentleness, hospitality? For if we gain these possessions, we shall find them going beforehand, to make a welcome for us there in the land of the meek.

With these thoughts let a man urge himself not to grow careless, especially if he considers that he is one of God's servants, and owes service to his master. Now as a servant would not dare to say, "Today I do not work because I worked yesterday," nor would count up the time that is past and rest in the coming days; but each day, as is written in the Gospel (cf. *Luke* 17:7–8), shows the same willingness, in order to keep his Lord's favor and avoid danger; so too let us too daily abide in our service, knowing that if we are slovenly for one day, He will not pardon us for the sake of the bygone time, but will be angry with us for slighting Him. So have we heard in Ezechiel (cf. *Ezech.* 3:20); so, too, Judas in one night destroyed all his toil in the foregone time. (Cf. *John* 6:71–72).

Therefore, children, let us hold fast the religious life and not grow careless. For in this we have the Lord working with us, as it is written, God cooperates unto good with everyone that chooseth the good. (Cf. *Rom.* 8:28). And to prevent negligence, it is well for us to ponder on the Apostle's saying: *I die daily.* (*1 Cor.* 15:31). For if we also so live as dying daily, we shall not sin. What is meant is this: that when we wake each day, we should think we shall not live till evening; and again, when we go to sleep, we should think we shall not wake, for our life is of its nature uncertain and is measured out to us daily by Providence. So thinking and so living from day to day, we shall not sin, nor shall we have any longing for anything, nor cherish wrath against anyone, nor lay up treasure on the earth; but as men who each day expect to die, we shall be poor, we shall forgive everything to all men. The desire of women and of evil pleasure we shall—not meet and master—but we shall turn away from it as a fleeting thing, striving always, and always looking to the Day of Judgment. (Cf. *Luke* 12:5). For the greater fear and the danger of torment always break the delight of pleasure and steady the wavering mind.

Having made a beginning and set out on the way of virtue, let us stretch out yet more to reach the things that are before us. Let none turn back like Lot's wife, especially as the Lord has said: *No man setting his hand to the plough and turning back is fit for the kingdom of heaven.* (*Luke* 9:62). Turning back simply means changing one's mind and caring again for worldly things.

And when you hear of virtue, do not fear nor feel the word strange; for it is not afar from us, not something that stands without; no, the thing is within us, and the doing it easy, if only we have the will. The Greeks go abroad and cross the sea to study letters, but we have no need to go abroad for the kingdom of Heaven, nor to cross the sea after virtue. For the Lord has told us beforehand: *The kingdom of heaven is within you.* (*Luke* 17:21). Virtue, therefore, needs only our will, since it is within us and grows from us. For virtue grows when the soul keeps the understanding according to nature. It is according to nature when it remains as it was made. Now it was made beautiful and perfectly straight. For this reason Josue, the son of Nave, commanded the people: Make straight your hearts to your ways. (Cf. *Josue* 24:23). For the straightness of the soul consists in the mind's being according to nature, as it was made; as, on the other hand, the soul is said to be evil when it bends and gets twisted away from what is according to nature. So the task is not difficult: if we remain as God made us, we are in virtue; if we give our minds to evil, we are accounted wicked. If, then, it were a thing that must be sought from without, the task would indeed be hard; but if it be within us, let us guard ourselves from evil thoughts and keep our soul for the Lord, as a trust we have received from Him, that He may recognize His work, finding it as it was when He made it.

Let us fight also not to be mastered by anger nor enslaved by concupiscence. For it is written that *the anger of man worketh not the justice of God. (James* 1:20). And *concupiscence, having conceived, bringeth forth sin; and sin, when it is completed, bringeth forth death.* (Cf. *James* 1:15).

CHAPTER SIX
Of the Assaults of Demons

LIVING this life, let us watch ceaselessly, and as it is written, guard our heart with all watchfulness. (Cf. *Prov.* 4:23). For we have enemies, terrible and unscrupulous, the wicked demons, and against them is our warfare, as the Apostle said, *not against flesh and blood, but against principalities and powers, against the rulers of the world of this darkness, against the spirits of wickedness dwelling in the high places.* (*Eph.* 6:12). Great is the number of them in the air around us, and they are not far from us. But there is much difference in them. It would be long to speak of their nature and differences, and such a discourse is for others greater than us; the only pressing and necessary thing now is to know their treacheries against us.

Let us first understand this, that the demons were not made as demons, for God made nothing bad. But they also were created beautiful, but fell from heavenly wisdom; and thenceforward, wandering about the earth, they have deceived the Greeks with their apparitions. They envy us Christians and move everything to hinder us from the way to Heaven, lest we mount to where they fell from. Therefore there is needed much prayer and self-discipline, that a man may receive from the Holy Ghost the gift of discerning spirits and may be able to know about them—which of them are less wicked, and which more, and in what kind of thing each of them is interested, and how each is defeated and cast out. For they have many treacheries and many moves in their plotting. The blessed Apostle and his followers knew this, saying: *We are not ignorant of his contrivings. (2 Cor.* 2:11). And we, from being tempted by them, must guide one another. Therefore, as having in part experience of them, I speak to you as my children.

If, then, they see any Christians, but especially monks, laboring gladly and making progress, they first attack them and tempt them by putting continual stumbling blocks in their way. These stumbling blocks are bad thoughts. We must not fear their suggestions, for by prayers and fastings and trust in the Lord they are defeated at once. Yet when defeated they do not cease, but come back again wickedly and deceitfully. For when they cannot mislead the heart with plainly unclean delights, they attack again in another way and try to frighten it by weaving phantoms, taking the forms of women, of beasts and reptiles, and gigantic bodies, and armies of soldiers. But even so, we must not fear their phantoms, for they are nothing and quickly disappear, especially if one fortify himself with faith and the Sign of the Cross. But they are daring and utterly shameless. For if here too they are beaten, they come on again in another way. They pretend to prophesy and to foretell things to come, and to show themselves taller than the roof and as vast phantoms to those whom they could not beguile with thoughts. And if even so they find the soul firm in faith and in the hope of its purpose, then they bring in their leader.

Often, he said, they appear in shape such as the Lord revealed the devil to Job, saying: *His eyes are like the look of the dawn. From his mouth come forth burning lamps, and fires are shot forth. From his nostrils comes the smoke of a furnace, burning with a fire of coals. His breath is coals, and flame proceeds from his mouth.* (Cf. *Job* 41:9–12). When the leader of the devils appears in this way, the wretch causes terror, as I said, boasting as the Lord described, saying to Job: *He esteemed iron as chaff, and bronze as rotten wood; he thought the sea a vessel for ointments, the deeps of hell a captive; he judged the deeps to be a place for walking* (cf. *Job* 41:18); and by the mouth of the Prophet: *The enemy said, I will pursue and will capture* (cf. *Ex.* 15:9); and by another: *I will grasp the whole world in my hand like a nest, and as deserted eggs will I seize it.* (Cf. *Is.* 10:14). And all such boastings and threatenings they make, seeking to deceive the devout. Here, again, we faithful must not fear his appearances nor heed his words. For he lies, and there is no truth at all in his speech. For he talks thus and makes so bold, ignoring how he was dragged away with a hook like a serpent by the Saviour, was haltered like a beast of burden, was ringed through the nostrils like a runaway, and his lips pierced with an armlet. (Cf. *Job* 40:19). The Lord has tethered him as a sparrow, to be mocked at by us. (Cf. *Job* 40:24). He and his demons are put like scorpions and snakes to be trodden under foot by us Christians. A proof of this is our now living this life in spite of him. For he that threatened to wipe up the sea and to grasp the world, now, behold, cannot hinder our devotion, cannot even stop me speaking against him. Therefore, let us not heed whatever he may say, for he lies, nor fear his lying visions. For it is no true light that is seen in them; rather, they bring a foretaste and likeness of the fire that was prepared for them. They seek to frighten men with that in which themselves shall burn. They appear, but at once they disappear again, having hurt no one, and taking with them the likeness of the fire that is to receive them. So we need not fear them on this account either, for by the grace of Christ all their practicings are to no purpose. They are treacherous and ready to take on them any part and any shape. Often, without appearing, they pretend to sing psalms and repeat sayings from the Scripture. Sometimes, when we are reading, they will repeat at once like an echo the very words we have read. When we are asleep, they wake us to prayers, and this persistently, scarcely letting us get to sleep. At times, too, they take the shape of monks and pretend to talk piously, in order to deceive by the likeness of form, and then lead whither they will those whom they have beguiled. But we must not heed them, though they wake us to pray, though they advise us to fast altogether, though they pretend to accuse and reproach us for things wherein once they were our accomplices. Not for piety nor for truth's sake do they do this, but in order to bring the simple into despair, and to say that asceticism avails not, and to make men disgusted with the monastic life as burdensome and most grievous, and to entangle those whose life is contrary to them.

Against such as these the prophet sent by God pronounces woe, saying: *Woe to him that giveth his neighbour a troubled drink to turn him back.* (Cf. *Hab.* 2:15). For such devices and thoughts turn men back in the way that leads to virtue. And Our Lord Himself, even when the demons spoke the truth (for they truly said, "Thou art the Son of God"), yet silenced them and forbade them to speak, lest after the truth they should oversow their own wickedness, and also to teach us never to heed them, even though they seem to speak truth, for it is unseemly that we who have the Holy Scriptures—and the freedom of Christ—should be taught by the devil, who kept not his own rank, but is minded now one way, now another. (Cf. *Jude*). Therefore, He forbids him to speak, even to quote the words of Scripture: *To the sinful one God said, Why do you relate my judgements and take my testament into your mouth?* (Cf. *Ps.* 49:16). For they do everything; they talk, they make an uproar, they pretend, they unsettle the mind, all to deceive the simple, making a din, laughing senselessly, hissing. And if one heed them not, they weep and wail as defeated.

The Lord, then, being God, silenced the demons. But we, learning from the Saints, must do as they did and imitate their courage. For they, when they saw these things, said: *When the sinner stood against me, I was dumb, and was humbled, and kept silence from good things.* (Cf. *Ps.* 38:2). And again: *But I, as a deaf man, heard not: and as a dumb man not opening his mouth: and I became as a man that heareth not.* (Cf. *Ps.* 37:14). Wherefore let us not listen to them; they are none of ours. Nor let us hearken, though they call us to prayer or speak of fastings. But rather, let us attend to our own purpose of holy living and not be cheated by them who do all deceitfully. We must not fear them, though they seem to assault us or threaten death, for they are powerless and can do nothing but threaten.

This much I have said of them in passing. But now we must not shrink from a fuller discourse about them; it will be safer for you to be warned.

CHAPTER SEVEN
The Devil's Powerlessness

SINCE Our Lord lived, the enemy is fallen, and his powers have lost their strength. Therefore, though he can do nothing, nevertheless, like a fallen tyrant, he does not rest, but threatens, though it be but words. Let each of you think of that, and he can despise the demons. If they were tied to such bodies as we are, they might then say, "We cannot find men who hide, but if we do find them, we hurt them." And we in that case might escape them by hiding and locking doors against them. But since they are not so, but can enter where doors are locked, and since they are found in all the air, they and their chief, the devil, and since they are evil-willed and ready to hurt—and as Our Lord said: *the father of evil, the devil, is a murderer from the beginning* (*John* 8:44)—and nevertheless, we live and carry on our life in defiance of them, it is evident that they have no power. Place does not hinder them from plotting; and they do not see us friendly to them, that they should spare us; and they have no love of justice, that they should amend. On the contrary, they are wicked and desire nothing so much as to injure those who seek virtue and honor God. The reason they do nothing is because they can do nothing, except threaten; if they could, they would not wait, but would do the evil at once, since their will is quite ready for it, especially against us. Look: here are we now gathered and talking against them; and they know that, as we advance, they grow weak. If, then, they had power, they would not have let one of us Christians live, for the service of God is an abomination to the sinner. As they can do nothing, they rather injure themselves in this, for they cannot do aught of what they threaten.

Again, this must be remembered, to end all fear of them. If any power belonged to them, they would not come in a crowd, nor cause phantoms, nor use devices and appearances; it would be enough that one alone should come and do what he could and would. Anyone who really has power does not destroy with phantoms nor frighten with crowds, but uses his power at once as he wills. But the demons, who have no power, play as on a stage, changing their forms and frightening children by the look of numbers and by their shapes; for all which they are the more to be despised as powerless. The real angel who was sent by God against the Assyrians needed not crowds, nor visible phantoms, nor clangings, nor clappings, but quietly used his power and destroyed a hundred and eighty-five thousand of them. Whereas helpless demons like these try to frighten, if only by shadows.

Now if anyone thinks of the case of Job and asks, "Why then did the devil go forth and do everything against him—strip him of his possessions, destroy his children and strike him with a grievous ulcer?" let such a one know that it was not the devil who had power, but God who gave Job into his hands to be tried. Because he had no power to do anything, he asked and received, and did it. Herein, therefore, is the more reason to despise the enemy, that though he desired, he was powerless against one just man. Had he had power, he would not have asked for it. He asked, not once, but a second time; plainly he is weak and helpless. And little wonder he was powerless against Job, when he could not destroy even his beasts unless God had permitted. Not even against swine has he power, for as it is written in the Gospel: *They entreated the Lord saying, Suffer us to depart into the swine. (Mark* 5:12). If they have no power over swine, much less have they over men made in the likeness of God.

God only must we fear, then; these creatures we must despise and nowise fear. Indeed, the more they do, the more effort must we make on our way in defiance of them. For the great weapon against them is a right life and confidence in God. For they dread the ascetics' fasting, watching, prayers, meekness, peacefulness, their scorn of wealth and of vainglory, their humility, love of the poor, alms-deeds, their mildness, and most of all, their devotion to Christ. This is why they do all they can that there may be none to trample on them: for they know the grace that the Saviour gave to His faithful against them when He said: *Behold I have given you power to trample on serpents and scorpions and on all the strength of the enemy. (Luke* 10:19).

CHAPTER EIGHT
The Devil's Prophecies

FURTHER, if they pretend also to prophesy, let no one heed. For often they tell us days beforehand of brothers who are coming to see us; and they do come. It is not from kindness to their hearers that they do this, but in order to induce these to trust them, and thereafter, having them in their power, to destroy them. Wherefore we must not listen to them, but even as they speak must repulse them; for we have no need of them. For what wonder is it if they whose bodies are of subtler nature than men's, when they have seen some of the brethren beginning a journey, outrun them and announce them? So does a horseman bring word, outstripping those who go on foot. So here, too, we need not marvel at them. They foreknow naught of what has not yet happened; God alone knows all things before they come to birth. But these, like thieves, run ahead and bring word what they have seen. Even at this moment to how many do they make known our doings, how we are assembled and hold discourse against them, before any goes from us to give the news! This, too, a fleet-footed boy might do, outstripping a slower.

What I mean is this: If someone begins to travel from the Thebaid or any other place, they do not know if he will travel till he starts. But when they see him on the way, they run ahead and bring word before he comes; and so it is that after some days the traveler comes. Yet often enough their news is false, for the travelers turn back.

So, too, at times they chatter about the water of the river. Seeing great rains falling in the parts of Ethiopia, and knowing that from there comes the flooding of the river, they run ahead and tell it before the water reaches Egypt. Men could tell it too, if they could run as these. And as David's scout (cf. *2 Kgs.* 18:24), mounting a height, saw better who was coming than one who stayed below; and as even he who ran ahead told before the rest not things unborn, but things that had come to pass and were on the way; so these choose to hurry and bring news

37

to others simply to deceive them. But if in the meantime Providence arrange aught concerning the waters or the travelers, as it can, then the demons have spoken falsely and they who heeded them are deceived.

It was thus that the Greek oracles arose and men were formerly deceived by the demons, but it is thus, too, that the deceit is ended henceforward. For the Lord came, who has made void the demons and all their wickedness. For of themselves they know nothing, but they see what knowledge others have, and like thieves take it and twist it. They are guessers rather than prophets. Therefore, if sometimes they foretell such things truly, even so no one need wonder at them. For physicians also who have experience of diseases, when they meet the same disease in others, can often tell beforehand, judging from experience. And again, seamen and farmers, looking at the state of the weather, from their experience prophesy that there will be a storm or fine weather. No one would say because of this that they prophesy by supernatural inspiration, but by experience and practice. Wherefore, if the demons too sometimes say these same things by conjecture, they are not to be admired or heeded on that account. For what profit is it to the hearers to learn from them days beforehand what is coming; or what manner of eagerness to know such things, even could one know them truly? For this makes not for virtue, neither is it any mark of goodness. For none of us is judged for that [which] he knows not, and none is blessed for that [which] he has learned and knows; but on these things each has to be judged—if he has held fast the Faith, and truly kept the Commandments.

Therefore, we must not make much of these things, nor live our life of hardship and toil for the sake of knowing the future, but in order to please God by living well. And we must pray, not in order to know the future, nor is that the reward we must ask for our hard life, but that Our Lord may be our fellow-worker in conquering the devil. But if ever we care to know the future, let us be pure in mind. For I am sure that, when a soul is pure on all sides and in her natural state, she becomes clear-sighted and can see more and further than the demons, having the Lord to show her, as was the soul of Eliseus when watching the doings of Giezi, and seeing the armies that stood by them. (Cf. *4 Kgs.* 5:26; 6:17).

CHAPTER NINE
How to Distinguish Good from Bad Visions

WHEN they come to you by night and want to tell the future, or say, "We are the angels," do not heed, for they lie. And if they praise your strict life, and call you blessed, do not you hearken nor deal with them at all. Rather, bless yourselves and bless the house, and pray, and you will see them disappear. For they are cowards and utterly dread the sign of our Lord's Cross, since it was on the Cross that the Saviour despoiled them and exposed them. (Cf. *Col.* 2:25). But if they stay unashamed, with dancing and changing shows, do you not fear nor shrink, neither give heed to them as being good spirits. For to distinguish the presence of the good and the bad is by God's gift possible and easy. A vision of holy ones is not troubled, *for he shall not contend, nor cry out, neither shall any man hear his voice* (cf. *Matt.* 12:19); but it falls so restfully and gently that instant gladness and joy and courage awake in the soul. For with the holy visitants is Our Lord, who is our joy and God the Father's might. The soul's thoughts remain untroubled and calm, so that she looks on her visitants enlightened in herself. There comes on her a longing for heavenly things and things to come, and she is ready to be wholly united to them if she might go with them. And if some, being human, tremble at the vision of good angels, then at once the angel dispels the fear by love, as did Gabriel for Zachary (cf. *Luke* 1:13), and the angel who appeared in the holy sepulchre for the women (cf. *Mark* 16:6), and he that said to the shepherds in the Gospel, *Fear not.* (Cf. *Luke* 2:10). For their fear is not from cowardice of soul, but from feeling the presence of higher natures. Such then is the vision of holy ones.

But the assault and appearance of the evil ones is troubled, with crashing and din and outcry, as might be the rioting of rough youths and thieves. From which comes at once terror of soul, disturbance and disorder of thoughts, dejection, hatred of ascetics, recklessness, sadness, the memory of one's family, the fear of death; and then a craving for evil, a contempt of virtue and an unsettling of the character. When, therefore, you see someone and are afraid, if the fear is immediately taken from you and instead of it comes joy unspeakable, cheerfulness, courage and recovery, and calmness of thought, and the rest that I have named, strength, and love of God, then be of good cheer, and pray, for the joy and the steadiness of the soul show the holiness of the Presence. So Abraham (cf. *John* 8:56), seeing Our Lord, rejoiced; and John (cf. *Luke* 1:41), at the voice of Mary, the Mother of God, leapt for joy.

But if, when any appear to you, there is tumult and noise from without and earthly shows and threatening of death and all that I have spoken of, then know that the visitation is from the wicked.

Let this likewise be a sign to you: when the soul continues in terror, the presence is of the enemy. For the demons do not take away men's fear, as the great archangel Gabriel did for Mary and for Zachary (cf. *Luke* 1:13, 30) and he who appeared to the women in the tomb; but rather, when they see them afraid, they increase their phantoms, the more to terrify them, that then they may come on them and mock them saying, *Fall down and adore us.* (Cf. *Matt.* 4:9). The Greeks they did thus deceive, for among them they were thus taken for false gods. But Our Lord has not left us to be deceived by the devil, since when he made such appearances to Him, He rebuked him saying, *Get behind me, Satan; for it is written, The Lord thy God shalt thou adore, and him only shalt thou serve.* (Cf. *Matt.* 4:10). Therefore, let the evil one be more and more despised by us. For what Our Lord said, He said for our sake, that the devils, hearing the same words from us, may be put to flight through the Lord, who in these words rebuked them.

We must not boast for having cast out devils, nor be proud for healings; nor must we admire only him who casts out devils and make naught of him who does not. But let a man study the strict living of each, and either copy and match it, or else better it. For to work signs is not ours. That is the Saviour's doing. So He said to the disciples, *Rejoice not because the devils are subject to you, but because your names are written in Heaven.* (Cf. *Luke* 10:20). For our names written in Heaven are a witness to our virtue and our life, but to cast out devils is simply a favor of the Saviour who gave it. Wherefore to those who boast of their miracles and not of their virtues, saying, *Lord, have we not cast out devils in thy name and wrought many miracles in thy name?* (Cf. *Matt.* 7:22), He answered, *Amen, I say to you, I know you not.* For the Lord knows not the ways of the unholy. (Cf. *Ps.* 1:6).

As I have said, it is absolutely necessary to pray to receive the grace of discerning spirits, that as it is written, we may not trust every spirit. (Cf. *1 John* 4:1).

I would now cease, saying nothing of my own, and being content with thus much only. But that you may not think these things are only my talk, but may be sure that I speak from experience and fact, for this reason, though I become as one unwise, yet the Lord who hears knows that my conscience is clean, and that not for myself but for your love and your profit do I repeat what I have seen of the practices of the demons. How often have they called me blessed, and I have cursed them in the name of the Lord. How often have they foretold about the water of the river, and I have said to them, "And what concern is that of yours?" Once they came threatening, and surrounded me with battle array, like soldiers. Sometimes they filled the house with horses and beasts and serpents, and I sang the psalm, *These in chariots, and these in horses, but we shall be magnified in the name of the Lord our God* (cf. *Ps.* 19:8), and at these prayers they were turned back by the Lord. Once in the dark they came with a show of light, saying, "We have come to light you, Antony." But I shut my eyes and prayed, and at once their unholy light was quenched. And a few months later, they came as if singing psalms and quoting the Scriptures, *and I as one deaf heard not.* (*Ps.* 37:14). Once they shook the monastery, but I prayed and remained unshaken in mind. And afterwards they came again, stamping, hissing and leaping. But as I prayed and reclined, singing psalms to myself, they at once began to wail and weep as if utterly exhausted, and I glorified God, who took away and made mockery of their daring and their fury.

Once a demon appeared to me, exceeding lofty, with phantom array, and dared to say, "I am the power of God, and I am His providence; what wilt thou that I bestow on thee?" Then I blew a breath at him, naming the name of Christ and endeavored to strike him; and it seemed to me that I had struck him, and instantly, vast as he was, he disappeared with all his demons at the name of Christ. Once when I was fasting, the deceiver came to me as a monk carrying phantom loaves, and gave me counsel, saying, "Eat, and cease from your many hardships; you also are a man, and you will lose your strength." I, knowing his craft, arose to pray, and he could not bear it, for he vanished, looking like smoke as he went out through the door. How often in the desert did he show me a vision of gold, that I might but touch it and look at it; and I sang a psalm against him, and it melted away. Often they struck me blows, and I said, *Nothing shall part me from the love of Christ* (cf. *Rom.* 8:35), and on that they struck each other instead. It was not I who stopped them and brought them to naught, but it was the Lord, who says: *I saw Satan like lightning falling from heaven. (Luke* 10:18). My children, I have transferred these things to myself, mindful of the Apostle's saying (*1 Cor.* 4:6), in order that you may learn not to faint in your hard life and not to fear the phantoms of the devil and his demons.

CHAPTER TEN
That We Need Not Fear Satan

SEEING that I have begun to discourse thus unwisely, take for your safety and encouragement this also. And believe me, for I do not lie. Once someone knocked at my door in the monastery, and going out

I saw a tall and mighty figure. Then on my asking, "Who are you?" he said, "I am Satan." I asked, "Why are you here?" and he said, "Why do the monks and all other Christians blame me for no cause? Why do they curse me every hour?" When I said, "Then why do you annoy them?" he answered, "It is not I that annoy them, but they disturb themselves, for I am become powerless. Have they not read that *the swords of the enemy have failed to the end, and their cities thou hast destroyed?* (*Ps.* 9:7). I have now no place, no weapon, no city. Everywhere are Christians, and now the desert too is grown full of monks. Let them watch themselves, and not curse me without cause." Then I, marveling at the grace of the Lord, said to him, "Liar though you always are and never speaking truth, yet this time you have spoken true, even against your will, for Christ has come and made you powerless and cast you down and disarmed you." He, hearing the Saviour's name and not enduring the burning heat thereof, disappeared.

Now if the devil himself confesses that he can do nothing, we ought utterly to condemn both him and his demons.

The enemy, then, with his hounds has all these wicked arts, but we who have learned his weakness are able to despise them. Therefore, let us not droop in mind in regard of this, nor ponder terrors in our soul, nor weave affrights for ourselves, saying, "But how if a demon come and overthrow me, or lift me and hurl me down, or appear suddenly and craze me with fear?" Such things must not enter our minds at all, nor must we be sad as though perishing. Rather we must be brave and glad, as men who are being saved. Let us bear in mind that with us is the Lord, who defeated them and brought them to naught. And let us always believe and ponder this, that, while Our Lord is with us, our enemies shall not touch us. For when they come, as they find us, so do they themselves become to us: they fit their phantoms to the mind they find in us. If they find us in fear and panic, at once they assail us, like thieves who find the place unguarded; and all that we of ourselves are thinking, that they do and more. For if they see us afraid and cowardly, they increase our fear yet more by phantoms and threats, and thereafter the wretched soul is punished in these ways. But if they find us glad in the Lord and pondering on the good things to come and thinking thoughts of God and accounting that all is in God's hand and that a demon avails naught against a Christian nor has power over any—seeing the soul safeguarded with such thoughts, they turn away in shame. So the enemy, seeing Job thus fenced about (cf. *Job* 1:21), fled from him; but finding Judas bare of these thoughts (cf. *John* 13:2), mastered him. Therefore, if we would despise the enemy, our thoughts must always be of God and our souls always glad with hope, and we shall see the toys of the demons as smoke and themselves fleeing instead of pursuing, for they are, as I said, very cowardly, always expecting the fire that is prepared for them.

This sign also keep by you to cut off fear of them: When any vision comes, do not begin by falling into panic, but whatever it be, first ask bravely, "Who are you, and whence?" and if it be a vision of the good, they will satisfy you and change your fear into joy. But if it is anything diabolical, at once it loses all strength, seeing your spirit strong; for simply to ask, "Who are you, and whence?" is a proof of calmness. So when the son of Nave questioned (cf. *Jos.* 5:13) he learned, and the enemy was discovered when Daniel (cf. *Dan.* 13:54, 58) questioned him.

BOOK THREE

Antony's Work for Others

———————●———————

CHAPTER ELEVEN
The Persecution under Maximinus

AS ANTONY made this discourse, all rejoiced. It increased the love of virtue in some, in some it cast out carelessness, and in others it ended self-conceit. All were persuaded to despise the plottings of the devil, admiring the grace which God had given to Antony for the discerning of spirits.

The monasteries in the hills were like tents filled with heavenly choirs, singing, studying, fasting, praying, rejoicing for the hope of the life to come, laboring in order to give alms, having love and harmony among themselves. And in truth it was like a land of religion and justice to see, a land apart. For neither wronger nor wronged was there; nor plaint of tax-gathering; but a multitude of ascetics, all with one purpose to virtue; so that, looking back on the monasteries and on so fair an array of monks, one cried aloud saying: *How lovely are thy dwellings, O Jacob, thy tents, O Israel; like shady groves, and like a garden by a river, and like tents that the Lord hath pitched, and like cedars beside the waters.* (*Num.* 24:5–6).

Antony himself retired as usual to his own monastery by himself and went on with his holy life, groaning daily at thought of the mansions of Heaven, longing for them and seeing the shortness of man's life. For when going to food and sleep and the other needs of the body, shame came on him, thinking of the spirituality of the soul. Often when he was to eat with many other monks, the thought of the spirit's food came back on him, and he excused himself and went a long way from them, thinking it shame that he should be seen eating by others. Yet he ate alone, for the needs of the body; and often too with the brethren, ashamed on their account, but emboldened by the words of help he gave them. He used to say that we should give all our time to the soul, rather than to the body. A little time indeed we must of necessity allow to the body, but in the main we must devote ourselves to the soul and seek its profit, that it may not be dragged down by the pleasures of the body, but rather that the body be made subject to the soul, this being what the Saviour spoke of: *Be not solicitous for your life what you shall eat, nor for your body what you shall put on. (Luke 12:22). And seek not what you may eat or what you may drink, and be not lifted up; for all these things do the nations of the world seek. But your Father knoweth that you have need of all these things. But seek ye first his kingdom, and all these things shall be added to you. (Cf. Luke 12:29–31).*

After this, the persecution which then befell under Maximinus overtook the Church. When the holy martyrs were taken to Alexandria, Antony also quitted his monastery and followed, saying, "Let us too go that we may suffer if we are called, or else may look on the sufferers." He had a longing to be martyred, but not wishing to give himself up, he ministered to the confessors in the mines and in the prisons. In the hall of judgment he was full of zeal for those who were called, stirring them to generosity in their struggles, and in their martyrdom receiving them and escorting them to the end. Then the judge, seeing the fearlessness of Antony and his companions and their zeal in this work, gave orders that none of the monks should appear in the judgment hall, nor stay in the city at all. All the others thought best to be hidden that day, but Antony cared so much for it that he washed his tunic all the more, and on the next day stood on a high place in front and showed himself plainly to the prefect. While all wondered at this, and the prefect saw as he went through with his escort, Antony himself stood fearless, showing the eagerness that belongs to us Christians; for he was praying that he too might be martyred, as I have said. He himself mourned because he was not martyred, but God was keeping him to help us and others, that to many he might be a teacher of the strict life that he had himself learned from the Scriptures. For simply at seeing his behavior many were eager to become followers of his way of life. Again, therefore, he ministered as before to the confessors, and as though sharing their bonds, he wearied himself in serving them.

When later the persecution ceased, and the Bishop, Peter of blessed memory, had died a martyr, Antony departed and went back to his monastery and abode there, a daily martyr to conscience, fighting the fights of the faith. He practiced a high and more intense asceticism; he fasted constantly; his clothing was hair within and skin without, and this he kept till his death. He never bathed his body in water for cleanliness, nor even washed his feet, nor would he consent to put them in water at all without necessity. Neither was he *ever* seen undressed, nor till he died and was buried did any ever see the body of Antony uncovered.

CHAPTER TWELVE
In the Heart of the Desert
(At Der Mar Antonios, Between the Nile and the Red Sea)

WHEN he retired and purposed to pass a season neither going forth himself nor admitting any, a certain captain of soldiers, Martinianus, came and disturbed him, for he had a daughter beset by a demon. As he stayed long, beating the door and asking him to come and pray to God for the child, Antony would not open, but leaned down from above and said, "Man, why do you cry to me? I am a man like yourself. But if you trust in Christ whom I serve, go, and as you trust, so pray to God, and it shall be done." And he at once believing and calling on Christ, went away with his daughter made clean from the demon. Many other things did the Lord through Antony, for He says, *Ask and it shall be given to you. (Luke* 11:9). For though he opened not the door, very many sufferers simply slept outside the monastery, and trusted and prayed sincerely and were cleansed.

As he saw that many thronged to him and that he was not suffered to retire in his own way as he wished, being anxious lest from what the Lord did through him, either he himself should be lifted up (cf. *2 Cor.* 12:6), or another should think about him above the truth, he looked around him and set out to go to the upper Thebaid, where he was not known. He had got loaves from the brethren and was sitting by the banks of the river watching if a boat should pass, that he might embark and go up with them. While he was thus minded, a voice came to him from above: "Antony, where are you going, and why?" He was not alarmed, being used to be often thus called; but listened and answered, "Since the crowds will not let me be alone, therefore I want to go to the upper Thebaid because of the many annoyances here, and especially because they ask me things beyond my power." And the voice said to him, "Though you should go up to the Thebaid, or, as you are considering, down to the pastures, you will have greater and twice as great burden to bear. But if you wish to be really alone, go up now to the inner desert." Antony said, "And who will show me the way, for I know it not?" And at once he was shown some Saracens setting out that way. Advancing and drawing near, Antony asked to go with them into the desert, and they welcomed him as though by the command of Providence. He traveled with them three days and three nights and came to a very high hill. There was water under the hill, perfectly clear, sweet and very cold; beyond was flat land, and a few wild date-palms.

Antony, as though moved by God, fell in love with the place, for this was the place indicated by the voice that spoke to him at the river bank. At the beginning he got bread from his fellow-travelers and abode alone on the hill, none other being with him, for he kept the place from then on as one who has found again his own home. The Saracens themselves, who had seen Antony's earnestness, used to travel by that way on purpose and were glad to bring him bread; he had besides a small and frugal refreshment from the date-palms. Afterwards, when the brethren learned the place, they were careful to send to him, as children mindful of their father. But Antony, seeing that by occasion of the bread some were footsore and endured fatigue, and wishing to spare the monks in this matter also, took counsel with himself and asked some of those who visited him to bring him a pronged hoe, an axe, and some corn. When they were brought, he went over the ground about the hill, and finding a very small patch that was suitable, he tilled it and sowed it, having water in abundance from the spring. This he did every year, and had bread thence; being glad that he should trouble no one on this account, but in all things kept himself from being a burden. But later, seeing that people were coming to him again, he grew a few vegetables also, that the visitor might have some little refreshment after the weariness of that hard road. At first the beasts in the desert used to often damage his crops and his garden when they came for water, but he, catching one of the beasts, said graciously to all, "Why do you harm me when I do not harm you? Begone, and in the name of the Lord do not come near these things again." And thereafter, as though fearing his command, they did not approach the place.

He then was alone in the inner hills, devoting himself to prayer and spiritual exercise. But the brethren who ministered to him asked that they might bring him each month olives and oil, for he was now an old man.

How many wrestlings he endured while he dwelt there we have learned from those who visited him: not against flesh and blood (*Eph.* 6:12), as it is written, but against opposing demons. For there also they heard tumults and many voices and clashing as of weapons, and at night they saw the hill full of wild beasts, and him they saw fighting as with visible foes and praying against them. His visitors he comforted, but he himself fought, bending his knees and entreating the Lord. And it was indeed a thing to admire, that being alone in such a wilderness, he was neither dismayed by the attacks of devils, nor with so many four-footed and creeping things there, did he fear their savageness, but according to the Scripture (*Ps.* 124:1), he trusted the Lord truly like Mount Sion, with a mind tranquil and untossed; so that rather the devils fled, and the wild beasts kept peace with him, as it is written.

Thus the devil watched Antony and gnashed his teeth against him, as David says in the psalm (*Ps.* 111:10), while Antony had consolations from the Saviour and abode unharmed by his wickedness and his many arts. He set wild beasts on him when watching at night. Almost all the hyenas in that desert, coming out from their dens, surrounded him. He was in their midst, and each with open mouth threatened to bite him. But knowing the enemy's craft, he said to them all, "If you have received power over me, I am ready to be eaten by you, but if you are sent by devils, delay not, but go, for I am Christ's servant." On this they fled, his words chasing them like a whip.

A few days after, while he was working (for he was careful to work), someone stood at the door and pulled the string of his work, for he was weaving baskets, which he gave to his visitors in exchange for what they brought. He rose and saw a beast resembling a man as far as the thighs, but with legs and feet like a donkey. Antony simply crossed himself and said, "I am Christ's servant; if you are sent against me, here I am," and the monster with its demons fled so fast that for very speed it fell and died. And the death of the beast was the demons' fall, for they were hasting to do everything to drive him back from the desert, and they could not.

CHAPTER THIRTEEN
The Teacher of Monks

ONCE, being asked by the monks to return to them and oversee them and their dwellings from time to time, he set out with the monks who had come to meet him. A camel carried bread and water for them, for all that desert is waterless and there is no drinkable water at all except in the one hill where they had drawn, where his monastery is. On the way, the water failed, and they were all like to be in danger, the heat being extreme. For having searched around and found no water, they were now unable even to walk, but lay down on the ground and let the camel go, giving themselves up. And the old man, seeing all in danger, was very grieved, and groaning, went a little way from them and prayed, bending his knees and lifting his hands. And at once the Lord made a spring come forth there where he was praying, and so all drank and were refreshed. Filling their water-skins, they sought the camel and found it, for it happened that the rope had wrapped round a stone and so was held fast; they brought it back and watered it, and putting the skins on it, finished their journey unharmed.

When he came to the outer monasteries, all welcomed him, seeing in him a father. And he, as though he had brought with him supplies from the mount, entertained them with discourse and imparted help. So there was joy anew in the hills, eagerness to advance, and each drew courage from the faith of the rest. He too rejoiced to see the zeal of the monks and to find that his sister had grown old in her virginity and was herself a guide to other virgins.

After some days he returned to his hill. From that time many came to him, and some who were sufferers dared the journey. For all monks who came to him he always had this advice: to trust in the Lord, and love Him, to keep themselves from bad thoughts and bodily pleasures, and not to be led astray by the feasting of the stomach, (as it is written in Proverbs), to flee vainglory, to pray always, to sing psalms before sleeping and after, to repeat by heart the commandments of the Scriptures and to remember the deeds of the Saints, that by their example the soul may train itself under the guidance of the Commandments. Especially did he advise them to give continual heed to the Apostle's word: *Let not the sun go down upon your wrath*, and to consider that this was spoken about all the Commandments alike, so that the sun should not go down, not simply on our anger, but on any other sin of ours, for that it is right and necessary that the sun condemn us not for any sin by day, nor the moon for any fall or even thought by night. To safeguard this it is well to hear and observe the Apostle, for he says: *Judge yourselves and prove yourselves. (2 Cor.* 13:5). Daily then let each take account with himself of the day's and the night's doings, and if he has sinned let him cease; and if he has not, let him not boast, but abide in the good and not grow careless, nor judge his neighbor, nor justify himself, as the blessed Apostle Paul said, till the Lord come who searcheth hidden things. For often we miss seeing what we do, and we do not know, but the Lord misses nothing. To Him therefore let us leave judgment; with each other let us have sympathy and bear one another's burdens; ourselves let us judge, and where we fail be earnest to amend. For a safeguard against sinning, use this manner of observing: let us each note and write down our deeds and the movements of the soul, as if to tell them to each other, and be sure that from utter shame of being known, we shall cease from sinning and even from thinking over anything bad. For who likes to be seen when he is sinning, or having sinned, does not rather lie, wishing to hide it? Just as we should do no foulness in sight of each other, so if we write our thoughts as if telling them to each other, we shall better guard ourselves from foul thoughts, for shame of being known. Let the written tale be to us instead of the eyes of our fellow monks, that, shamed as much at writing as at being seen, we may not even think evil, and molding ourselves in this way, we shall be able to master the body, to please God and to trample on the snares of the enemy."

CHAPTER FOURTEEN
Miracles

THIS was his instruction to those who visited him: To sufferers he gave compassion and prayed with them, and often the Lord heard him in many ways. He neither boasted when he was heard, nor murmured when not, but always gave thanks to God and urged the sufferers to be patient and to know that healing belonged not to him nor to any man, but to God who doeth when He will and to whom He will. The sufferers took the old man's words in place of healing, since they had learned to suffer with patience and not with shrinking, and the cured learned not to thank Antony, but God alone.

A man named Fronton from Palatium had a terrible disease, for he was biting his tongue, and his eyes were in danger. He came to the hill and begged Antony to pray for him. When he had prayed, he said to Fronton, "Depart and you shall be healed." Fronton objected and for days stayed in the house, while Antony continued saying, "You cannot be healed while you stay here. Go, and when you reach Egypt, you shall see the sign that is wrought on you." The man believed and went, and as soon as he came in sight of Egypt, he was freed from his sickness and made well, according to the word of Antony, which he had learned from the Saviour in prayer.

A girl from Busiris in Tripoli had a dreadful and distressing sickness, a discharge from eyes, nose and ears, which turned to worms when it fell to the ground; and her body was paralyzed and her eyes unnatural. Her parents, hearing of monks who were going to Antony, and having faith in the Lord who healed the woman troubled with an issue of blood (*Matt.* 9:20), asked to accompany them with their daughter, and they consented. The parents and their child remained below the hill with Paphnutius, the confessor and monk. The others went up, but when they wished to tell about the girl, Antony interrupted them and described the child's sufferings and how they had traveled with them. On their asking that these also might come to him, he would not allow

53

it, but said, "Go, and you will find her cured if she is not dead. For this is not my work, that she should come to a wretched man like me, but healing is the Saviour's, who doeth His mercy in all places to them that call on Him. To this child also the Lord hath granted her prayer, and His love has made known to me that He will heal her sickness while she is there." So the marvel came to pass, and going out they found the parents rejoicing and the girl in sound health.

Two of the brethren were traveling to him when the water failed, and one died and the other was dying; he had no longer strength to go [on], and lay on the ground awaiting death. But Antony, sitting on the hill, called two monks who happened to be there and urged them, saying, "Take a jar of water and run down the road towards Egypt, for two were coming, and one has just died, and the other will if you do not hasten. This has just been shown me in prayer." The monks therefore went and found the one lying a corpse and buried him; the other they revived with water and brought him to the old man, for the distance was a day's journey. If anyone asks why he did not speak before the other died, he asks amiss in so speaking. For the sentence of death was not from Antony, but from God, who so decreed about the one and revealed concerning the other. In Antony this only is wonderful, that while he sat on the hill and watched in heart, the Lord revealed to him things afar.

For another time also, as he was sitting there and looking up, he saw in the air someone borne along, and great rejoicing in all that met him. Wondering at such a choir and thinking of their blessedness, he prayed to learn what this might be. And at once a voice came to him that this was the soul of the monk Amun in Nitria. He had lived as an ascetic till old age. Now the distance from Nitria to the hill where Antony was thirteen days' journey. Those who were with Antony, seeing the old man in admiration, asked to know and heard from him that Amun had just died. He was well known because he often visited there and because through him also many miracles had come to pass, of which this is one. Once, when he had need to cross the river called the Lycus, the waters being in flood, he asked his companion Theodore to keep far from him that they might not see each other naked in swimming the river. Theodore went, but he was again ashamed to see himself naked. While, therefore, he was ashamed and pondering, he was suddenly carried to the other side. Theodore, himself a devout man, came up, and seeing that Amun was first and unwetted by the water, asked to know how he had crossed. And seeing that he did not wish to speak, he seized his feet, declaring that he would not let him go till he had heard. Amun, seeing Theodore's obstinacy, especially from his speech, asked him in turn not to tell anyone till his death, and then told him that he had been carried across and set down on the other side, that he had not walked on the water, and that this was a thing not possible to men, but only to the Lord and those to whom He granted it, as He did to the great Apostle Peter. (*Matt.* 14:29). And Theodore told this after Amun's death.

Now the monks to whom Antony spoke of Amun's death noted the day, and when, thirty days later, the brethren came from Nitria, they inquired and found that Amun had fallen asleep at the day and hour when the old man saw his soul carried up. And both these and the others were all amazed how pure was the soul of Antony, that he should learn at once what happened thirteen days away and should see the soul in its flight.

Again, Archelaus the Count once met him in the outer hills and asked him only to pray for Polycratia, the renowned and Christ-like virgin of Laodicea, for she was suffering much in her stomach and side, through her great mortifications, and was weak throughout her body. Antony therefore prayed, and the Count made a note of the day when the prayer was made, and departing to Laodicea, found the virgin well. Asking when and on what day she was freed from her sickness, he brought out the paper on which he had written the time of the prayer; and when he heard, he immediately showed the writing on the paper, and all recognized with wonder that the Lord had freed her from her pains at the moment when Antony was praying and invoking the goodness of the Saviour on her behalf.

Often he spoke days beforehand of those who were coming to him, and sometimes a month before, and of the cause for which they came. For some came simply to see him, some through sickness, some suffering from devils. And all thought the toil of the journey no trouble or loss, for each returned feeling helped. Antony, while he said and saw such things, begged that none should admire him in this regard, but rather should admire the Lord, who grants to us men to know Him in our own measure.

Another time, when he had gone down to the outer monasteries and was asked to enter a ship and pray with the monks, he alone perceived a horrible, pungent smell. The crew said that there was fish and pickled meat in the boat and that the smell was from them, but he said it was different; and even as he spoke, came a sudden shriek from a young man having a devil, who had come on board earlier and was hiding in the vessel. Being charged in the name of our Lord Jesus Christ, the devil went out, and the man was made whole, and all knew that the foul smell was from the evil spirit.

Another came to him, one of the nobles, having a devil. This demon was so dreadful that the possessed man did not know he was going to Antony; also he used to eat the filth of his own body. Those who brought him begged Antony to pray for him, and Antony, pitying the youth, prayed and watched the whole night with him. Towards dawn, the youth suddenly sprang on Antony, pushing him. His friends were indignant, but Antony said, "Do not be angry with the youth; it is not he, but the demon in him, for being rebuked and commanded to depart into waterless places, he became furious and has done this. Therefore, glorify God, for his attacking me in this way is a sign to you of the demon's going." And when Antony had said this, the youth was at once made whole and then, in his right mind, recognized where he was and embraced the old man, thanking God.

CHAPTER FIFTEEN
Visions

MANY other such things are related by numbers of monks to have been done through him, and their stories agree. Yet these are not so marvelous as the greater wonders that he saw. Once when he was about to eat and stood up to pray, about the ninth hour, he felt himself carried away in spirit; and, a thing strange, as he stood, he saw himself as though out of himself and being guided by others through the air, also foul and terrible beings stationed in the air and seeking to hinder his passage. As his guides resisted, the others demanded a reckoning, if he were not liable to them. But when they would have taken an account from his birth, Antony's guides stopped them, saying, "All from the time of his birth the Lord has wiped out, but from the time he became a monk and promised himself to God, you can take account." Then, as they accused him but proved nothing, the path became free and unhindered for him, and he saw himself approaching and reentering himself, and so once more he was Antony. Then, forgetting to eat, he remained the rest of the day and all the night groaning and praying. For he was in amazement to see how many we fight against and with what great labors we have to pass through the air, and he remembered that this is what the Apostle said: *According to the ruler of the power of the air.* (Cf. *Eph.* 2:2). For herein has the enemy his power, in fighting and trying to stop those who pass through. For which cause he specially exhorted us: *Take ye up the armor of God that ye may be able to withstand in the evil day* (*Eph.* 6:13), *that having no ill to say about us* (*Titus* 2:8), the enemy may be put to shame. And let us who have learned this remember the Apostle's words: *Whether in the body I know not, or out of the body, I know not; God knoweth.* (*2 Cor.* 12:2). But Paul was rapt to the third heaven and heard words unspeakable, and returned; whereas Antony saw himself entering the air and struggling till he was proved free.

Another favor he had from God. When he sat alone in the

mountain, if ever he looked into any matter with himself and could not see his way, it was revealed to him by Providence in prayer. He was one of the blessed who are taught of God (*John* 6:45), as it is written. So later, when he had had a discussion with some visitors about the life of the soul and the kind of place it will have hereafter, in the following night one called him from above, saying, "Antony, rise and go out and look." He went out (for he knew which voices to obey) and looking up saw a great figure, formless and terrible, standing and reaching to the clouds, and people going up as if on wings. And the figure was stretching out his hands, and some he stopped, and others flew above and, passing by him, rose without trouble thereafter. At these he gnashed his teeth, but exulted over those who fell. Then a voice came to Antony, "Understand the vision." And his mind being opened, he understood that it was the passing of souls and that the great figure standing was the enemy who hates the faithful. Those who are in his power he seizes and stops them from passing, but those who have not yielded to him he cannot seize, but they pass him by. Having seen this, he took it as a reminder, and strove the more to advance forward each day.

He did not willingly relate these things to others. But when he had long prayed and admired them in his own heart and his companions questioned and pressed him, he was forced to speak, being unable, as a father, to hide these things from his children, thinking also that while his own conscience was clear, the telling might be a help to them, teaching that the religious life bears good fruit and that often there is comfort for its hardships in its visions.

BOOK FOUR

Antony's Last Years

———————•———————

CHAPTER SIXTEEN
His Devotion to God's Church

ANTONY was by disposition long suffering and humble of soul. Being what he was, he yet reverenced the law of the Church exceedingly, and he would have every cleric honored above himself. He was not ashamed to bow his head before bishops and priests, and if ever a deacon came to him to seek help, he spoke what was needed to help him, but in regard to prayers he gave place to him, thinking it no shame that he too should be taught. For often he would ask questions and beg to hear his companions and acknowledge that he was helped if one said something useful. His face had a grace in it great and beyond belief. And he had this further gift from the Saviour: if he was with a company of monks and someone wished to see him who did not know him before, as soon as he arrived, he would pass over the others and run straight to Antony as if drawn by his eyes. Not by appearance or figure was he different from others, but by his ordered character and the purity of his soul. For his soul being at peace, he had his outer senses also untroubled, so that from the joy of the soul his face also was joyous, and from the body's movements one saw and knew the state of his soul, according to the Scripture: *When the heart is merry, the face is glad; when in grief, the face is gloomy. (Prov.* 15:13). So Jacob knew that Laban was devising a plot and said to his wives: *Your father's countenance is not as yesterday and the day before. (Gen.* 31:5). So Samuel knew David, for he had eyes that moved joy and teeth white as milk (cf. *1 Kgs.* 16:12). And so too was Antony known, for he was never troubled, his soul being tranquil; he was never gloomy, his mind being glad.

To the Faith his devotion was wonderful. He never held communion with the Meletian schismatics, knowing their wickedness and rebellion from the beginning, nor had friendly converse with the Manichees, nor any other heretics, save only to warn them to return to their duty, believing and teaching that their friendship and society was a harm and ruin to the soul. So also he loathed the Arian heresy and taught all neither to go near them nor partake in their ill-faith. Once when some of the Ariomanites came to him and he questioned them and found them misbelievers, he drove them from the hill, saying that their words were worse than the poison of serpents.

Again when the Arians lied about him, that he believed as they, he was grieved and angry with them. Then, urged by the bishops and all the other brethren, he came down from the hill, and entering Alexandria, denounced the Arians, saying this was the last heresy and the forerunner of Antichrist. And he taught the people that the Son of God is not a creature, neither is He begotten out of nothingness, but that He is the eternal Word and Wisdom of the Father's being. "Therefore, it is impious to say there was a time when He was not; for the Word was always co-existing with the Father. Wherefore, do ye have no fellowship at all with these most impious Arians, *for there is no fellowship of light with darkness.* (Cf. *2 Cor.* 6:14). For you are devout Christians, but these who say that the Son and Wisdom of God the Father is a creature differ nothing from Gentiles, worshipping the creature before God the Creator. Be ye sure that the whole creation is aroused against these men, because they count among creatures the Creator and Lord of all, in whom all things were made."

The people all rejoiced to hear so great a man anathematize the heresy which attacks Christ. And all the citizens ran together to see Antony. Greeks, too, and even their so-called priests came to the church, saying, "We ask to see the man of God for so all called him. For there also the Lord through him cleansed many from demons and healed the mad. Many Greeks asked only to touch the old man, believing they should be helped. Naturally, in those few days as many became Christians as else one would have seen in a year. Some thought that he was annoyed by the crowds, and therefore were keeping the people from him, but he, untroubled, answered, "These are no more numerous than the demons with whom we wrestle in the hills."

When he was leaving[1] and we were setting him on his way, a woman from behind shouted, "Wait, man of God, my daughter is grievously troubled with a devil; wait, I beseech, lest I hurt myself running." The old man hearing and being asked by us, waited willingly. When the woman drew near, the child was hurled to the ground. Antony prayed and spoke the name of Christ, and the child rose up healed, the unclean spirit being gone out of her. The mother blessed God, and all gave thanks. And he too rejoiced, departing to the hill as to his own home.

CHAPTER SEVENTEEN
The Gift of Understanding

HE WAS extremely prudent. The wonderful thing was that, not having learned letters, he was yet a quick-witted and clever man. Once two Greek philosophers came to him, thinking that they could

---

1. Socrates of Constantinople, *Hist.* IV, c. 25, relates an incident of this journey: It is said that earlier Antony had met this Didymus in the time of Valens, when he went down to Alexandria from the desert because of the Arians, and that finding the intelligence of the man he said to him, "Let not the loss of your bodily eyes trouble you, Didymus; for the eyes that are failing you are only such as flies and gnats also can see with. But rejoice that you have the eyes wherewith angels see, by which God is seen, and His light is received."

experiment on Antony. He was then in the outer hills. But understanding the men from their looks, he went out to them and said through an interpreter, "Why, O philosophers, have you toiled all this way to a foolish man?" And when they answered that he was not foolish, but very wise, he said to them, "If you have come to a fool, your labor is useless; but if you think me wise, then become as I, for we ought to imitate what is good. If I had gone to you, I would have imitated you; as you have come to me, become as I, for I am a Christian." They departed in wonder, for they saw that even demons feared Antony.

Some others of the same kind met him again in the outer hills and thought to mock him because he had not learned letters. Antony said to them, "And what say you, which is first, the mind or letters? And which is the cause of which, the mind of letters, or letters of the mind?" When they answered that the mind is first and is the inventor of letters, Antony said, "Then to one whose mind is sound, letters are needless." This answer astounded both them and the listeners. They went away marveling to see such wisdom in a plain man.[2] For he had not the rough character of one who is reared in the hills and grows old there, but he was both gracious and courteous. His speech was seasoned with the wisdom of God, so that none had against him, but rather, all rejoiced on his account who went to see him.

Later, some others came. They were of those who among the Greeks seem to be wise. When they asked from him an account of our faith in Christ and tried to argue about the preaching of the Cross of God and wished to scoff, Antony waited for a little, and first pitying them for their ignorance, said through an interpreter (who could render his words excellently), "Which is nobler: to confess the Cross, or to attribute adulteries and impurities to those who among you are called

---

2. One of the philosophers came to the holy Antony and said, "Father, how do you keep up without the comfort of books?" And Antony said, "My book is nature, and whenever I will, I can read the words of God." (Socrates of Constantinople, *Hist.* IV, c. 23.).

gods? For to say what we say is a sign of manly courage, a proof of contempt of death, but yours is a yielding to lewdness. Next, which is better: to say that the Word of God was not changed, but remaining the
same, took to him a human body to save and help men, in order that,
sharing our human birth, he might make men sharers of the divine and
spiritual nature, or to liken the divine to senseless things, and for that
cause to worship beasts and serpents and images of men? For these are
the things worshipped by you who are wise. And how do you dare to
scoff at our saying that Christ has appeared as man, when you make
the soul come from Heaven, saying that it had strayed and fell from
the vault of Heaven into the body?—and would that it were only into
the body of man, and not shared with beasts and serpents. Our faith
declares the coming of Christ to save men, but you talk amiss of the
soul unbegotten. We believe the power of Providence and His love of
men, that this also is not impossible with God; but you, calling the soul
an image of the spirit, impute falls to it and make fables of how it can
be changed. And now through the soul you are making the spirit too a
thing changeable. For as was the image, so needs must be that of which
it is the image. And when you thus deem about the spirit, bear in mind
that you are blaspheming also the Father of the Spirit.

"And touching the Cross, which would you say is better: when
plotted against by wicked men to endure the Cross and not shrink
from any manner of death whatever, or to tell tales of the wanderings
of Osiris and Isis, and the plots of Typhon, and the flight of Kronos,
and swallowings of children and slaying of fathers? For this among you
is wisdom. And if you mock at the Cross, why do you not marvel at the
Resurrection? For those who tell of the one wrote the other, too. Or
why, when you remember the Cross, do you say nothing of the dead
who were raised, the blind who saw, the paralytics who were cured and
the lepers made clean, the walking on the sea and the other signs and
wonders which show Christ, not as man, but as God? To me it seems
that you are utterly unfair to yourselves and that you have not honestly
read our Scriptures. But do you read them and see that the things which

Christ did prove Him to be God dwelling with us for men's salvation.

"But do you also tell us your own teachings. Though what could you say about brute things except brutishness and savagery? But if, as I hear, you wish to say that these things are spoken among you in figure, and you make the rape of Persephone an allegory of the earth and Hephaestus of the fire, and Hera of the air, and Apollo of the sun, and Artemis of the moon, and Poseidon of the sea; nonetheless, you are again worshipping that which is no god; you are serving the creature instead of the God who created all. For if you have made up these tales because of the loveliness of the world, you are right to go as far as admiring it, but not to make gods of creatures, lest you give to things made, the honor of the Maker. In that case, it is time you should hand over the architect's honor to the house he has built, or the general's honor to the soldier. Now, what do you say to all this?—that we may see if the Cross has anything that deserves to be scoffed at."

As they were quite at a loss, turning this way and that, Antony smiled and said again through the interpreter, "All this is clear even at first sight. But since you lean rather on proofs and arguments and because you have this art, you want us also not to worship God without reasoned proofs. Do you first tell me this: How comes sure knowing of things, and especially knowledge about God? Is it through reasoned proof, or through a faith which acts; and which is the earlier, the faith that acts, or proof by reasoning?" And when they answered that the faith that acts comes earlier, and that this is the sure knowledge, Antony said, "You say well, for that faith comes from the very build of the soul, but the art of logic from the skill of those who framed it. It follows that, to those who have an active belief, reasoned proofs are needless and probably useless. For what we know by faith, that you are trying to establish by argument. And often you cannot even put in words what we know, so that the action of faith is better and surer than your sophist's proofs.

"Now, we Christians hold not our secret in the wisdom of Greek reasonings, but in the power of a faith which is added to us by God through Christ Jesus. For proof that this is a true account, look how without learning letters we believe in God, knowing from His works, His providence over all things. And for our faith being a force which acts, look how we lean on the belief in Christ; whereas you lean on sophistical debates, and yet your monstrous idols are coming to naught, while our faith is spreading everywhere. And you with your syllogisms and sophisms do not draw any from Christianity to Hellenism; we, teaching faith in Christ, despoil your superstition, for all are learning that Christ is God and the Son of God. You with all your beauty of speech do not stop the teaching of Christ, but we by naming Christ crucified drive away all the demons whom you fear as gods. And where the Sign of the Cross comes, magic fails and poisons do not work.

"For tell me, where are now your oracles, where the incantations of the Egyptians, where the phantoms of magicians? When did all these cease and fail, but at the coming of the Cross of Christ? And is it the Cross then that deserves scorn, and not rather the things which by it have been made void and proved powerless? For this is another wonderful thing, that your teaching was never persecuted, but was honored by cities publicly, while the Christians are persecuted, and yet it is we and not you that flourish and grow. Your teachings, praised on all sides, guarded on all sides, perish; while the faith and teaching of Christ, mocked by you and persecuted by kings, has filled the world. For when did the knowledge of God so shine out? When did chastity and the virtue of virginity so show itself, or when was death so scorned as since the Cross of Christ came? And this none doubts who looks at the martyrs scorning death for Christ's sake, or looks at the virgins of the Church, who for Christ's sake keep their bodies pure and undefiled.

"These are sufficient proofs to show that for serving God, faith in Christ is the only true faith. Even now, behold, you who seek conclusions from reasonings, you have no faith. But we do not prove, as our teacher said, in persuasive words of Greek wisdom; we win men by faith, which lays hold of real things before argument can logically establish them (cf. *1 Cor.* 2:4). See, there are some standing here suffering from demons (they were people who had come to him beset by demons, and bringing them into the midst he said): Either do you make them clean by your syllogisms and by any art or magic you wish, calling on your idols, or if you cannot, then cease attacking us, and see the power of the Cross of Christ?" Having said this, he invoked Christ, and signed the sufferers with the Sign of the Cross twice and thrice. And at once the men stood up, whole now and in their right mind and blessing God. And the so-called philosophers were astonished and really stupefied at his wisdom and at the miracle that was done. But Antony said, "Why do you wonder over this? It is not we that do it, but Christ, who does these things through those who believe in Him. Believe, then, you also; and you will see that what we have is not tricks of words, but belief through a love that is active unto Christ, which if you also have, you will no longer seek proofs by reasonings, but will think faith in Christ sufficient by itself."

This was Antony's discourse. The men wondered at it and departed embracing him and acknowledging that they had been helped.

CHAPTER EIGHTEEN
The Arian Persecution

THE renown of Antony reached even to kings. For on hearing of these things, Constantine Augustus and his sons, Constantius Augustus and Constans Augustus, wrote to him as to a father and begged to receive answers from him. He, however, did not value these writings nor rejoice over the letters, but was just what he had been before the kings wrote to him. When the letters were brought to him, he called the monks and said, "Do not admire if a king writes to us, for he is a man, but admire rather that God has written the law for men, and has spoken to us by His own Son." He wished not to receive the letters, saying that he knew not what to answer to such. But being urged by the monks because the kings were Christians and they might be scandalized as though he made them outcasts, he allowed them to be read. And he wrote back, welcoming them because they worshiped Christ, and advised them, for their salvation, not to think much of things present, but rather to remember the coming judgment, and to know that the only true and eternal king is Christ. He begged them also to be lovers of men, to care for justice and to care for the poor. And they were glad to get his letter. So was he beloved by all, and so did all wish to hold him as a father.

With this character, and thus answering those who sought him, he returned again to the mount in the interior and continued his usual life. Often when sitting or walking with visitors he would become dumb, as it is written in Daniel. (Cf. *Dan.* 10:15). After a time he would resume his former discourse with the brethren, but they perceived that he was seeing some vision. For often in the mountain he saw things happening in Egypt, and described them to the Bishop Serapion, who was within and saw Antony occupied with the vision. Once as he sat working, he became as in ecstasy, and in the vision he groaned constantly. Then after a time he turned to his companions groaning; and trembling, he prayed, bending his knees and abiding a long time; and when he arose, the old man was weeping. Then the others trembled and were much afraid and begged him to tell, and long they urged him till he was compelled to speak. Then with a great groan he said, "Ah, my children, better is it to die than that there happen what I have seen in this vision." And when they asked again, he said with tears, "Wrath shall overtake the Church, and she shall be delivered up to men who are like to senseless beasts. For I saw the table of the Lord, and around it mules standing on all sides in a ring and kicking what was within, as might be the kicking of beasts in a wild frolic. You heard surely," he said, "how I was groaning, for I heard a voice saying, 'My altar shall be made an abomination.'"

So the old man said, and two years after came this present onset of the Arians and the plundering of the churches, wherein, seizing by force the vessels, they had them carried away by pagans; when, too, they forced the pagans from the workshops to their meetings and in their presence did what they would on the sacred table. Then we all understood that the kicking of the mules had foreshown to Antony what the Arians are now doing, brutishly as beasts. When he saw this vision, he comforted his companions, saying, "Do not lose heart, children, for as the Lord has been angry, so later will He bring healing. And the Church shall quickly regain her own beauty and shine as before. And you shall see the persecuted restored and impiety retiring to its own hiding places and the True Faith in all places speaking openly with all freedom. Only, defile not yourselves with the Arians. For this teaching is not of the Apostles, but of the demons and their father the devil; and indeed from no source, from no sense, from a mind not right it comes, like the senselessness of mules."

CHAPTER NINETEEN
His Spiritual Influence

SUCH was the life of Antony. We must not disbelieve when all these wonders are wrought through a man. For it is the promise of the Saviour, who said: *If you have faith as a grain of mustard seed, you shall say to this mountain, Depart hence, and it shall depart; and nothing shall be impossible to you.* (*Matt.* 17:19). And again: *Amen, amen I say to you, if you ask the Father anything in my name he will give it to you. Ask and you shall receive.* (*John* 16:23, 24). And it is He who said to His disciples and to all that believe in Him: *Heal the sick; cast out devils; freely you have received, freely give.* (*Matt.* 10:8).

Antony healed, therefore, not as one commanding, but praying and using the name of Christ, so that it was plain to all that the doer was not he, but the Lord, who through Antony showed His tenderness for men and healed the sufferers. Only the prayer was Antony's, and the ascetic life for the sake of which he had settled on the mountain, glad in the contemplation of heavenly things, grieved that so many disturbed him and dragged him down to the outer hills. For the judges all wanted him to come down from the mount, since it was impossible for them to go there because of the pleaders who followed them. But they asked him to go that they might only see him. He disliked and declined the journey to them. But they would hold their ground and send the prisoners up to him with soldiers, that by reason of these, he might perhaps come down. So being constrained and seeing them lamenting, he used to go to the outer hills, and his toil was not wasted, for to many he was a help and his coming a benefit. He helped the judges, counseling them to value justice above all else and to fear God and to know that with what judgment they judge, with such shall they be judged. (*Matt.* 7:2). Yet he loved his abode in the hills above all other.

Once when he was thus constrained by those in need, and the officer of the soldiers had begged him by many messengers to come down, he went and discoursed a little on matters of salvation and on their own needs, and then was hastening back. On the captain asking him to stay longer, he answered that he could not be long with them and satisfied him by a beautiful comparison, saying, "As fish that are long on dry land die, so monks who linger among you and spend much time with you grow lax. Therefore, we have to hasten to the hills as the fish to the sea, lest if we linger, we should forget the inner life." The officer who heard this and much more from him said in admiration that surely this was a servant of God, for whence came wisdom so high and so great to a mere man, unless he were beloved of God?

There was one officer, named Balakios, who sharply persecuted us Christians in his zeal for the abominable Arians. Since he was so cruel as to beat virgins and strip and flog monks, Antony sent to him and wrote a letter to this intent: "I see wrath approaching you; cease, therefore, persecuting Christians, lest the wrath overtake you, for even now it is nigh upon you." Balakios, laughing, threw the letter on the ground and spat on it, and insulting the bearers, told them to take this message back to Antony: "Since you are anxious about the monks, I will now pay you a visit also." And five days had not passed when the wrath overtook him. For Balakios and Nestorius, the prefect of Egypt, went out to the halting place of Chaireos, the first from Alexandria; and they were both riding on horses. These belonged to Balakios, the quietest he had. But before they reached the place, they began to play with each other, as horses do, and suddenly the quieter of the two, on which was Nestorius, biting Balakios, threw him down and fell upon him, and so tore his thigh with its teeth that he was carried back to the city at once and died in three days. And all men marveled how what Antony had foretold was quickly fulfilled.

In such wise did he warn the cruel. But others who came to him he brought to such a mind that they forgot straightway their disputes at law and esteemed those blessed who withdraw from the world. But if any were wronged, he so defended them that one would think that he himself, and not other persons, had been wronged. He had such influence for good over all, that many who were soldiers and many of the wealthy laid aside the burdens of their life and became monks. He was, in fact, like a healer given to Egypt by God. For who went to him in sorrow and did not return in joy? Who came mourning for his dead and did not quickly put aside his grief? Who came in anger and was not changed to kindness? Who sought him desperate in his poverty, and hearing him and seeing him, did not learn to despise wealth and take comfort from poverty? What monk grown careless but became stronger from visiting him? What youth ever came to the mount and looked on Antony but soon renounced pleasure and loved self-denial? Who came to him tempted by devils and was not freed? Who came with troublous thoughts and gained not peace of mind?

For this was another great thing in Antony's holiness, that having, as I have said, the grace of discerning spirits, he knew their movements and was not ignorant to what object each of them leans and impels. And not only was he himself not befooled by them, but others who were beset in their thoughts he taught how they might defeat their snares, explaining the weakness and the wickedness of the tempters. Each, therefore, as though anointed by him for the fight, went down emboldened against all the contrivings of the devil and his demons.

Again, how many maidens who had suitors, seeing Antony only from afar, remained virgins for Christ? From foreign lands, too, men came to him, and having received help with the rest, returned as if sent forth by their father. And since he died, all are like fatherless orphans, comforting each other with the bare memory of him, and cherishing his teachings and his counsels.

CHAPTER TWENTY
His Death

THE manner of the end of his life I ought also to tell, and you to hear eagerly, for this also is a pattern to imitate. He was visiting as usual the monks in the outer hills, and learning of his end from Providence, he spoke to the brethren saying, "This is the last visiting of you that I shall make, and I wonder if we shall see each other again in this life. It is time now for me to be dissolved, for I am near a hundred and five years." Hearing this, they wept, clasping and embracing the old man. But he talked joyously, as one leaving a foreign town to go to his own, and bade them "not to fail in their labors nor lose heart in their strict life, but live as dying daily; and, as I have said before, to be earnest to guard the heart from unclean thoughts; to vie with the holy; not to go near the Meletian schismatics, for you know their wicked and profane heresy; nor to have any fellowship with the Arians, for the impiety of these is plain to all. Be not troubled if you see judges protecting them, for their triumph will end; it is mortal and short-lived. Therefore, do ye keep yourselves clean from these and guard the tradition of the Fathers, and above all the loving faith in our Lord Jesus Christ, which you have learned from the Scriptures and have often been put in mind of by me."

When the brethren pressed him to stay with them and die there, he would not for many reasons, as he implied without saying, but on this account chiefly: To the bodies of religious men, especially of the holy martyrs, the Egyptians like to give funeral honors and wrap them in fine linens, but not to bury them in the earth, but to place them on couches and keep them at home with them, thinking by this to honor the departed. Antony often asked the bishops to tell the people about this, and likewise shamed laymen and reproved women, saying it was not right nor even reverent, for that the bodies of the patriarchs and prophets are preserved even till now in tombs, and the very body of Our Lord was put in a sepulchre and a stone set against it hid it till He rose the third day. He said this to show that he does wrong who after death does not bury the bodies of the dead, holy though they be. For what is greater or holier than the Lord's body? Many, therefore, hearing him, buried thenceforward in the ground and thanked God that they had the right teaching.

Now knowing this, and fearing lest they might so treat his body also, Antony hastened and took leave of the monks in the outer hills, and returning to the inner hills where he was used to dwell, he fell sick after a few months. He called those who were there (they were two who lived in the house, who had been fifteen years in the religious life, and ministered to him because of his great age) and said to them: "I am going the way of my fathers, as the Scripture says (cf. *Josue* 23:14), for I see myself called by the Lord. Be you wary and undo not your long service of God, but be earnest to keep your strong purpose, as though you were but now beginning. You know the demons who plot against you, you know how savage they are and how powerless; therefore, fear them not. Let Christ be as the breath you breathe; in Him put your trust. Live as dying daily, heeding yourselves and remembering the counsels you have heard from me. And let there be no communion between you and the schismatics, nor the heretical Arians. For you know how I also have avoided them for their false and anti-Christian heresy. So do you also be earnest always to be in union first with the Lord and then with the Saints, that after death, they also may receive you into everlasting tabernacles as known friends. Ponder these things, and mean them. And if you have any care for me, and remember me as your father, do not allow anyone to take my body to Egypt, lest they should deposit it in houses, for that is the reason why I entered the mountains and came here. And you know how I have always reproached those who do this and bade them stop the practice. Therefore, care for my body yourselves and bury it in the earth, and let my words be so observed by you that no one shall know the place but yourselves only. For in the Resurrection of the dead I shall receive it back from the Saviour incorruptible. Distribute my garments; the one sheepskin give to Athanasius the bishop, and the cloak I used to lie on, which he gave me new, but it has worn out with me; and the other sheepskin give to Serapion the bishop, and do you have the hair-cloth garment. And now God save you, children, for Antony departs and is with you no more."

Having said this and been embraced by them, he drew up his feet; then gazing as it seemed on friends who came for him, and filled by them with joy, for his countenance glowed as he lay, he died and was taken to his fathers. Then they, as he had given them orders, cared for his body and wrapped it up and buried it there in the earth, and no man yet knows where it is laid save only those two. And they who received the sheepskins of the blessed Antony and the cloak that he wore out, each guard them as some great treasure. For to look on them is like looking on Antony, and to wear them is like joyfully taking on us his teachings.

This is the end of Antony's life in the body, as that was the beginning of his religious life. And if this is but little to tell of such virtue as his, yet from this little do you judge what manner of man was Antony, the man of God, who from youth to such great age held unchanged his keen quest of a better life, who never for old age yielded to the desire of varied meats, nor for failing strength of body changed his form of dress nor even bathed his feet with water. And yet in all respects he was to the end untouched by decay. He saw well, his eyes being sound and undimmed; and of his teeth he had not lost one, only they were worn near the gums, through the old man's great age. In feet and hands, too, he was quite healthy, and altogether he seemed brighter and more active than all those who use rich diet and baths and many clothes.

That he was everywhere spoken of and by all admired and sought even by those who had not seen him—these things are proof of his virtue and of a soul dear to God. For Antony was known not for his writings, nor for worldly wisdom, nor for any art, but simply for his service of God. That this is God's gift none could deny. For how was he heard of even to Spain and to Gaul, to Rome and to Africa, he sitting hidden in the hills, unless it were God who everywhere makes known His own people, who also had in the beginning announced this to Antony? For though they themselves act in secret and wish to be unnoticed, yet the Lord shows them as lanterns to all, that even from this the hearers may know that the Commandments are able to be fulfilled, and so may take courage on the path of virtue.

Now, therefore, read this to the other brethren, that they may learn what should be the life of monks and may believe that our Lord and Saviour Jesus Christ glorifies them that glorify Him, and not only brings to the kingdom of Heaven those who serve Him to the end, but even here (though they hide themselves and seek retirement) He makes them everywhere known and spoken of for their own goodness and for the helping of others. And if need arise, read it also to the pagans, that perhaps thus they may learn not only that Our Lord Jesus Christ is God and the Son of God, but also that through Him the Christians, who serve Him sincerely and who piously trust in Him, not only prove that the demons whom the Greeks think gods are no gods, but trample on them and drive them out as deceivers and corrupters of men, through Christ Jesus our Lord, to whom is glory for ages of ages. Amen.

THE HOLY RULE OF
SAINT BENEDICT

————•————

Edited by William Edmund Fahey, Ph.D.

THE HOLY RULE OF SAINT BENEDICT

PREFACE TO THE HOLY RULE OF SAINT BENEDICT

LIGHT ON THE MOUNTAIN— THE LAST ROMAN FATHER AND THE BIRTH OF CATHOLIC EUROPE

By William Edmund Fahey, Ph.D.

———————•———————

There was a man of venerable life, who was blessed in both grace and name. From his boyhood, he had the heart of a mature man. In his way of life he outstripped his years for he would not give himself over to sensual pleasure. On earth he could have indulged himself with liberty, but he looked dimly upon the glory of this world and did not desire its vanities.

Born in the region of Nursia to honorable parents, he was sent to Rome for an education in the humanities. Yet when he saw how many—though thoroughly educated— were leaping into a lewd life, he held back his foot, which was just beginning to cross the threshold of this world. He was duly afraid that worldly learning would trip him up and cast him into the godless abyss. So, he set aside his studies, forsook his father's house and inheritance, and desired to please God alone. . . . Thus, he left Rome schooled with learned ignorance and nourished by an unlearned wisdom.

So opens our near contemporary account of the life of St. Benedict. The majority opinion is that this biography was penned half a century after the death of Benedict by Pope St. Gregory the Great, himself a Benedictine. That account, or "life of Benedict," can be found in the second book of Gregory's *Dialogues*, a long, conversational narrative in which the lives of many Italian holy men were set down. Although the second book is often isolated and reprinted as if a Vita or Biography, students should be aware that the narrative of Benedict's life was part of a larger story in the work. St. Gregory had access to records and personal accounts of Benedict left by his disciples: indeed, Gregory interviewed four of St. Benedict's original disciples before retelling the saint's life. Prior to Gregory's account, there is only a short hymn to St. Benedict. Students must keep in mind that St. Gregory's account is not a modern biography, but, rather like a textual icon, an image of a man who succeeded in imitating Christ.

The details of this "life" reveal a man making a transition from the monastic spirit of the East to something new, Roman, and Western. St. Benedict is held to have been born about 480. His family was wealthy, free, and perhaps noble. The education to which he had access and small details known about his social circle point to an aristocratic background, but secular Rome—even the inspirational idea of Rome as the center of life and culture, *Roma aeterna*—was not to be the center of Benedict's life.

The young Benedict left his liberal studies for an education in the Abruzzi mountains, some fifty miles from Rome, and with him came a loyal nurse or household slave. Benedict lived in loose communion with a group of men residing at a church dedicated to St. Peter. Here may be seen the origins of the long-standing tradition which has tied the Benedictines with the See of Peter. Soon after his time with this community, Benedict moved ten miles further to the highlands near

Subiaco, where he lived close to the ruins of a villa of Nero. In a small cave, above a lake, Benedict dwelt in solitude, but not out of communion. He placed himself under the direction of Romanus of Subiaco, a monk from a nearby community directed by the Abbot Adeodatus. Though receiving only brief attention in the narrative of St. Gregory, this phase of life may account for Benedict's sober assessment of the various forms of monasticism, found in the first chapter of his *Rule*—the anchorite (who largely lives alone, in the eastern fashion); the Sarabaites (who live in small groups without clear laws or direction); the gyrovagues (who live a vagabond life and are ruled largely by passionate impulses); and the cenobites (who live in community under the dual authority of a rule and an abbot). To varying degrees, Benedict learned by trial, error, and observation what each life meant. *Experience*, therefore, not theoretical knowledge, lies at the heart of Benedictine monasticism. In the end, his hard-won experience pointed him and others over the centuries towards the life of the cenobites as the most fruitful and realistic form of monasticism for most ordinary men and women.

Although St. Benedict lived for three years in the cave (*Sacro Speco*) near Subiaco, his solitude did not prevent men from learning about his character and holiness. He was approached by a small neighboring community and pressed to be its spiritual director. From Gregory's description, this community sounds like what Benedict would term Sarabaites. They soon grew to detest Benedict's desire for consistent rules and authority. In the end, they attempted to poison him and, having failed, traded the father of western monasticism for the rule of individual whim. Benedict returned to the region of Subiaco, where he continued in his own prayer life and contemplation, and the journey towards greater self-mastery. Gregory's "life" concentrates on Benedict's interior life, but reveals that he not only remained in communion, but established twelve monastic communities. The greatest was Monte Cassino, eighty miles south-east of Rome. Here, in the ruins of a temple dedicated to Apollo, Benedict established another community. This site, if not always the locus of this early confederation under the direction of St. Benedict, quickly became a center of spiritual authority, the kind of power with which secular leaders in the world have ever been fascinated. It was here that Benedict was visited by Totila, the masterful king of the Ostrogoths. It was here that Benedict died in 543. At his death, a strong network living under a single rule had been established and the ideals of western monasticism indelibly pressed upon the soul of Europe. What is more, it is here that the birth of a culture formed by Christian principles was given a tone on structure to endure through the centuries. Indeed, it is not an overstatement to say that the *Regula Sancti Benedicti*—the rule of St. Benedict—was a founding document for Christendom, second only to Sacred Scripture for its influence on individuals and institutions during the middle ages.

Readers of the *Rule* should keep in mind several features found in the "life" of St. Benedict by Gregory the Great. First, we find a man who learns and acts upon experience, not literary or even theological knowledge. Although the text of the *Rule* is enlivened by Sacred Scripture and the writings of the Fathers, what may go unnoticed is the experience of a spiritual master so clearly born into the Roman world of laws and traditions. Benedict's Roman heritage added a particular structure to his thoughts and encouraged him to articulate the spiritual life in a specific way: with constant reference to tested Roman concepts of law, family, fatherhood, love of community, and the military life. Second, miracles abound in Gregory's *Dialogue*, but most miracles are either directly parallel to those of Christ or deal with utterly ordinary things—pots, pans, tools, food, and very common temptations of men and women. So too, the *Rule* is marked by an attention to detail in the most ordinary things. Indeed, the ordinary is elevated and made the sublime arena of the spiritual struggle: no desert or mountain or ruined temple is envisioned, only the everyday life of work and prayer and human needs. Yet the grand drama found in both the "life" and the *Rule* is the drama of the human will and how the human will can and must be subordinated to the will of God the Father for abiding human happiness and true progress to be made.

The *Regula* or *Rule* is the only work St. Benedict left for posterity. It is a singular gift: it is, of course, a written document—a kind of constitution, and yet behind the spare word is the imprint of Benedict's whole *way of living* and his manner of understanding and upholding a way of life that forged a union between the Roman and the Christian. The *Rule* is Benedict's union of contemplation and action. It is arguably western Christendom's most glorious example of one man's imitation of his master—Christ—and that imitation leading to a complete incarnation. For Benedict, to follow a monastic *regula* was to imitate Christ through the simple subordination of the will to legitimate Christian authority—the authority found in words and in a person; one must never lose sight that the *Rule* is an imitation of Christ, the Word.

A *regula*, or rule, for Benedict is made up of a systematic gathering of "precepts"—as he calls them in the prologue. Here he borrows heavily from the wisdom literature of the Old Testament, such as Proverbs and Ecclesiastes and elsewhere, aimed at the education of youth: "He that instructeth his son shall be praised in him, and shall glory in him in the midst of them of his household. He that teacheth his son, maketh his enemy jealous, and in the midst of his friends he shall glory in him." (*Eccles.* 30:2–3). Such texts are not systematic to most eyes, but to simple souls an education in the virtues, an education that comes through such morsels of thought, easily taken and slowly digested, is nourishment for the body and soul. St. Benedict clearly had a paternal instinct in grasping and staying close to the ancient tradition of living according to maxims short enough to be internalized, but thoughtful enough to be read again and again.

Parallel to his reliance upon the scriptural pillar of wisdom literature, St. Benedict depends also upon the great classical, and especially Roman, tradition of a father actively mastering his household and in so doing creating a true economy in the literal sense—a regulated household and a community of good living. His organization of the monastery is considerably informed by the aristocratic love for detailed organization that one finds in some of the oldest Latin authors. Men such as Marcus Porcius Cato (234–149 B.C.) and Marcus Terentius Varro (116–27 B.C.) provided a codification of the Roman practice of setting out in handbook form the rules of a household. Cato had stated emphatically that "when it is clear and indisputable what labor lies before you, you must set out how it is to be done in an orderly way." Unspoken traditions obviously continued to flourish, but the Roman impulse was always to codify and set out the basic truths of how to live. These truths were grounded in experience, not theory. As Varro put it, rules were derived from "what I observed in my own practice, what I read, and what I learned from the most experienced men." Like his Roman antecedents, Benedict established his *regula* because he saw clearly that such a set of "household rules" was needed for Christian life. In producing his *Rule*, he wrote after reflecting upon years of personal experience, a lifetime spent meditating on the Word of God and in consultation with the minds of his monastic forbearers. The Hebraic and Roman traditions of fatherly guidance are perfectly wed in the *Rule*.

It is by the "labor of obedience," as St. Benedict says, that the son returns to the heavenly father. To Benedict the word "obedience" had a richness obscured to us by the dust of language. *Oboedire* in Latin meant not only "to submit" or "obey," but chiefly "to harken" or "to listen with care." Reflection *and* action were called for by this single expression. Again, is this not what fathers traditionally called for from their households? No good father wishes for mere "obedience" from his children (though at times this must be enforced). Rather, a father wishes that his charges will reflect on his words and act in accord with them, not because his children are slavish drones, but because he as father is responsible for seeing that their minds and hearts are fully in accord with his own pursuit of truth and holiness. Rules are the path towards such thoughtful action and self-mastery.

"The labor of obedience" in English may seem negative to modern readers. Readers of Virgil will recall the attractiveness of the word *labor*.

The word had none of the drudgery that "labor" increasingly carries in English. The "labor of obedience" was an opportunity to be seized! It was good and thoughtful work, not mechanical, but fully human and noble. The mind, soul, heart, and body were all called to purposeful engagement. That engagement was the kind set in motion by a father. And, as St. Benedict, the Roman tradition, and Holy Scripture all assert, it is labor that would end in glory. Again, the old Roman pursuit of personal glory can be seen in the *Regula* but now transfigured by a new piety and transformed by Christian teaching.

As in the "life," the *Rule* bears witness to St. Benedict's attention to order, detail, and tradition—all very Roman, given depth by the Hebraic wisdom literature and personal immediacy by an encounter with Christ. Benedict speaks even more directly than the authors of Proverbs and Ecclesiastes. He speaks as father to son, as Christian disciple to brother disciple, understanding himself, and by extension all abbots, as on the same journey as the greenest monk towards a celestial *patria*.

Readers of the *Rule* should, therefore, understand the layers of western tradition behind the precise guidelines concerning food, sleep, reading, the calendar, travel, the treatment of illness, and corporal punishment. If one keeps in mind the synthesis of Roman aristocratic leadership and Hebraic wisdom literature, these sections are clearly of a piece not only with the guidelines on monastic officers (such as the porter, prior, and of course abbot), but also Christian meditations on the virtues.

Many readers will also approach the *Regula* with some notion that the Benedictine tradition is summarized in the motto—*Ora est Labora*, "Prayer *is* work." This belief is gravely mistaken. Nowhere in St. Benedict's *Rule* or subsequent literature does one find this expression. Pray and work are not equivalent in Benedictine's view. More confusing still is the common notion that the Benedictine life is, in sum, a balance between work and prayer: *Ora et Labora*, "Prayer *and* Work." This so-called motto does appear in writings by and about the Benedictines—starting in the later nineteenth century with the writings of Abbot Maurus Wolter, but again, the *Rule* never uses such an expression. It is best to read the *Rule* and let Benedict speak in his own words. He saw himself as compelled by the love of Christ to build something: *Constituenda est ergo nobis dominici scola servitii* ("We must, therefore, establish a school of the Lord's service"). This new institution Benedict was establishing surely involved work, but for all Benedict's appreciation of labor he nevertheless viewed it as lower in the hierarchy of goods. In the Roman world, *scola* or "school" was something set apart from work—as sacred things are apart from the profane. Indeed, the word also meant "leisure." If one carefully counts the hours, Benedict did not imagine the need to work much more than about five hours— hardly comparable to what we think of as "work" since the industrial revolution. Work is part of the human condition and it has its dignity in the Roman and Benedictine world—hard work at times, but like most work in a traditional society, work was to be done at a humane pace and done for the sake of higher things. The expression "school of service" is an apparent paradox—for *servitium* denoted the condition of slavery. Yet it is slavery or service for the Lord. A school of "service," yes, but the service was to Christ and His heavenly Father through the grace of the Holy Spirit. Read in the context of the *Rule*'s prologue, the "school of the Lord's service" was a new institution: communal, traditional, Roman, but built around the study of Sacred Scripture, the pursuit of wisdom, loyalty to Christ, and all for the praise of God. All things were done for the sake arriving at the Kingdom of Christ, but by enjoying the fruits of that Kingdom in ordinary time through contemplation, especially that which was nourished in common prayer and discovered in the careful reading of Scripture (*lectio divina*).

Finally, readers should be aware that St. Benedict drew heavily, sometimes word for word, on other monastic texts, as well as Scripture (Indeed, modern translations—including the one that follows— obscure the experience of reading the *Rule*). There were no quotation marks or citations of Scriptural passage to let the reader know Benedict was quoting the Bible. A mature reader who had passages of Scripture in his mind would know the reference. Some readers no doubt detected the shift in style from Benedict's Late Latin to the strange many-layered words of the Latin translation of the Bible, but it was hard to be sure—in fact, the need for such surety is really a modern preoccupation. Benedict and his monks aimed to allow the Word of God to penetrate the heart, mind, soul, and imagination. The words of a Christian writer should be shot through with the words of Scripture and the Fathers.

One of the greatest non-scriptural inspirations for St. Benedict was the *Regula Magistri*—the "Rule of the Master." As modern editions with commentaries on the Latin have made clear, large portions of the rules have been lifted directly from the *Rule of the Master*. Noteworthy are the little changes and additions which come only from Benedict. These appear always as humane touches and the softening of a prior, but stiff, template. The character of St. Benedict emerges clearly at such moments. Many rules laid out guidelines for kitchen service and the details of guidelines such as are found in chapter 35 may bore first-time or inattentive readers. But consider this little aside, an addition to material that Benedict found elsewhere:

> An hour before meal time let the weekly servers each receive a drink and a piece of bread over the prescribed portion. In this way, they may serve their brethren at meal time without murmuring or undue strain.

Here we see the Abbot Benedict emerge and the essence of his humane character revealed. Behind the law-giver is the abbot or father, and he reveals himself as a kind and attentive father. The heady principle of charity in the kitchen may be inspirational, but perhaps too intellectual, too theologically distant; the regulation of times and food allotments scarcely moves most readers; but how can this passage, born of real experience of human frailty, not warm the heart of anyone who has borne responsibility or sought to serve others day in and day out? A drink and a welcome morsel are natural goods on which the supernatural can more effectively transform the ordinary. It is in little details such as this that readers will find the heart of Benedict's *Rule*.

Further Reading

The bibliography of works on St. Benedict and his *Rule* is vast. Readers who enjoy plumbing the depths of online resources should start with the largest Benedictine site, a veritable library created by the monks of St. John's in Collegeville, Minnesota (www.osb.org).

The suggestions below are guided by a sense that many traditional or early works have been forgotten in the rush to publish new material. Thus, what follows is a mixture of basic readings—the "standards"—as well as neglected classics.

The Rule: translated editions and some recent commentaries

> *The Rule of Saint Benedict—A Commentary* by the Right Rev. Dom Paul Delatte, Abbot of Solesmes and Superior General of the Congregation of Benedictines in France, trans. Dom Justin McCann, O.S.B. (Latrobe, PA: St. Vincent's Archabbey Press, 1950). This commentary, written before the First World War, remains the crowning achievement of traditional Benedictine spirituality. It is now rarely cited and difficult to find.

> *The Rule of Saint Benedict in English and Latin*, trans. and ed. by Abbot Justin McCann, O.S.B. (reprinted Roman Catholic Books: Fort Collins, CO, n.d.) Abbot McCann's edition is one of the few that breaks the text into the traditional dated sections for reading according to the Benedictine calendar, three times a year. The notes are a wealth of grammatical and cultural detail.

> *The Holy Rule—Notes on St. Benedict's Legislation for Monks* by Dom Hubert Van Zeller (New York: Sheed and Ward, 1958).

> *The Rule of Saint Benedict—A Doctrinal and Spiritual Commentary* by Dom Adalbert de Vogüé, O.S.B. (Spencer, MA: Cistercian Publications, 1983).

Benedict's Rule—A Translation and Commentary, ed. Fr. Terrence Kardong, O.S.B. (Collegeville, MN: The Liturgical Press, 1996). The academic fruit of fifteen years research, Fr. Kardong's translation and commentary presents the latest findings regarding textual and theological studies of the *Rule*.

Biographies of St. Benedict: One early life exists, that written shortly after his death by Pope St. Gregory the Great as part of his larger work, *The Dialogues*. Book Two of the Dialogues is dedicated to the life of Benedict.

> St. Gregory the Great, *The Life of St. Benedict*, trans. Hilary Costello and Eoin de Bhaldraithe, with commentary by Adalbert de Vogüé, O.S.B. (Petersham, MA: St. Bede's, 1993).
>
> St. Gregory the Great, *The Life of St. Benedict*, trans. and commentary by Terrence G. Kardong, O.S.B. (Collegeville, MN: The Liturgical Press, 2009).
>
> St. Gregory the Great, *The Dialogues*, trans. by Odo John Zimmerman, O.S.B. (Washington, D.C.: The Catholic University Press of America, 1959). Some readers may wish to look at the "life" of St. Benedict in context. Dom Zimmerman's is the standard modern translation.

Modern biographies and reflections

> Dom Fernand Cabrol, O.S.B., *St. Benedict* (London: Burns, Oates, & Washbourne, 1934).
>
> Adalbert de Vogüé, O.S.B., *St. Benedict: The Man and His Work* (New York: Fordham University Press, 2006).
>
> Pope Pius XII, *Flugens Radiatur* (March 21, 1947). In this encyclical letter, Pius XII presents a summary of St. Benedict's life and spirituality, followed by points that should inspire Catholics in the modern age.

There are many fine works which attempt to give a sense of the theology, spirituality, and very culture that spring forth from the Benedictine way. The works below provide keen readers with an overview of some of the best from the past two centuries:

Abbot Aelread Carlyle, O.S.B. *Our Purpose and Method* (Elgin, Scotland: Pluscarden Abbey Press, 1987). In this brief book, Abbot Carlyle sets out the vision of his Anglican Benedictine community on the island of Caldey, off the coast of southwest Wales. In 1913 the entire community entered the Roman Catholic Church. The book was thought by Bl. Columba Marmion to be an excellent introduction to the Benedictine way.

Michael Casey, O.S.C.O., *Strangers to the City: Reflections on the Beliefs and Values of the Rule of St. Benedict* (Brewster, MA: Paraclete Press, 2005).

Abbot Prosper Guéranger, *The Liturgical Year*, 15 vols. (London: Stanbrook Abbey, 1918). For those who wish to observe how St. Benedict's simple codification of the cycle for the Divine Office grew into an effulgent meditation on the liturgy throughout the year, this work by Dom Guéranger is essential. Dom Guéranger, Abbot of Solesmes, almost single-handed brought the Benedictine Order out of the ashes in France during the middle of the nineteenth century, when Benedictine communities had fallen from approximately 1500 in the eighteenth century to only 30 when Dom Guéranger was a young man.

To appreciate the rich spirituality and energy for broader Catholic renewal that Dom Guéranger and his community at Solesmes generated, readers should seek out *The Spirit of Solesmes—The Christian Life in the Works of Dom Prosper Guéranger, Abbes Cécile Bruyère, and Dom Paul Delatte*, ed. Sr. Mary David Totah, O.S.B. (Petersham, MA: St. Bede's Publications, 1997).

Dwight Longenecker, *St. Benedict and St. Thérèse—The Little Rule and the Little Way* (Huntington, IN: Our Sunday Visitor, 2002).

Bl. Columba Marmion, *Christ the Ideal of the Monk—Spiritual Conferences on the Monastic and Religious Life* (London: Sands and Co., 1926). Born in Ireland, Bl. Columba eventually became the Abbot of monastery at Mardesous, Belgium. Of his many works, *Christ the Ideal of the Monk* is his most explicitly Benedictine. In addition to his own tradition, Bl. Columba was also a careful reader of St. Thomas Aquinas and well-read in the rich tradition of spirituality found in the other religious orders.

Bl. John Henry Newman, *The Benedictine Order* (London: Catholic Truth Society, 1914). This short work was derived from his inspiring essays "The Benedictine Centuries" and "The Mission of St. Benedict and Benedictine Schools".

Dom Hubert Van Zeller, O.S.B. *Approach to Monasticism* (New York: Sheed and Ward, 1960). Building on the work that went into his translation and commentary of the *Rule*, Dom Hubert sets forth a practical and frank discussion of the monastic life. The object is to de-romanticize the Benedictine life and present to aspirants, veterans, and scholars of the monasticism a study which allows that life to be understood in decisive vocational terms: a life to be chosen and lived, not to be passively endured out of fear, inadequacy, or indecision.

The majority of the books listed above concentrate on spirituality and most have a non-academic intent. The following works, while originally written for scholars, will prove profoundly interesting to students of St. Benedict.

Dom Cuthbert Butler, O.S.B., *Benedictine Monachism: Studies in Benedictine Life and Rule* (London: Longman, Green and Co., 1919).

Dom David Knowles, *The Benedictines* (New York: Sheed and Ward, 1929). This short pamphlet by one of England's best known Benedictine scholars of the last century has not been surpassed as a pithy, but erudite introduction.

Dom Jean Leclercq, O.S.B., *The Love of Learning and the Desire for God* (New York: Fordham University Press, 1960). To list this amongst academic titles may discourage broad readership, which would be unfortunate, since Dom Leclercq's style and breadth will engage all audiences. This book has been the starting point and inspiration for much of the post-World War II scholarship on St. Benedict and the culture he helped to establish.

Oblates

Oblates in the modern age are typically those lay men and women who formally and according to a rite of the Church associate themselves with a Benedictine monastery and live out their lives—according to their place in the world—under the *Rule of St. Benedict* and are guided by Benedictine spirituality. While oblates have always been a part of the Benedictine family, in recent decades their numbers have now far surpassed those of cloistered monks and nuns. A cursory search at a bookstore or through internet sources will reveal the numerous works generated in the last few years by oblates and monks guiding oblate communities. The list below is provided only of those lesser known or older works which should receive a wider readership.

Anon., *Manual for the Use of the Oblates of the Order of St. Benedict Affiliated to the Abbey, Fort Augustus* (Fort Augustus Abbey, Fort Augustus, Scotland, 1893).

Anon., *Manual for Oblates of St. Benedict*—Prepared by monks of St. John's Abbey under the direction of the National Conference of Oblate Directors (Collegeville, MN: St. John's Abbey Press, 1955).

Alcuin Deutch, O.S.B., *Manual for Oblates of St. Benedict* (Collegeville, MN: St. John's Abbey Press, 1937).

T. F. Lindsay, *The Holy Rule for Laymen* (London: Burns, Oates and Washbourne, 1947).

Dwight Longenecker, *Listen, My Son—St Benedict for Fathers* (Leominster: Gracewing, 2000).

Dom Norbert Schachinger, O.S.B., *The Lay Apostle after the Heart of St. Benedict* (Collegeville, MN: St. John's Abbey Press, 1931).

THE RULE OF ST. BENEDICT:
A NOTE ON THE TRANSLATION

THE translation that follows is a revision and in many place new translation of that made by Boniface Verheyen, O.S.B. (1843–1923). Fr. Boniface was a Benedictine of St. Benedict's Abbey in Atchison, Kansas. He held the office of Prior under the dynamic Abbot, Innocent Wolf, O.S.B.. Fr. Verheyen's translation was created for the novices in Atchinson.

While benefitting from Fr. Verheyen's version, the present translation takes advantage of the last century of textual scholarship on the Rule, avoids elevation of tone when the Latin does not suggest it, and—it is hoped—restores some sense of the personality evident in Benedict's prose style. The following examples should allow readers to gauge the degree of revision:

> To thee, therefore, my speech is now directed, who, giving up thine own will, takest up the strong and most excellent arms of obedience, to do battle for Christ the Lord, the true King. (Prologue, Verheyen original).

> It is to you that I direct my words, whoever you may be. My hope is that you will renounce your own will, and then take up the strong and most excellent arms of obedience, and so do battle for Christ the Lord, the true King. (Prologue, Fahey version).

If we do not venture to approach men who are in power, except with humility and reverence, when we wish to ask a favor, how much must we beseech the Lord God of all things with all humility and purity of devotion? (Chapter 20, Verheyen original).

When we wish to ask a favor of men who are in power, we do not dare to approach them, except with humility and reverence. How much more, then, should we beseech the Lord God of the universe with all humility and purity of devotion? (Chapter 20, Fahey version).

PROLOGUE

———— • ————

L ISTEN, O my son, to the precepts of your master. Incline the ear of your heart; willingly receive and faithfully follow the advice of your loving Father, so that through the labor of obedience you may return to Him from whom you had departed through the sloth of disobedience.

It is to you that I direct my words, whoever you may be. My hope is that you will renounce your own will, and then take up the strong and most excellent arms of obedience, and so do battle for Christ the Lord, the true King.

The crucial first step is this: to beg of Him by most ardent prayer that He perfect whatever good work you have started, so that He who has so kindly numbered us among His children need never be grieved by our evil deeds. For at all times we should serve Him with the gifts He has bestowed upon us. If we do this, we can be sure that He will not disinherit His children, as an angry father does, nor, like a dread lord, enraged at our evil deeds, hand us over to everlasting punishment as if we were wicked servants, who would not follow Him to glory.

Let us then rise at length, since the Scripture stirs us up, saying: "It is now the hour for us to rise from sleep" (*Rom*. 13:11); and having opened our eyes to the deifying light, let us hear with awestruck ears what the divine voice, crying out daily, admonishes us, saying: "Today, if you shall hear his voice, harden not your hearts." (*Ps*. 94:8; 95:8, Vulg.). And again: "He that hath ears to hear, let him hear what the Spirit saith to the churches." (*Rev*. 2:7). And what else does He say?—"Come, children, hearken unto me, I will teach you the fear of the Lord." (*Ps.* 33:12; 34:12, Vulg.). "Run whilst you have the light of life, that the darkness of death overtake you not." (*John* 12:35).

And the Lord seeking His workman in the multitude of the people, to whom He proclaims these words, says again: "Who is the man that desireth life and loveth to see good days?" (*Ps.* 33:13; 34:13, Vulg.). If hearing this you answer, "I am he," then God will respond: "If thou wilt have true and everlasting life, keep thy tongue from evil, and thy lips from speaking guile; turn away from evil and do good; seek after peace and pursue it." (*Ps.* 33:14–15; 34:14–15, Vulg.). And when you have done these things, my eyes will be upon you, and my ears open to your prayers. And before you call upon me I will say: "Behold, I am here." (*Is.* 58:9).

What, dearest brethren, can be sweeter to us than the voice of our Lord inviting us to be with Him? Behold, in His devoted care for us, the Lord shows us the way of life. Therefore, having our loins girt with faith and the performance of good works, let us walk in His ways under the guidance of the Gospel, that we may be found worthy of seeing Him who has called us to His kingdom. (Cf. *1 Thess.* 2:12).

If we desire to dwell in the tabernacle of His kingdom, we cannot reach it in any way unless we run there by good works. But let us ask the Lord with the Prophet, saying to Him: "Lord, who shall dwell in Thy tabernacle, or who shall rest in Thy holy hill?" (*Ps.* 14:1; 15:1, Vulg.).

After this question, brethren, let us listen to the Lord answering and showing us the way to this tabernacle, saying: "He that walketh without blemish and worketh justice; he that speaketh truth in his heart; who hath not used deceit in his tongue, nor hath done evil to his neighbor, nor hath taken up a reproach against his neighbor" (*Ps.* 14:2–3; 15:2–3, Vulg.), who has brought to naught the foul demon tempting him, casting him out of his heart with his temptation, and has taken his evil thoughts while they were yet weak and has dashed them against Christ. (Cf. *Ps.* 14:4; 15:4, Vulg.; *Ps.* 136:9;

137:9, Vulg.). Such men as these fear the Lord. They are not puffed up by their good works. Instead, they hold that the actual good which is in them does not have its origin in themselves, but comes from the Lord; thus, they magnify the Lord working in them (cf. *Ps.* 14:4; 15:4, Vulg.), saying with the Prophet: "Not to us, O Lord, not to us; but to Thy name give glory." (*Ps.* 113:9; 115:1, Vulg.). So also the Apostle Paul did not credit himself for his preaching, but says: "By the grace of God, I am what I am." (*1 Cor.* 15:10). And likewise, he says: "He that glorieth, let him glory in the Lord." (*2 Cor.* 10:17).

Hence, the Lord also says in the Gospel: "He that heareth these my words and doeth them, shall be likened to a wise man who built his house upon a rock; the floods came, the winds blew, and they beat upon that house, and it fell not, for it was founded on a rock." (*Matt.* 7:24–25). The Lord, fulfilling these words, now waits daily for us to respond to His holy admonition through our very actions. Therefore, our days are lengthened and a truce granted for the amendment of our evil ways; as the Apostle says: "Knowest thou not that the patience of God leadeth thee to penance" (*Rom.* 2:4)? For our compassionate Lord says: "I desire not the death of the sinner, but that he be converted and live." (*Ezek.* 33:11).

So, brethren, we have asked the Lord who it is that shall dwell in His tabernacle, and we have heard the conditions for dwelling there. If we fulfill those duties, we shall be heirs of the kingdom of heaven. Therefore, our hearts and our bodies must be ready to do battle under holy obedience to his commands. Let us ask the Lord that He supply for us by the help of His grace what is impossible for us by nature. And if, flying from the pains of hell, we desire to reach life everlasting, then—while there is yet time, and we are still in the flesh, and while we are able to fulfill all these things in the light of this life—we must make haste to do now what will profit us forever.

We must, therefore, establish a school of the Lord's service, and in its founding, we hope to introduce nothing harsh or burdensome. But even if, to correct vices or to preserve charity, sound reason dictates something that should prove somewhat stringent, do not suddenly fly off in dismay from the way of salvation; the first stage of this path is always narrow. But as we advance in our religious life and in our faith, we shall race along the way of God's commandments with bursting hearts and unspeakable sweetness of love; so that never departing from His guidance and persevering in His doctrine within the monastery until death, we may share in the sufferings of Christ through patience, and thus be found worthy to be companions with Him in His kingdom. Amen.

THE HOLY RULE OF SAINT BENEDICT

CHAPTER ONE
On the Kinds or the Life of Monks

IT IS CLEAR that there are four kinds of monks. The first kind is the Cenobite, that is, the monastic, who serves under a rule and an Abbot.

The second kind are the Ancorites, or Hermits, that is, those who, no longer in the first fervor of their conversion, but tested by long monastic practice and helped by the experience of many brethren, have already learned to fight against the devil. Going forth from the battle line of the brethren having been well-trained for hand-to-hand combat in the desert, they are now able—by the strength of their own hand and arm and with the assistance of God—to cope without the support of others against the vices of the flesh and evil thoughts.

A third and most vile class of monks is that of Sarabaites, who have been tried by no rule nor the mastery of experience, as gold is tried in the fire (cf. *Prov.* 27:21), but are as soft as lead. And in their actions they still keep faith with the world, while their tonsure exposes them as liars before God. Living in twos and threes, or even singly, without a shepherd, enclosed, not in the Lord's sheepfold, but in their own, they make the gratification of their desires their law. What they wish to do, they call holy, but what they dislike, they consider unlawful.

The fourth class of monks are those called Gyrovagues, who spend their whole lives wandering from one province to another, staying three or four days at a time in different monastic cells as guests. Always roving and never stable, they indulge their own passions and the cravings of gluttony, and they are in every way worse than the Sarabaites. It is better to pass all these over in silence than to speak of their most wretched life.

Therefore, passing these over, let us go on with the help of God to set out the guidelines for those most valiant kind of monks, the Cenobites.

CHAPTER TWO
What Kind of Man the Abbot Ought to Be

AN ABBOT who is worthy of ruling over a monastery ought always to be mindful of what he is called—a Superior—and make his actions reflect his very name. For he is believed to hold the place of Christ in the monastery, since he is called by His name, according to the saying of the Apostle: "Ye have received the spirit of adoption of sons, whereby we cry *Abba*—Father." (*Rom.* 8:15). Therefore, the Abbot should never teach, authorize, or command anything contrary to the laws of the Lord (God forbid this should happen); but his commands and teaching should be kneaded like the leaven of divine justice into the minds of his disciples.

Let the Abbot always bear in mind that at the dread Judgment of God he must give an account both of his own teaching and of the obedience of his disciples. And let the Abbot know that whatever lack of profit the Father of the Family shall find in the sheep, will be laid to the blame of the shepherd. On the other hand, he will be blameless, if he gave all a shepherd's care to his restless and disobedient flock, and took all pains to correct its corrupt manner of life; so that their shepherd, acquitted at the Lord's judgment seat, may say to the Lord with the Prophet: "I have not hid Thy justice within my heart. I have declared Thy truth and Thy salvation." (*Ps.* 39:11; 40:11, Vulg.). "But they despising have rejected me." (*Is.* 1:2; *Ezek.* 20:27). Then at length overpowering death will be the penalty of those sheep who rebelled against his charge.

When, therefore, anyone takes the name of Abbot he should govern his disciples by a twofold teaching: namely, he should show them all that is good and holy by his deeds rather than by his words—demonstrating the commandments of God to his thoughtful disciples through words, but declaring the divine precepts to those of hard-hearts or those of more simple minds through his works. And let him show by his actions, that whatever he teaches his disciples as being contrary to the law of God must not be done, "lest perhaps when he hath preached to others, he himself should become a castaway" (*1 Cor.* 9:27), and lest he himself committing sin, God one day should say to him: "Why dost thou declare My justices, and take My covenant in thy mouth? For thou hast hated discipline, and hast cast My words behind thee." (*Ps.* 49:16–17; 50:16–17, Vulg.). And: "Thou who sawest the mote in thy brother's eye, didst not see the beam in thine own." (*Matt.* 7:3).

Let him make no distinction of persons in the monastery. Let him not love one more than another, unless it be someone found exemplary in good works and obedience. Let not a free-born be preferred to a former slave, unless there be some other reasonable cause. But if from a just reason the Abbot deems it proper to make such a distinction, he may do so in regard to the rank of anyone whomsoever; otherwise let everyone keep his own place; for whether bound or free, we are all one in Christ (cf. *Gal.* 3:28; *Eph.* 6:8), and we all bear an equal burden serving in the army of Our Lord, "for there is no respect of persons with God." (*Rom.* 2:11). We are distinguished in his sight for this respect alone: when we are found to excel others in good works and in humility. Therefore, let the Abbot have equal charity for all, and impose a uniform discipline upon all according to merit.

For in his teaching the Abbot should always observe that principle of the Apostle in which he says: "Reprove, entreat, rebuke" (*2 Tim.* 4:2), that is, mingling gentleness with severity, as the occasion may call

107

for, let him show the rigor of a master or the kindly affection of a father. He must sternly rebuke the undisciplined and restless; but he must exhort the obedient, meek, and patient to advance in virtue. But we charge him to rebuke and punish the negligent and haughty. Let him not shut his eyes to the faults of offenders, but on their first appearance let him do his utmost to cut them out from the root at once, remembering the fate of Heli, the priest of Silo. (Cf. *1 Sam.* 2:11–4:18). The well-disposed and those of sensitive minds, let him correct on the first and second occasions only with verbal warnings; but let him chastise the wicked and the hard of heart, and the proud and disobedient on the very first offense with the rod and other bodily punishments, knowing that it is written: "The fool is not corrected with words." (*Prov.* 29:19). And again: "Strike thy son with the rod, and thou shalt deliver his soul from death." (*Prov.* 23:14).

The Abbot ought always to remember what he is and what he is called, and to know that to whom much has been entrusted, from him much will be required; and let him understand what a difficult and arduous task he has assumed in governing souls and accommodating himself to a variety of dispositions. Let him so adjust and adapt himself to everyone—with one, encouraging remarks, with another, reproofs, and with another type persuasive arguments, according to each one's character and intelligence—that he not only suffer no loss in his flock, but may rejoice in the increase of a worthy fold.

Above all things the Abbot must not neglect or undervalue the welfare of the souls entrusted to him, because he has been distracted by fleeting, earthly, perishable things; but let him always dwell on the fact that he has undertaken the government of souls, for which he will have to render an account. And in case he is tempted to complain about the lack of earthly resources, let him remember what is written: "Seek ye first the kingdom of God and His justice, and all these things shall be added unto you." (*Matt.* 6:33). And again: "There is no want to them that fear Him." (*Ps.* 33:10; 34:10, Vulg.). And let him know that he who undertakes the government of souls must prepare himself to render an account for them; and whatever the number of brethren he has under his charge, let him be sure that on the Day of Judgment he will, without doubt, have to give an account to the Lord for all these souls, as well as his own. And thus, while he should be ever fearful of the Shepherd's future assessment of the sheep entrusted to him, and while he is vigilant over the account he will need to give about other men, he is made solicitous also for his own sake. And so, by the warnings he uses to correct others, he himself will be purified of his own faults.

CHAPTER THREE
On Calling the Brethren for Counsel

WHENEVER weighty matters are to be transacted in the monastery, let the Abbot call together the whole community, and make known the matter which is to be considered. Having heard the brethren's counsel, let him weigh the matter with himself and do what he thinks best. It is for this reason, however, we said that all should be called for council, because the Lord often reveals to the younger what is best. Let the brethren, however, give their counsel with humble deference, and let them not presume stubbornly to defend their own opinions, but let the matter depend rather on the Abbot's will, so that all obey him in what he considers best. But as it is proper for disciples to obey their master, so also it is proper for the master to dispose all things with prudence and justice.

Therefore, let all follow the Rule as their guide in everything, and let no one rashly depart from it. Let no one in the monastery follow the will of his own heart, and let no one dare to dispute insolently with his Abbot, either inside or outside the monastery. If anyone dare to do so, let him be placed under the correction prescribed by the Rule. Let the Abbot himself, however, do everything in the fear of the Lord and with careful regard for the Rule, knowing that, without a shadow of a doubt, he will have to render to God, the most just Judge, a full account of all his decisions. If, however, matters of less importance, having to do with the welfare of the monastery, are to be treated of, let him take the counsel of the Seniors only, as it is written: "Do all things with counsel, and thou shalt not repent when thou hast done." (*Sir.* 32:24).

CHAPTER FOUR
The Tools of Good Works

1) In the first place to love the Lord God with one's whole heart, whole soul, whole strength.
2) Then, one's neighbor as one's self. (Cf. *Matt.* 22:37–39; *Mark* 12:30–31; *Luke* 10:27).
3) Then, not to kill.
4) Not to commit adultery.
5) Not to steal.
6) Not to covet. (Cf. *Rom.* 13:9).
7) Not to bear false witness. (Cf. *Matt.* 19:18; *Mark* 10:19; *Luke* 18:20).
8) To honor all men. (Cf. *1 Pet.* 2:17).
9) Not to do unto another, what one would not have done to oneself. (Cf. *Tob.* 4:16; *Matt.* 7:12; *Luke* 6:31).
10) To deny one's self in order to follow Christ. (Cf. *Matt.* 16:24; *Luke* 9:23).
11) To chastise the body. (Cf. *1 Cor.* 9:27).
12) Not to cling to soft living.
13) To love fasting.
14) To relieve the poor.
15) To clothe the naked.
16) To visit the sick. (Cf. *Matt.* 25:36).
17) To bury the dead.
18) To provide help in times of trouble.
19) To console the sorrowing.

20) To keep aloof from worldly ways.

21) To prefer nothing to the love of Christ.

22) Not to give way to anger.

23) Not to foster a desire for revenge.

24) Not to nurse guile in one's heart.

25) Not to make a false peace.

26) Not to forsake charity.

27) Not to swear, lest perchance one swear falsely.

28) To speak the truth with heart and tongue.

29) Not to return evil for evil. (Cf. *1 Thess.* 5:15; *1 Pet.* 3:9).

30) To do no wrong, but patiently to bear the wrong done us.

31) To love one's enemies. (Cf. *Matt.* 5:44; *Luke* 6:27).

32) Not to curse them that curse us, but rather to bless them.

33) To bear persecution for justice sake. (Cf. *Matt.* 5:10).

34) Not to be proud.

35) Not to be a winebibber. (Cf. *Titus* 1:7; *1 Tim.* 3:3).

36) Not to be a gorger.

37) Not to be sluggish.

38) Not to be slothful. (Cf. *Rom.* 12:11).

39) Not to be a murmurer.

40) Not to be a detractor.

41) To put one's hope in God.

42) To attribute any good one sees in oneself to God, and not to oneself.

43) But as to recognize that evil is one's own doing and impute it as such.

44) To fear the Day of Judgment.

45) To be in dread of hell.

46) To desire eternal life with all spiritual longing.

47) To keep death before one's eyes daily.

48) To keep a constant watch over the actions of one's life.

49) To hold as certain that God sees one everywhere.

50) To dash at once against Christ the evil thoughts which rise in one's heart,

51) and to disclose them to our spiritual father.

52) To guard one's tongue against bad and wicked speech.

53) Not to love much speaking.

54) Not to encourage idle conversation or say things fit for buffoonery.

55) Not to love excessive or boisterous laughter.

56) To listen willingly to holy reading.

57) To apply one's self often to prayer.

58) To confess one's past sins to God daily praying with sighs and tears, and to amend them for the future.

59) Not to fulfill the desires of the flesh. (Cf. *Gal.* 5:16).

60) To hate one's own will.

61) To obey the commands of the Abbot in all things, even though he himself (God forbid) act otherwise, mindful of that precept of the Lord: "What they say, do ye; but what they do, do ye not." (*Matt.* 23:3).

62) Not to desire to be called holy before one is so; but to be holy first, that one may be truly so called.

63) To fulfill daily the commandments of God in one's actions.

64) To love chastity.

65) To hate no one.

66) Not to be jealous; not to give way to envy.

67) Not to love strife.

68) To flee vainglory.

69) To honor the community's elders.

70) To love the community's younger members.

71) To pray for one's enemies in the love of Christ.

72) To make peace with an adversary before the setting of the sun

73) And never to despair of God's mercy.

Behold, these are the tools of the spiritual craft, which, if used without ceasing day and night and returned on Judgment Day, will earn for us from the Lord that reward which He hath promised: "The eye hath not seen, nor the ear heard, what things God hath prepared for them that love Him." (*1 Cor.* 2:9). But the workshop in which we labor with diligence is the enclosure of the monastery and stability in the community.

CHAPTER FIVE
On Obedience

THE first step in humility is obedience without delay. This is characteristic of those who hold nothing dearer to them than Christ. Whether it is on account of the holy servitude they have embraced, or the fear of hell, or the glory of life everlasting, these are unable to tolerate any delay in responding to the order of their superior. As soon as the order is given, they act upon it as if God Himself had issued the command. Of these men the Lord says: "At the hearing of the ear he hath obeyed Me." (*Ps.* 17:45; 18:45, Vulg.). And again He says to the teachers: "He that heareth you heareth Me." (*Luke* 10:16).

Men such as these, therefore, quit their own affairs instantly and forsake their own will. They disengage their hands, putting aside what they were doing and, with the ready step of obedience, follow the voice of him who commands with determination. Thus are fulfilled, as if in the same moment, both matters—the order commanded by the master and the action completed by the disciple—united and more quickly accomplished through swiftness sparked by the fear of God, for both are pushed on by their desire for attaining everlasting life. They, therefore, seize upon the narrow way about which the Lord says: "Narrow is the way which leadeth to life." (*Matt.* 7:14), so that, not living according to their own will, nor obeying their own desires and passions, but walking according to the judgment and command of another, they live in monasteries, and desire an Abbot to be over them. Such as these truly live up to that saying of the Lord: "I came not to do My own will, but the will of Him that sent Me." (*John* 6:38).

This obedience, however, will be acceptable to God and agreeable to men then only, if what is commanded is done without hesitation, delay, lukewarmness, grumbling, or complaint, because the obedience which is rendered to superiors is rendered to God. For He Himself said: "He that heareth you, heareth Me." (*Luke* 10:16). And obedience must be offered by the disciples with a good will, "for the God loveth a cheerful giver." (*2 Cor.* 9:7). For if the disciple obeys with an ill will, and murmurs, not only with lips but also in his heart, even though he fulfill the command, his action will not be acceptable to God, who regards the heart of the murmurer. And for such an action he will gain no benefit; rather he incurs the punishment of murmurers, unless he amend his ways and offer reparation.

CHAPTER SIX
On Silence

LET US do what the Prophet says: "I said, I will take heed of my ways, that I sin not with my tongue: I have set a guard to my mouth, I was dumb, and was humbled, and kept silence even from good things." (*Ps.* 38:2–3; 39:2–3, Vulg.). Here the prophet shows that, if at times we ought to refrain from good words for the sake of silence, how much more ought we to abstain from evil words on account of the punishment due to sin.

Therefore, because of the importance of silence, let permission to speak be seldom granted to perfect disciples even for discourse which is good and holy and aimed at edification, for it is written: "In much speaking thou shalt not escape sin." (*Prov.* 10:19). And elsewhere: "Death and life are in the power of the tongue." (*Prov.* 18:21). For it belongs to the master to speak and to teach; after all, it is appropriate for the disciple to be silent and to listen. If, therefore, anything must be asked of the superior, let it be asked with all humility and respectful submission. But coarse jests, and words that are pointless or that are only a prompt for laughter, we condemn in every situation by a permanent ban; nor do we do permit the disciple to open his lips for such conversation.

CHAPTER SEVEN
On Humility

B RETHREN, the Holy Scripture cries out to us saying: "Every one that exalteth himself shall be humbled; and he that humbleth himself shall be exalted." (*Luke* 14:11, 18:14). Since, therefore, it says this, it shows us that every exaltation is a kind of pride. The Prophet shows that he guards himself against this, saying: "Lord, my heart is not puffed up; nor are my eyes haughty. Neither have I walked in great matters nor in wonderful things above me." (*Ps.* 130:1; 131:1, Vulg.). Why is this? "If I was not humbly minded, but exalted my soul; as a child that is weaned is towards his mother so shalt Thou reward my soul." (*Ps.* 130:2; 131:2, Vulg.).

Which is why, brethren, if we wish to arrive at the summit of humility, and speedily to reach that heavenly exaltation to which to which one only climbs by humility in this present life, then, mounting by our actions, we must erect the ladder akin to the one that appeared to Jacob in his dream, upon which angels were shown ascending and descending. (Cf. *Gen.* 28:12). Without a doubt, we understand this ascending and descending to be nothing else but that we descend by self exaltation and ascend by humility. The ladder thus erected is our life in the present world, which, when we are humble of heart, the Lord raises up to heaven. In fact, we could say that our body and our soul are the two sides of this ladder; and into these sides the divine calling has inserted various steps of humility or discipline, which we must mount.

The first step of humility, then, is that a man always have the fear of God before his eyes (cf. *Ps.* 35:2; 36:2, Vulg.), shunning all forgetfulness. Likewise, he must be ever mindful of all that God hath commanded and perpetually reflecting upon the reality that those who despise God will burn in hell for their sins, while life everlasting is prepared for those who fear God. And while he guards himself hour after hour against sin and vices—that is thoughts, words, deeds, and his own will—let him also be quick to cut off the desires of the flesh.

Let a man consider that God is ever observing him from Heaven, and that his works are everywhere beheld by the gaze of the Divinity, and that angels report them to Him every hour. The Prophet tells us this when he shows that God ever discerns our thoughts, saying: "The searcher of hearts and reins is God." (*Ps.* 7:10). And again: "The Lord knoweth the thoughts of men." (*Ps.* 93:11; 94:11, Vulg.). Likewise, he says: "Thou hast understood my thoughts afar off." (*Ps.* 138:3; 139:3, Vulg.). And: "The thoughts of man shall give praise to Thee." (*Ps.* 75:11; 76:11, Vulg.). Therefore, in order that he may always be on his guard against evil thoughts, let the humble brother always say in his heart: "Then I shall be spotless before Him, if I shall keep myself from iniquity." (*Ps.* 17:24; 18:24, Vulg.).

Truly, we must understand that we are forbidden to do our own will, since the Scripture says to us: "And turn away from thy evil will." (*Sir.* 18:30). And thus, too, we ask God in prayer that His will may be done in us. (Cf. *Matt.* 6:10). We are, therefore, rightly taught not to do our own will, when we take notice of Scriptures warning: "There are ways that to men seem right, but in the end plungeth man into the depths of hell." (*Prov.* 16:25). So too, we are filled with dread at what is said of the negligent: "They are corrupted and become abominable in their pleasure." (*Ps.* 13:1; 14:1, Vulg.). But as regards desires of the flesh, let us believe that God discerns our every thought, since the Prophet says to the Lord: "All my desire is before Thee." (*Ps.* 37:10; 38:10, Vulg.).

We must, therefore, guard thus against evil desires, because death lies waiting near the entrance of pleasure. And that is why the Scripture commands: "Go not after thy lusts." (*Sir.* 18:30). If, therefore, the eyes of the Lord observe the good and the bad (cf. *Prov.* 15:3) and the Lord always looks down from heaven on the children of men, to see whether there be anyone that understands or seeks God (cf. *Ps.* 13:2; 14:2, Vulg.); and if our actions are reported to the Lord day and night by the angels who are appointed to watch over us daily, we must ever be on our guard, brethren, as the Prophet says in the psalm, so that God never see us "gone astray to evil and become unprofitable" (*Ps.* 13:3; 14:3, Vulg.), and although he has spared us presently, because of his devoted care, he does look to us to alter our lives for the better, and he will say to us in the future: "These things thou hast done and I was silent." (*Ps.* 49:21; 50:21, Vulg.).

The second step of humility is, when a man loves not his own will, nor is pleased to fulfill his own desires but by his deeds carries out that saying of the Lord: "I came not to do My own will but the will of Him that sent Me." (*John* 6:38). Likewise Scripture has it: "Self-will hath its punishment, but necessity winneth the crown."[1]

The third step of humility is, that for the love of God a man subject himself to a Superior in all obedience, imitating the Lord, of whom the Apostle says: "He became obedient unto death." (*Phil.* 2:8).

The fourth step of humility is, that, if this obedience involves hard and annoying things, no, even more if obedience entails personal offense, one should embrace patience with an even temper, and not grow weary or give up, but hold out, as the Scripture says: "He that shall persevere unto the end shall be saved." (*Matt.* 10:22). And again: "Let thy heart take courage, and wait thou for the Lord."

---

1. This reference has no Scriptural antecedent. As with many of the Fathers, St. Benedict often cites references from memory. The maxim he gives here cannot be found in the Bible. Benedict is either following one of his favorite sources, *The Rule of the Master*, or simply giving a well-known proverb the luster of Sacred Scripture.

(*Ps.* 26:14; 27:14, Vulg.). To demonstrate that a faithful man ought even to bear all things—even personal offenses for the Lord, Scripture says in the voice of the afflicted: "For Thy sake we suffer death all the day long; we are counted as sheep for the slaughter." (*Rom.* 8:36; *Ps.* 43:22; 44:22, Vulg.). And secure in the hope of the divine reward, they go on joyfully, saying: "But in all these things we overcome because of Him that hath loved us." (*Rom.* 8:37). And likewise in another place the Scripture says: "Thou, O God, hast proved us; Thou hast tried us by fire as silver is tried; Thou hast brought us into a net, Thou hast laid afflictions on our back." (*Ps.* 65:10–11; 66:10–11, Vulg.). And to show us that we ought to be under a Superior, it continues, saying: "Thou hast set men over our heads." (*Ps.* 65:12; 66:12, Vulg.). And fulfilling the command of the Lord through patience in the face of both adversities and injuries, those who are struck on the one cheek will turn also the other. When someone takes their coat they give their cloak also; and when forced to go one mile they go two. (Cf. *Matt.* 5:39–41). With the Apostle Paul they endure false brethren and "bless those who curse them" (*2 Cor.* 11:26; *1 Cor.* 4:12).

The fifth step of humility is to hide from his Abbot none of the evil thoughts that enter into his heart or the evils committed in secret, but humbly to confess them. Concerning this the Scripture exhorts us, saying: "Reveal thy way to the Lord and trust in Him." (*Ps.* 36:5; 37:5, Vulg.). And it says further: "Confess to the Lord, for He is good, for His mercy endureth forever." (*Ps.* 105:1; *Ps.* 106:1, Vulg.; *Ps.* 117:1; *Ps.* 118:1, Vulg.). And the Prophet likewise says: "I have acknowledged my sin to Thee and my injustice I have not concealed. I said I will confess against myself my injustice to the Lord; and Thou hast forgiven the wickedness of my sins." (*Ps.* 31:5; 32:5, Vulg.).

The sixth step of humility is when a monk is content with the meanest and worst of everything, and in all that is enjoined him considers himself a bad and worthless workman, saying with the Prophet: "I am brought to nothing and I knew it not; I am become as a beast before Thee, and I am always with Thee." (*Ps.* 72:22–23; 73:22–23, Vulg.).

The seventh step of humility is when he not only declares with his tongue that he is the lowest and vilest of men, but also believes it in the depths of his soul. Thus he will humble himself and say with the Prophet: "I am but a worm and no man, the reproach of men and the outcast of the people." (*Ps.* 21:7; 22:7, Vulg.). "I have been exalted and humbled and confounded." (*Ps.* 87:16; 88:16, Vulg.). And also: "It is good for me that Thou hast humbled me, that I may learn Thy commandments." (*Ps.* 118:71, 73; 119:71, 73, Vulg.).

The eighth step of humility is when a monk does nothing but what is encouraged by the common rule of the monastery and the example of the experienced members of the community.

The ninth step of humility is when a monk holds his tongue from speaking, and out of consideration of the virtue of silence does not speak until he is asked; for the Scripture argues that "in a multitude of words thou shalt not avoid sin" (*Prov.* 10:19); and that "the talkative man does not prosper on the earth." (*Ps.* 139:12; 140:12, Vulg.).

The tenth step of humility is when a monk is not easily clever at jokes or keen to laugh, for it is written: "The fool exalteth his voice in laughter." (*Sir.* 21:23).

The eleventh step of humility is that when a monk speaks, he speaks gently and without laughter, humbly and with gravity, with few and well-chosen words, and that he not raise his voice, for it is written: "The wise man is known by the fewness of his words."

The twelfth step of humility is that a monk is not only humble of heart, but in his whole bearing he always displays humility to those who met up with him; namely, at the Work of God, in the oratory, in the monastery, in the garden, on a journey, in the field, or wherever he may be. Whether sitting, walking, or standing, let him always have his head bowed down, his eyes fixed on the ground, ever considering himself guilty of his sins, thinking that he is already standing before the dread judgment seat of God, and always saying to himself in his heart what the publican in the Gospel said, with his eyes fixed on the ground: "Lord, I am a sinner and not worthy to lift up mine eyes to heaven"

(*Luke* 18:13); and again with the Prophet: "I am bowed down and humbled exceedingly." (*Ps.* 37:7–9; Ps. 38:7–9, Vulg.; *Ps.* 118:107; *Ps.* 119:107, Vulg.).

When, at last, he has ascended all these steps of humility, the monk will soon arrive at that love of God, which being perfect, casteth out fear. (*1 John* 4:18). By virtue of this love, all rules which he initially observed not without fear, he will now begin to keep without any effort; and he will do so with the natural grace of a habit, no longer from the fear of hell, but from the love of Christ—from the very habit of goodness and a delight in virtue. The Lord will make all this manifest in him through His Holy Spirit, once this worker is cleansed of vices and sins.

CHAPTER EIGHT
On the Divine Office during the Night

THE brethren will rise during the winter season, that is, from the calends of November till Easter, at the eighth hour of the night (as one would reasonably calculate it); so that, having rested until just past midnight, they may rise after they have fully digested their supper. The time, however, which remains over after the night Office will be employed in study by those of the brethren who still have some parts of the psalms and the lessons to learn.

But from Easter to the aforesaid calends, let the hour for celebrating the night Office be so arranged, that after a very short interval, during which the brethren may go out for the necessities of nature, the morning Office, which is to be said at the break of day, may follow shortly thereafter.

CHAPTER NINE
How Many Psalms Are to Be
Said at the Night Office

D URING the winter season, after the essential opening words—
Deus, in adjutorium meum intende; Domine, ad adjuvandum me festina—there is next to be said three times, *Domine, labia mea aperies, et os meum annuntiabit laudem tuam.* (*Ps.* 50:17; 51:17, Vulg.). To this the 3rd psalm and the *Gloria* are to be added. After this the 94th psalm is to be chanted with its antiphon, or at least chanted. Next let a hymn follow, and after that six psalms with antiphons. After these and the versicle have been said, let the Abbot give the blessing. Once everyone is seated on the benches, let three lessons be read alternately by the brethren from the book on the lectern. Between lessons let three responsories be said. Let two of the responsories be said without the *Gloria*, but after the third lesson, let the cantor intone the *Gloria*. When the cantor begins to sing it, let all rise at once from their seats in honor of and with reverence for the Blessed Trinity.

Let the divinely inspired books of both the Old and the New Testaments be read at the night Offices, as well as the expositions of them which have been written by the most eminent orthodox and Catholic Fathers.

After these three lessons with their responsories, let six more psalms follow, to be sung with *Alleluia*. After these let the lessons from the Apostle be said by heart, then the verse, the petition of the litany, that is, *Kyrie eleison*. And so let the night Office come to an end.

CHAPTER TEN
How the Office Is to Be Said
during the Summer Season

F ROM Easter till the calends of November let the same number of psalms be recited in the manner described above, except that on account of the shortness of the nights, no lessons should be read from the book. In place of these three lessons, let one from the Old Testament be said by heart. Let a short responsory follow this, and let all the rest be performed as was stated; namely, that never fewer than twelve psalms be said at the night Office, exclusive of the 3rd and the 94th psalm.

CHAPTER ELEVEN
How the Night Office Is to Be
Said on Sundays

FOR the night Office on Sunday the monks should rise earlier. At this Office let the following regulations be observed, namely: after six psalms and the verse have been sung, as we arranged above, and all have been properly seated on the benches in their order, let four lessons with their responsories be read from the book, as we said above. In the fourth responsory only, let the *Gloria* be intoned by the chanter, and as soon as he begins it let all rise with reverence.

After these lessons let six other psalms with antiphons and the verse follow in order as before. After these let there be said three canticles from the Prophets, selected by the Abbot, and chanted with *Alleluia*. When the verse also has been said and the Abbot has given the blessing, let four other lessons from the New Testament be read in the order above mentioned. But after the fourth responsory, let the Abbot intone the hymn *Te Deum laudamus*. When this hath been said, let the Abbot read the lesson from the Gospel, all standing with reverence and awe. When the Gospel has been read let all answer *Amen*, and immediately the Abbot will follow up with the hymn *Te decet laus*, and when he has given the blessing Morning Prayer will begin.

Let this order of the night Office be observed on Sunday the same way in all seasons, in summer as well as in winter, unless for some reason (God forbid) the brethren should rise too late, then some of the lessons or the responsories would have to be shortened. Let every precaution be taken that this does not occur. If it should happen, let him through whose neglect it came about make due satisfaction for it to God in the oratory.

CHAPTER TWELVE
How Morning Prayer Is to Be Said

A T MORNING prayer on Sunday, let the 66th psalm be said first simply, without an antiphon. After that let the 50th psalm be said with *Alleluia*; after this let the 117th and the 62nd be said; then the blessing and the praises, one lesson from the Apocalypse, said by heart, a responsory, the Ambrosian hymn, the verse and the canticle from the Gospel, the litany, and it is finished.

CHAPTER THIRTEEN
How Morning Prayer Is to Be
Said on Week Days

O N WEEK days let Morning Prayer be celebrated in the follow- ing manner, to wit: Let the 66th psalm be said without an anti- phon, drawing it out a little as on Sunday, that all may arrive for the 50th, which is to be said with an antiphon. After this let two other psalms be said according to custom; namely, the 5th and the 35th on the second day, the 42nd and the 56th on the third day, the 63rd and the 64th on the fourth day, the 87th and the 89th on the fifth day, the 75th and the 91st on the sixth day, and on Saturday the 142nd and the canticle from Deuteronomy, which should be divided into two *Glorias*. On the other days, however, let canticles from the Prophets, each for its proper day, be said as the Roman Church skillfully sings it. After these let the psalms of praise follow; then one lesson from the Apostle, to be said from memory, the responsory, the Ambrosian hymn, the verse, the canticle from the Gospel, the litany, and it is finished.

Never end Morning Prayer or Vespers unless the Lord's Prayer is said in the hearing of all by the Superior. This is established because the thorns of scandal are likely to spring up. By virtue of the promise which the brethren make when they say, "Forgive us as we forgive" (*Matt.* 6:12), they may cleanse themselves of failings of this kind.

At the other hours which are to be said, let only the last part of this prayer be said aloud, so that all may answer, "But deliver us from evil." (*Matt.* 6:13).

CHAPTER FOURTEEN
How the Night Office Is to Be Said on the Feasts of the Saints

ON THE feasts of the saints and all other solemnities let the night Office be performed as we said it should be done for Sunday; except that the psalms, the antiphons, and the lessons proper for that day should be said; but let the arrangement mentioned above be maintained.

CHAPTER FIFTEEN
At What Times the Alleluia Is to Be Said

FROM holy Easter until Pentecost let the *Alleluia* be said without exception, both with the psalms and with the responsories; but from Pentecost until the beginning of Lent let it be said every night at the Night Office with the six latter psalms only. However, on all Sundays outside of Lent, let the canticles, Morning Prayer, Prime, Terce, Sext, and None be said with *Alleluia*. Let Vespers, however, be said with the antiphon; but let the responsories never be said with *Alleluia*, except from Easter to Pentecost.

CHAPTER SIXTEEN
How the Work of God Is to Be Performed during the Day

A S THE Prophet says: "Seven times a day I have given praise to Thee" (*Ps.* 118:164; 119:164, Vulg.), we will fulfill this sacred sevenfold number if we perform the duties of our service at the time of Morning Prayer, Prime, Terce, Sext, None, Vespers, and Compline; for he was speaking of these hours when he said: "Seven times a day I have given praise to Thee." (*Ps.* 118:164; 119:164, Vulg.). In fact, the same Prophet says of the night watches: "At midnight I arose to confess to Thee." (*Ps.* 118:62; 119:62, Vulg.). At these times, therefore, let us offer praise to our Creator "for the judgments of His justice;" namely, at Morning Prayer, Prime, Terce, Sext, None, Vespers, and Compline; and let us rise at night to acknowledge Him. (Cf. *Ps.* 118:164, 62; 119:164, 62, Vulg.).

CHAPTER SEVENTEEN
How Many Psalms Are to Be Sung at These Hours

W E HAVE now arranged the order of the psalmody for the Night and the Morning Offices; now let us arrange for the remaining Hours. At the first Hour let three psalms be said separately, and not under one *Gloria*. Let the hymn for the same Hour be said after the verse *Deus, in adjutorium* (*Ps.* 69:2; 70:2, Vulg.), before the psalms are begun. Then, after the completion of three psalms, let one lesson be said, a verse, the *Kyrie eleison*, and the collects.

At the third, the sixth, and the ninth Hours, the prayer will be said in the same order; namely, the verse, the hymn proper to each Hour, the three psalms, the lesson, the verse, the *Kyrie eleison*, and the collects. If the community is large, let these Hours be sung with antiphons; but if small, let them be said straight through.

Let the Office of Vespers be limited to four psalms and their antiphons; after these psalms a lesson is to be recited, next a responsory, the Ambrosian hymn, a verse, the Canticle from the Gospel (the *Magnificat*), the Litany, the Lord's Prayer, and the collects.

Let Compline end with the saying of three psalms, which are to be said straight on without an antiphon, and after these the hymn for the same Hour, one lesson, the verse, *Kyrie eleison*, the blessing, and the collects.

CHAPTER EIGHTEEN
In What Order the Psalms Are to Be Said

FIRST of all, the daytime Hours should begin with this verse: *Deus, in adjutorium meum intende; Domine, ad adjuvandum me festina* (*Ps.* 69:2; 70:2, Vulg.), and the *Gloria*, followed by the hymn proper to each Hour. At Prime on Sunday there are to be said four sections of the 118th psalm. At the other Hours—namely, Terce, Sext, and None—let three sections of the same psalm be said. But at Prime on Monday let three psalms be said—namely, the first, the second, and the sixth; and thus each day at Prime until Sunday, let three psalms be said each time in consecutive order up to the 19th psalm, yet so that the 9th psalm and the 17th be each divided into two *Glorias*; and thus it will come about that at the night Office on Sundays we always begin with the 20th psalm.

At Terce, Sext, and None, on Monday, however, let the nine remaining sections of the 118th psalm be said, three sections at each of these Hours. The 118th psalm having thus been parceled out for two days—namely, Sunday and Monday—let there be sung on Tuesday for Terce, Sext, and None, three psalms each, from the 119th to the 127th, that is, nine psalms. These psalms will always be repeated at the same Hours until Sunday—the arrangement hymns, lessons, and versicles should nevertheless remain the same each day, so that on Sunday one always begins with the 118th psalm.

Let Vespers be sung daily with the four psalms sung in a richer mode. Let these psalms begin with the 109th to the 147th, but omitting those which are set aside for the other Hours—namely, from the 117th to the 127th, and the 133rd, and the 142nd. All the rest are to be said at Vespers; and as the psalms fall three short, those of the aforesaid psalms are to be divided as they are somewhat long—namely, the 138th, the 143rd, and the 144th. But because the 116th is short, let it be joined to the 115th. The order of the psalms for Vespers having thus been arranged let the rest, namely, the lessons, the responsories, the hymns, the verses, and the canticles, be said as we have directed above.

At Compline, however, let the same psalms be repeated every day—namely, the 4th, the 90th, and the 133rd.

Having arranged the order of the Office, let the remainder of the psalms be distributed equally into seven Night Offices; this is to be done by dividing the longer ones into two and making sure that twelve are fixed for each night. We wish to be absolutely clear that, if this distribution of the psalms should displease anyone, he should arrange them as he deems appropriate, so long as he takes particular care that the whole Psalter of one hundred and fifty psalms be said every week, and that it always start again from the beginning at during the Night Office (vigil) for Sunday. This is enjoined since monks who in a single week chant less that the whole Psalter with the customary canticles show themselves to be slothful in the service of their devotion. For we read that our holy forefathers promptly fulfilled in one day what I hope we lukewarm monks may be capable of performing over the course of a whole week.

CHAPTER NINETEEN
On Properly Reciting the Psalter

WE BELIEVE that God is present everywhere and that the eyes of the Lord behold the good and the bad in every place. (Cf.

Prov. 15:3). We particularly believe this when we take part in the Work of God. Let us, therefore, always be mindful of what the Prophet says, "Serve ye the Lord with fear." (*Ps.* 2:11). And again, "Sing ye wisely." (*Ps.* 46:8; 47:8, Vulg.). And, "In the sight of the angles I will sing praises to Thee." (*Ps.* 137:1; 138:1, Vulg.). Therefore, let us consider how we ought to behave in the sight of God and His angels, and let us stand while singing, so that our mind may be in harmony with our voice.

CHAPTER TWENTY
On Reverence at Prayer

WHEN we wish to ask a favor of men who are in power, we do not dare to approach them, except with humility and reverence. How much more, then, should we beseech the Lord God of the universe with all humility and purity of devotion? And let us be assured that it is not in many words, but in the purity of heart and tears of compunction that we are heard. For this reason prayer ought to be short and pure, unless, perhaps it is lengthened by the inspiration of divine grace. Yet prayers offered in community should always be short, and let all rise together as soon as the superior gives the signal.

CHAPTER TWENTY-ONE
On the Deans of the Monastery

IF THE community is large, let brethren of good repute and holy life be chosen from among them and be appointed Deans; and let them take care of their deaneries in everything according to the commandments of God and the directions of their Abbot. Let only men be chosen as Deans whom the Abbot can confidently share his burdens. Let them not be chosen for their rank, but for the merit of their life and their humble mastery of wisdom. And if any of them, puffed up with pride, should be found blameworthy, he should be corrected once and again and even a third time. If, however, he still refuses to amend his ways, let him be deposed, and one who is worthy be placed in his stead. We establish the same regulation for the Prior.

CHAPTER TWENTY-TWO
How the Monks Are to Sleep

LET THE brethren sleep separately, each in a separate bed. Let them receive bedding appropriate to their mode of life, as the Abbot directs. If possible, let all sleep in one chamber; but if the number does not allow this, let them sleep in tens or twenties with the seniors who have charge of them. Let a candle be kept burning constantly in the cell till morning.

Let them sleep clothed and girded with belts or cords so that they may be always ready; but let them not have knives at their sides while they sleep, lest perchance while asleep they are wounded in their dreams. When the sign is given, they must rise without delay. Then let them hasten to outstrip each other going to the Work of God, yet be sure that this is done with all gravity and decorum. Let the younger brethren not have their beds beside each other, but intermingled with the older ones; and rising to the Work of God, let them gently encourage one another and so thwart the typical excuses of the drowsy.

CHAPTER TWENTY-THREE
On Excommunication for Faults

IF A BROTHER is found stubborn or disobedient or proud or murmuring, or if he is opposed to anything in the Holy Rule and a scoffer of the commandments of his Superiors, let him be admonished by his Superiors once and again in secret, according to the command of our Lord. (Cf. *Matt.* 18:15–16). If he does not amend his ways let him publically be taken to task before the entire community. If he does not reform even then, let him be placed under excommunication—but only if he is capable of coming to terms with this punishment, On the other hand, if he is behaving like a scoundrel, let him undergo corporal punishment.

CHAPTER TWENTY-FOUR
What the Manner of
Excommunication Should Be

THE severity of excommunication or punishment ought to be proportionate to the gravity of the offense. To determine that is left to the judgment of the Abbot. If, however, anyone of the brethren is detected in smaller faults, let him only be excluded from eating at the common table.

The following shall be the practice with respect to one who has been excluded from the common table: he is not allowed to intone a psalm or an antiphon, nor to read a lesson in the oratory until he has given satisfaction. Let him take his meal alone, after that of the brethren. So, if, for instance, the brethren take their meal at the sixth hour that brother will take his at the ninth, and if the brethren take theirs at the ninth, he will take his in the evening, until by due satisfaction he obtains his pardon.

CHAPTER TWENTY-FIVE
On Graver Faults

BUT a brother who is found guilty of a graver fault should be excluded from both the table and the oratory. Let none of the brethren join his company or speak with him. Let him work alone at his assignments, continuing in his penitential sorrow, mindful of that terrible sentence of the Apostle which says, "such a man is delivered over for the destruction of the flesh, that the spirit may be saved in the day of the Lord." (*1 Cor.* 5:5). Let him take his food alone, and let the Abbot determine the amount and time of his meal; and let him not be blessed by anyone passing by, nor even the food that is given him.

CHAPTER TWENTY-SIX
On Those Who without the Abbot's Permission
Associate with the Excommunicated

IF ANY brother presume to associate with an excommunicated brother in any way, or to speak with him, or to send him a message, without the permission of the Abbot, let him incur the same penalty of excommunication.

CHAPTER TWENTY-SEVEN
How Concerned the Abbot Should
Be about the Excommunicated

LET THE Abbot show all care and concern towards offending brethren because "they that are in health need not a physician, but they that are sick." (*Matt.* 9:12). Therefore, like a wise physician he ought to use every opportunity to send secret consolers—namely, discreet elderly brethren—to console the wavering brother, as it were, in secret, and induce him to make humble satisfaction; and let them cheer him up "lest he be swallowed up with overmuch sorrow" (*2 Cor.* 2:7); but, as the same Apostle says, "confirm your charity towards him" (*2 Cor.* 2:8); and let everyone pray for him.

The Abbot must take the utmost pains and strive with all prudence and zeal so that none of the flock entrusted to him perish. For the Abbot must know that he has taken upon himself the care of infirm souls, not a tyranny over the strong. Let him fear the threat of the Prophet by which the Lord says: "What ye saw to be fat, that ye took to yourselves, and what was diseased ye cast away." (*Ezek.* 34:3–4). And let him imitate the loving example of the Good Shepherd, who, leaving the ninety-nine sheep on the mountains, went to seek the one that had gone astray. He had such pity on its weakness that He mercifully placed it on His sacred shoulders and thus brought back to the fold. (Cf. *Luke* 15:5).

CHAPTER TWENTY-EIGHT
On Those Who Having Often
Been Corrected Do Not Amend

IF A BROTHER has often been corrected and has even been excommunicated for a fault and does not amend, let a more severe correction be applied to him—namely, he should be beaten with rods.

But if even then he does not reform, or if (God forbid) he is puffed up with pride and attempts to defend his actions, then let the Abbot act like the wise physician. After he has applied the soothing lotions and ointments of encouragement, the medicine of the Holy Scriptures, and if, as a last resource, he has attempted the cautery of excommunication and the blows of the rod, and observes that even after all this his efforts are of no avail, let him apply for that brother at last what is more potent than all these measures: his own prayer and those of the brethren, so that the Lord who is all-powerful may work a cure of the sick brother.

But if he is not healed even in this way, then finally let the Abbot dismiss him from the community, as the Apostle says: "Put away the evil one from among you" (*1 Cor.* 5:13); and again: "If the faithless one depart, let him depart" (*1 Cor.* 7:15); for one diseased sheep must not infect the whole flock.

CHAPTER TWENTY-NINE
Whether Brethren Who Leave the Monastery Ought to Be Received Again

IF A BROTHER, who through his own fault leaves the monastery [*some manuscripts add*: or is expelled], desires to return, let him first promise full amendment of the fault for which he left. Then let him be received taking the lowest rank; by this means his humility will be tried. If he should leave again, let him be received up to a third time, after which point he should know that all possibility of readmission will be denied him.

CHAPTER THIRTY
How Young Boys Are to Be Corrected

EVERY age and aptitude should have its proper discipline. Whenever, therefore, children or youths or those too immature really to understand how grave a penalty excommunication is—when such as these are guilty of a serious fault, let them undergo severe fasting or be disciplined with a solid whipping so that they may be come to their senses.

CHAPTER THIRTY-ONE
The Kind of Man the Cellarer of the Monastery Ought to Be

LET A wise man be chosen from the community as Cellarer of the monastery. He should be of mature character, temperate, not a great eater, not conceited, nor irritable, the kind who does hold a grudge, neither stingy nor wasteful, but a man who fears God, and who could be like a father to the whole community.

Let him have the care of everything, let him do nothing without the order of the Abbot, let him do what has been bid of him and not grieve the brethren. If a brother should happen to request anything of him unreasonably let him not upset the brother with harsh rebuke, but politely and with humility refuse him who wrongfully made the request. Let him be watchful of his own soul, always mindful of the saying of the Apostle: "For they that have ministered well, shall purchase for themselves a good reward." (*1 Tim.* 3:13). Let him provide for the sick, the children, the guests, and the poor, with all care, knowing that, without doubt, he will have to give an account of all these things on judgment day. Let him regard all the vessels of the monastery and all its goods, as if they were sacred vessels of the altar. Let him neglect nothing and let him not give way to avarice, nor let him be wasteful nor a squanderer of the goods of the monastery; but let him do all things in due measure and according to the bidding of his Abbot.

Above all things, let him be humble; and if he hath not the things to give, let him answer with a kind word, because it is written: "A good word is above the best gift." (*Sir.* 18:17). Let him have under his charge everything that the Abbot has entrusted to him, and not presume to meddle with matters forbidden him. Let him give the brethren their apportioned allowance without a fuss or delay, that they may not be scandalized. And he should be mindful of what the Divine Word declares that he deserves who "shall scandalize one of these little ones." (Cf. *Matt.* 18:6).

Let him be given assistants if the community is large so that, with their help, he too may fulfill the Office entrusted to him with an even temper. Let the things that are needed should be distributed, and all the requests should be made at the proper times, so that nobody may be disturbed or annoyed in the house of God.

CHAPTER THIRTY-TWO
On the Tools and Goods of the Monastery

L ET THE Abbot appoint brethren on whose habits and character he can rely to supervise the property of the monastery—including tools, clothing, and things generally. Let the abbot assign to them, as he shall deem proper, all the things which must be collected after use and stored away. Let the Abbot keep a list of these articles, so that, when the brethren in turn succeed each other in these trusts, he may know what he gives out and what he receives back. If anyone, however, treats the goods of the monastery slovenly or carelessly let him be reprimanded and if he does not amend let him come under the discipline of the Rule.

CHAPTER THIRTY-THREE
*Whether Monks Ought to Have
Anything of Their Own*

T HE following vice must be torn out of the monastery by its very roots: that no one may presume to give or receive anything without the command of the Abbot. Neither should anyone regard anything whatever as his own—neither a book, nor a writing tablet, nor a pen, nor anything else whatsoever, since monks are permitted to hold neither their bodies nor their wills by their own power. Instead, everything that is necessary, they must hope to receive from the Father of the monastery; nor should they be allowed to have anything which the Abbot did not give or permit him to have. Let all things be common to all, as it is written; and let no one claim or presume to take anything as his own. (Cf. *Acts* 4:32). Now then, if anyone should be found to indulge this most detestable vice, he is to be warned once and then a second time. If he does not amend his ways, let him be subjected to punishment.

CHAPTER THIRTY-FOUR
*Whether All Should Receive in Equal
Measure What Is Necessary*

IT IS WRITTEN: "Distribution was made to everyone according as he had need." (*Acts* 4:35). We do not mean to cite this in support of indulgent favoritism—God forbid—but rather because one should take into account infirmities. Let him who needs less thank God and not be sad, but let him who needs more be humble when he considers his weakness, and feel special for the indulgence shown him. If this is observed, all the members of the community will be at peace.

Above all, let not the evil of murmuring appear in the smallest expression or gesture for any reason whatever. If anyone be found guilty of that matter, let him be placed under very severe discipline.

CHAPTER THIRTY-FIVE
On the Weekly Servers in the Kitchen

LET THE brethren serve each other so that no one be excused from the work in the kitchen, except on account of sickness or his attending to some important task. For then, greater merit and more charity will be acquired. Help should be given to the weak, however, so that they may do this work out sadness; the size of the community and the circumstances of the place will, of course, dictate the level of help. If the community is large, let the Cellarer be excused from the kitchen, or if, as we have said, any are engaged in more urgent work; let the rest serve each other in charity.

Let him who is to rotate out of the weekly service, do the cleaning on Saturday. Let him wash the towels with which the brethren wipe their hands and feet. Let the outgoing brother as well as the one just starting wash the feet of all. Let the outgoing brother return the utensils of his service to the Cellarer clean and in good condition. Let the

Cellarer give the same to the incoming brother taking stock what he gives out and what he receives back.

An hour before meal time let the weekly servers each receive a drink and a piece of bread over the prescribed portion. In this way, they may serve their brethren at meal time without murmuring or undue strain. On solemn feast days, however, let them abstain until after Mass.

As soon as the morning Office on Sunday is ended, let the incoming and outgoing servers of the week cast themselves upon their knees in the oratory before all, asking their prayers. Let him who is rotating out of the weekly service, say the following verse: *Benedictus es, Domine Deus, qui adjuvisti me et consolatus es me. (Dan.* 3:52; *Ps.* 85:17; *Ps.* 86:17, Vulg.). The one rotating out says this three times and receives the blessing, and then the one who is starting should say: *Deus in adjutorium meum intende; Domine, ad adjuvandum me festina. (Ps.* 69:2; 70:2, Vulg.). And let this also be repeated three times by all. After he has been blesssed let him enter upon his weekly service.

CHAPTER THIRTY-SIX
On the Sick Brethren

CARE must be taken of the sick before all other things and above all other things, for truly when they are served, Christ is served, just as he said, "I was sick and you visited Me." (*Matt.* 25:36). And "As long as you did it to one of these My least brethren, you did it to Me." (*Matt.* 25:40). But let the sick themselves also consider that they are served for the honor of God, and let them not annoy their brethren who serve them with excessive demands. Yet they must be patiently borne with, because from such as these a more bountiful reward is gained. Let the Abbot's greatest care be, therefore, that they suffer no neglect.

Let a room be set apart for the sick brethren, and a God-fearing, diligent, and careful attendant be appointed to serve them. Let the use of the bath be offered to the sick as often as it is useful, but let it be granted more rarely to the healthy and especially the young. Also, let the use of meat be granted to the sick and to the very weak for their recovery. But when they have been restored let them all abstain from meat in the usual manner.

But let the Abbot exercise the utmost care so that the sick are not neglected by the Cellarer or the attendants, because whatever his disciples do amiss is his responsibility.

CHAPTER THIRTY-SEVEN
On the Aged and Children

ALTHOUGH human nature is by itself moved to feelings of compassion for these times of life—namely, old age and childhood—still, the authority of the Rule should make accommodations for them as well. Let their natural weakness be always taken into account and let the strictness of the Rule not be observed in their case with respect to food. Instead, let there be a tender regard on their behalf and let them eat before regular hours.

CHAPTER THIRTY-EIGHT
On the Weekly Reader

READING must not be lacking when the brethren sit at table for meals, but no one should randomly select a text and read it. Rather, let him who is to read for the whole week formally begin his Office on Sunday. After Mass and Communion let him ask all to pray that God may preserve him from the spirit of pride. And let the following verse be said three times by all in the oratory, with the reader himself beginning it: *Domine, labia mea aperies, et os meum annuntiabit laudem tuam* (*Ps.* 50:17; 51:17, Vulg.), and thus having received the blessing let him commence reading.

Let a profound silence be observed at the table so that no whispering or any voice be heard except that of the reader alone. While they are eating and drinking, let the brethren so help each that no one need ask for anything. If, however, something is desired, let it be asked for by means of a sign of any kind rather than a sound. And let no one presume to ask any questions there, either about the book or anything else, in order that no occasion to speak be given (*Eph.* 4:27; *1 Tim.* 5:14), unless, perhaps, the Superior wishes to say a few words for edification.

Let the brother who is reader for the week take a little bread and wine before he starts to read, on account of Holy Communion; otherwise, it may prove too hard for him to fast so long. Afterward, however, he should take his meal in the kitchen with the weekly cooks and the servers. Finally, the brethren are not to read or to sing according to their rank, but rather according to their ability to edify those listening.

CHAPTER THIRTY-NINE
Of the Quantity of Food

MAKING allowance for the dietary limitations of individuals, we believe that for the daily meal (both at the sixth and the ninth hour) two kinds of cooked food are sufficient at every table. With this arrangement, someone who cannot eat of one, may make his meal of the other. Let two kinds of cooked food, therefore, be sufficient for all the brethren. And if there be fruit or fresh vegetables, a third may be added. Let a pound of bread suffice for each day, whether there be only one meal or both dinner and supper. If they are to eat supper, let a third part of the pound be reserved by the Cellarer and be given at supper.

If, however, their work has been especially strenuous, it is left to the discretion and power of the Abbot to add something, if he deem it appropriate, with the provision that there never be an occasion for excess, for a monk should never be overtaken by indigestion. For nothing is so contrary to Christians as excess, as our Lord says: "See that your hearts be not weighed down with excess and inebriation." (*Luke* 21:34).

Let the same quantity of food, however, not be served out to young children; they should receive less than the adults. Frugality must always be observed.

With the exception of the very weak and the ill, all should entirely abstain from eating the flesh of four-footed animals.

CHAPTER FORTY
On the Quantity of Drink

"EVERY one hath his proper gift from God, one after this manner and another after that." (*1 Cor.* 7:7). Thus, it is with some uneasiness that we determine the measure of consumption for others. Nevertheless, making allowance for the weakness of the infirm, we think one hemina of wine a day is sufficient for each man. But let those to whom God has given the strength for abstinence know that they will have their special reward. If the circumstances of the place, or the work, or the heat of summertime should require more, let that be at the discretion of the Superior who must above all things see to it that immoderation and drunkenness do not creep in.

Although we read that wine is not generally speaking proper for monks, yet, because monks in our times cannot be persuaded of this, let us at least agree to this, that we do not drink to satiety, but sparingly; because "wine maketh even wise men fall off." (*Sir.* 19:2). But when the poverty of the place does not even permit the amount described above, but much less or none at all, let those who live there bless God and murmur not. This we charge above all: that they live without murmuring.

CHAPTER FORTY-ONE
At What Times the Brethren
Should Take Their Meals

FROM holy Easter till Pentecost let the brethren dine at the sixth hour and take supper in the evening. From Pentecost on, however, during the whole summer, if the monks have no work in the fields and the excess of the heat doth not interfere, let them fast on Wednesday and Friday until the ninth hour; but on the other days let them dine at the sixth hour. This sixth hour for dinner is to be continued, if they have work in the fields or the heat of the summer is intense. Let the Abbot provide for this; and so let him manage and adjust everything so that souls can be saved, and that the brethren accomplish all their work without having a reasonable cause to murmur. From the ides of September until the beginning of Lent let them always dine at the ninth hour. During Lent, however, until Easter, let them dine in the evening. But let this evening hour be so arranged that they will not need lamp-light during their meal; in fact, let everything be finished while there is still daylight. In sum, let the hour of meals throughout the year, whether for dinner or for supper, be so arranged that everything is done by daylight.

CHAPTER FORTY-TWO
That No One Speak after Compline

AT ALL times monks ought to study silence. This is especially true during the hours of the night. Therefore, on every day, whether it is a day of fasting or a day or not, this shall hold as the rule. If it has been a non-fast day then, as soon as they have risen from their evening meal, let everyone sit together in one place, and let one monk read from the *Conferences of John Cassian* or from *The Lives* of the Fathers, or something else that will edify those listening. The Heptateuch or the Books of the Kings, however, should not be read because it would not be advantageous for tired and weak minds to hear that part of the Scripture at this hour; they should, however, be read at other times.

On the other hand, if it was a fast-day, then, a short interval after Vespers has been said, let them gather for the reading of the *Conferences*, as we have said. Four or five pages should be read, or as much as the hour will permit, in that way all will assemble in that place during the drawn out time of the reading. This should also allow anyone who had been assigned to some specific task to join the community. When, therefore, everyone has assembled in one place, then let them say Compline, and after they leave from Compline, no one should be granted permission to say anything further to anyone.

If, however, anyone is found trying to bend this rule, let him undergo serious punishment. The exceptions to the rule are responses to the needs of guests, or if the Abbot should perhaps give a command to someone. But let even this be done with the utmost gravity and moderation.

CHAPTER FORTY-THREE
On Those Who Are Tardy in Coming to the
Work of God or to Table

A S SOON as any monk hear the signal for the Divine Office he should leave whatever he was working on and hasten there with all speed. Yet he should move with gravity, so that there may be no occasion silliness. Therefore, let nothing be preferred to the Work of God.

If anyone arrives at the Night Office after the *Gloria* of the 94th psalm—which is why we wish it to be slowly and with pauses—he should not stand in his place in the choir; but let him stand last of all, or in the place which the Abbot has set apart for those who are careless. In that way he may be seen by him and by all, until, the Work of God has ended, and he will make satisfaction by public penance. We have made a determination they should stand in the last place or apart from the rest for the following reason: that they may correct their ways prompted by the shame of being seen by all. For if they remained outside the oratory, there might be some who would go back to sleep, or who would sit outside and idle their time in telling stories, and so give a "chance to the devil." (*Eph.* 4:27; *1 Tim.* 5:14). It is better that he come in, therefore. He will not miss the whole hour, and will amend himself for the future.

At the day hours, however, whoever does not arrive for the Work of God after the verse and the *Gloria* of the first psalm, which is said after the verse, should stand in the last place, according to the rule which we stated above. Let him not attempt to join the choir of the chanters until he has made satisfaction, unless the Abbot's permission has given him leave to do so, with the understanding that he atone the fault afterwards.

If anyone does not come to table before the verse, so that all may say the verse and pray together and then sit down to table at the same time, let him be corrected for this once or twice, if he failed to come through his own fault and negligence. If he does not improve his ways after this, he should not be permitted to eat at the common table. Instead, he should eat alone, separated from the company of all; and his portion of wine should be taken from him, until he has made satisfaction and has changed his ways. The same rule should apply to anyone who is not present also at the verse which is said after the meal.

And let no one presume to take food or drink before or after the appointed time. But if anything should be offered to a brother by a superior and he refuses to accept it and then afterwards he desires what he had earlier refused—or, for that matter is he desires anything else—let him receive nothing at all, until he makes due satisfaction.

CHAPTER FORTY-FOUR
Of Those Who Are Excommunicated—
How They Make Satisfaction

WHOEVER is excommunicated for graver faults from the oratory or the table *should* lie outstretched in silence before the door of the oratory the entire time that Work of God is celebrated in the oratory, but let him cast himself face down on the ground, completely prone at the feet of the entire community as they exit the oratory. And let him do this until the Abbot determines that it is enough. When the Abbot bids, let him come and cast himself at his feet, and then at the feet of all so that they may pray for him. Then, if the Abbot orders it, let him be received back into the choir in the place which the Abbot shall determine. Certainly, he should not presume to intone a psalm or a lesson or anything else in the oratory, unless the Abbot again orders it. What is more, at all the Hours, when the Work of God is finished, let him cast himself on the ground in the place where he stands, and thus let him make satisfaction, until the Abbot orders him to conclude his penance.

But those who for lesser faults are excommunicated from the table only should make satisfaction in the oratory, until the Abbot gives the order; let them so continue until he gives his blessing and says, "It is enough."

CHAPTER FORTY-FIVE
On Those Who Commit a Fault in the Oratory

IF ANYONE make a mistake while intoning a psalm, a responsory, an antiphon, or a lesson, but does not humbly make satisfaction on the spot in the presence of all, let him suffer a greater punishment, because he would not correct by humility what he did amiss through negligence. Children simply should receive a whipping for such a fault.

CHAPTER FORTY-SIX
On Those Who Fail in Any Other Matters

IF ANYONE does something wrong while engaged in any work—in the kitchen, in the cellar, in serving, in the bakery, in the garden, at any art or work in any place whatever—or if he breaks or loses anything, or transgresses in any way whatever, and he does not immediately come before the Abbot and the community, and of his own accord confess his offense and make satisfaction, and all this comes to the attention through the observation of another monk, let the offending monk be subjected to a greater correction.

If, however, the reason for his sin comes from some hidden spiritual issue, let the monk disclose it to the Abbot alone, or to his spiritual seniors, who know how to heal their own wounds, and those of others, while not exposing or making them public.

CHAPTER FORTY-SEVEN
On Giving the Signal for the
Time of the Work of God

LET IT BE the Abbot's care that the time for the Work of God be announced both by day and by night. He is either to announce it himself, or to entrust this charge to a careful brother that everything may be done at the proper time.

Let those who have been ordered, intone the psalms or the antiphons according to rank after the Abbot. No one, however, should presume to sing or read unless he is able so to perform this office so that those listening may be edified; and let it be done with humility, gravity, and reverence by the one whom the Abbot ordered.

CHAPTER FORTY-EIGHT
On the Daily Work

IDLENESS is the enemy of the soul. Therefore, the brethren ought to be employed in manual labor at certain times, at others, in *lectio divina*. Hence, we believe that the time for each activity will be properly ordered as follows: namely, that from Easter till the calends of October, they go out in the morning from the first till about the fourth hour, to do the necessary work, but that from the fourth till about the sixth hour they devote to reading. After the sixth hour, however, when they have risen from table, let them rest in their beds in complete silence; or if, perhaps, anyone desires to read for himself, let him read in such a way that he not disturb others. Let the Office of None be said somewhat earlier, about the middle of the eighth hour; and then let them work again at what is necessary until Vespers.

If, however, the needs of the place, or poverty should require that they do the work of gathering in the harvest themselves, they should not be downcast; for they are true monks, if they live by the work of their hands as did our forefathers and the Apostles. Let everything be done in moderation, however, on account of the faint-hearted.

From the calends of October till the beginning of Lent, let them apply themselves to reading until the end of second hour. At the second hour let Terce be said, and then let all be employed in the work which has been assigned to them till the ninth hour. When, however, the first signal for the hour of None hath been given, let each one put aside his work and be ready for the sound of the second signal. But after their meal they should devote themselves to reading or the psalms.

During the days of Lent let them be employed in reading from morning until the third hour, and till the tenth hour let them do the work which assigned to them. During these days of Lent let all received books from the library, and let them read them from beginning to end. These books are to be given out at the start of Lent.

Above all, let one or two of the seniors be appointed to go about the monastery during the time when the brethren are devoted to reading, and they should take notice in case a lazy brother be found giving himself up to idleness or gossip, and not applying himself seriously to *lectio*. Such a monk is not wasting his one time, but he is also distracting others. If such a monk be found (which God forbid), let him be corrected once and a second time. If he doth not change his ways, let him come under the correction of the Rule in such a way that others may fear. Finally, a brother should not spend time conversing with another brother except at the appropriate time.

On Sunday also let all devote themselves to reading, except those who are appointed to the various functions. But if anyone should be so careless and slothful that he will not or cannot meditate or read, let some work be given him to do, that he may not be idle.

As to the weak and the sickly brethren, let such work or craft be assign that they are not idle, but neither are they so wearied with the strain of work that they are driven away. Their weakness must be taken into account by the Abbot.

CHAPTER FORTY-NINE
On the Keeping of Lent

THE life of a monk ought always to be a Lenten observance. Since, however, few have that sort of strength, we advise that at least during these days of Lent he guard his life with every kind of purity and that at the same time he wash away all his neglect of other season during these holy days. This will then be worthily done, if we restrain ourselves from all vices. Let us devote ourselves to tearful prayers, to reading and compunction of heart, and to abstinence.

During these days, therefore, let us add something to the usual amount of our service in the form of special prayers and abstinence from food and drink so that each one can freely offer to God "with the joy of the Holy Ghost" (*1 Thess.* 1:6) something above and beyond the expected measure—namely, let him deprive his body somewhat of food, drink, sleep, chattiness, merriment—and let him await holy Easter with the joy of spiritual desire.

Everyone, however, should make known to his Abbot what he is offering up; it should be done with his approval and blessing, because what is done without permission of a spiritual father will be considered presumption and vain glory, and not merit. Therefore, let everything be done with the approval of the Abbot.

CHAPTER FIFTY
On Brethren Who Work a Long Distance from the Oratory or Are on a Journey

THE brethren who work at a great distance and cannot come to the oratory at the appointed time—in cases where the Abbot has made a careful determination that this is in fact the situation—should perform the Work of God where they are working, and do so on bended knee with a godly fear. In like manner let those who are sent on a journey not allow the appointed Hours to pass by, but let them say the Office by themselves as best they can and not neglect the duty of divine service.

CHAPTER FIFTY-ONE
On the Brethren Who Do Not Go Very Far Away

BRETHREN who are sent out on any business and are expected to return to the monastery the same day should not presume to eat away from the monastery, even though they are urged to do so, unless for some reason permission is granted by the Abbot. If they act otherwise, let them be excommunicated.

CHAPTER FIFTY-TWO
On the Oratory of the Monastery

LET THE oratory be what it is called, and let nothing else be done or stored there. When the Work of God is finished, let all go out with utmost silence and let reverence be shown to God. In this way, a brother who perhaps desires to pray by himself is not hindered by another's misconduct. And if a monk at some other time desires to pray in private, let him enter with simplicity and pray, not with a loud voice, but with tears and fervor of heart. In sum, anyone who does not say his prayers in this way, should not be permitted to stay in the oratory after the Work of God is finished, lest another monk, as we said, be disturbed.

CHAPTER FIFTY-THREE
Of the Reception of Guests

LET ALL guests who arrive be received as Christ, because He himself will say: "I was a stranger and you took Me in." (*Matt.* 25:35). And let due honor be shown to all, especially to those "of the household of the faith" (*Gal.* 6:10) and to pilgrims.

When, therefore, a guest is announced, let him be met by the Superior and the brethren with every mark of charity. The first order of business is that they must pray together; then they are united with one another in peace. The kiss of peace should not be given before prayer has first been said, on account of the wiles of the devil. In the greeting let all humility be shown to the guests, whether arriving or departing: With the head bowed down or even the whole body prostrate on the ground, let Christ be adored in them as He is also received.

When the guests have been received, let them be accompanied to prayer, and after that let the Superior, or whomever he commands, sit down with them. Let the divine law be read to the guest that he may be edified, after which let every kindness be shown him. Let the fast be broken by the Superior in deference to the guest, unless, it happens to be a day of solemn fast, which cannot be broken. The brethren, however, keep the customary fast. The Abbot should pour the water on the hands of the guests. And the Abbot and the whole brotherhood should wash the feet of all the guests. When they have been washed, let them say this verse: "We have received Thy mercy, O God, in the midst of Thy temple." (*Ps.* 47:10; 48:10, Vulg.). Let the greatest care be taken, especially in the reception of the poor and pilgrims, because Christ is received especially in them; whereas the dread respect for the wealthy itself obtains for them respect.

Let the kitchen of the Abbot and the guests set apart so that the brethren may not be disturbed. Guests arrive at uncertain times and are never wanting in the monastery. Let two brothers who are able to fulfill this Office well go into the kitchen for a year. Let help be given them as they need it, that they may serve without murmuring; and when they have not enough to do, let them go out again for work where it is commanded them. Let this course be followed, not only in this Office, but in all the Offices of the monastery—that whenever the brethren need help, it be given them, and that when they have nothing to do, they again obey orders. Moreover, let also a God-fearing brother have assigned to him the apartment of the guests, where there should be sufficient number of beds made up; and let the house of God be wisely managed by the wise.

On no account let anyone who is not ordered to do so, associate or speak with guests; but if he meet or see them, having saluted them humbly, as we have said, and asked a blessing, let him pass on saying that he is not allowed to speak with a guest.

CHAPTER FIFTY-FOUR
Whether a Monk Should Receive
Letters or Anything Else

O N NO account should a monk receive letters, pious tokens, or little gifts of any sort, either from parents or any other person, nor from his brothers, without the permission of the Abbot. Nor may they send them. And even if anything is sent him by his parents, he should not presume to accept it without first making it known to the Abbot. And if the Abbot grants that the gift may be accepted, it remains in Abbot's power to give it to whom he pleases. The brother to whom it was sent should not become sad, that "no chance be given to the devil." (*Eph.* 4:27; *1 Tim.* 5:14). Should anyone presume to act otherwise, however, let him fall under the discipline of the Rule.

CHAPTER FIFTY-FIVE
On the Clothing and the
Footgear of the Brethren

C LOTHING should be given to the brethren according to the circumstances of the place and the nature of the climate in which they live, because in cold regions more in needed, while in warm regions less. The abbot should, therefore, take such things into consideration. We are of the belief that for a temperate climate a cowl and a tunic for each monk are sufficient—a woolen cowl for winter and a thin or worn one for summer. Monks should also have a workman's apron, and sandals and a pair of boots to protect their feet.

Monks should not worry about the color or the texture of all these things. Let them be the sort that can be obtained locally and bought rather cheaply. Let the Abbot, however, pay attention to the size, so that these garments are not too small, but rightly fitted.

When a monk receives new clothes, he should promptly return the old ones, to be put away in the store room for the poor. For it is sufficient for a monk to have two tunics and two cowls, for wearing at night and for washing. Anything over and above that amount is super-fluous and should be taken away. So, too, let them return sandals and whatever is old, when they receive anything new.

Those who are sent out on a journey should receive leggings from the wardrobe, which, on their return, they will place back, washed. The cowls and the tunics taken on the journey should also be a little better than the ones they usually wear. These all they receive from the ward-robe when they set out on a journey, and give back when they return.

For their bedding, let a straw mattress, a blanket, a coverlet, and a pillow be sufficient. The Abbot should frequently examine these to determine if anyone is hiding private possessions there. And if anything is found that a monk did not receive with the permission of the Abbot, let him fall under the severest discipline. And that this vice of private ownership may be torn out by the roots, the Abbot should provide each monk the kind of things that he requires—namely, a cowl, tunic, san-dals, boots, belt, knife, pen, needle, towel, writing tablet; that all pre-tence of being needy may be removed. With respect to this matter, let the following sentence from the Acts of the Apostles always be kept in mind by the Abbot: "And distribution was made to every man accord-ing as he had need." (*Acts* 4:35). And so, let the Abbot should give attention to the infirmities of the needy, not for the ill will of the envi-ous. Yet in all his decisions, let the Abbot think of the judgment of God.

CHAPTER FIFTY-SIX
On the Abbot's Table

THE Abbot's table should always be with the guests and travel-ers. When, however, there are no guests, let it be in his power to invite any of the brethren he desires. Let him provide, however, that one or two of the seniors always remain with the brethren for the sake of discipline.

CHAPTER FIFTY-SEVEN
On the Craftsmen of the Monastery

IF THERE be craftsmen in the monastery, let them work at their art in all humility, provided that the Abbot gives his permission. But if any of them should grow proud on account of his craftsmanship and be of the opinion that he is personally bestowing a special grace to the monastery, let him be removed from his work and not return to it, unless after he has humbled himself, the Abbot again permits it. But if any of the work of the craftsmen is to be sold, let those assigned to oversee the transaction not attempt to practice any fraud. Let them always be mindful of Ananias and Saphira, lest, perhaps, they (or any others who practice fraud in things belonging to the monastery) end by suffering in their souls the death which these suffered in the body. (Cf. *Acts* 5:1–11). What is more, let not the vice of avarice creep into the way prices are determined, but let the price always be set a little lower than it can be given by men in the world, That God May Be Glorified in All Things. (Cf. *1 Pet.* 4:11).

CHAPTER FIFTY-EIGHT
On the Manner of Admitting Brethren

EASY admission should not be given granted to someone who is in the early stages of discerning a religious vocation, but, as the Apostle says, "Try the spirits, whether they be of God." (*1 John* 4:1). Therefore, if the newcomer perseveres in knocking, and after four or five days seems with patience to bear the wrongs he experiences and the difficulties of admission, and yet he persists in his request, then let admission be granted him, and let him live for a few days in the guest quarters.

After that period, however, let him live in the novice quarters, and there let him meditate, eat, and sleep. Let a senior also be appointed for him, who is skilled at winning souls; he will observe him with great care and see whether he really seeks God—whether he is eager for the Work of God, for obedience and for humiliations. Let him be shown all the hard and rugged things through which we pass on to God.

If he promises to persevere in stability, let this Rule be read to him in order after the lapse of two months, and let it be said to him: "Behold the law under which you desire to fight. If you can keep it, enter; if, however, you cannot, depart freely." If he still perseveres, then let him be taken back to the aforementioned apartment of the novices, and let him be tried again in all patience. And after the lapse of six months let the Rule be read over to him, that he may know for what purpose he enters. And if after four months, he still remains firm, let the same Rule be read to him again. Now if he carefully reflects on the matter and can promise to keep everything, and to do everything that is commanded him, then let him be received into the community, but he must understand that he is now placed under the law of the Rule, and that from that day forward it is no longer permitted to him to wrest his neck from under the yoke of the Rule, which after so long a deliberation he was at liberty either to refuse or to accept.

In the oratory when all are present, the one about to be received should promise his stability, the conversion of morals, and obedience. This promise is made before God and His saints so that should that man ever act contrary to our way of life, he clearly understands that he will be condemned by Him whom he mocks.

Let him write out his promise in the name of the saints whose relics are there, and of the Abbot there present. Let him set down promise in his own hand; or at least, if he does not know how to write, let another write it at his request, then, let the novice make his mark, and with his own hand place it upon the altar. After he has placed it there, the novice should next begin the verse: "Uphold me, O Lord, according to Thy word and I shall live; and let me not be confounded in my expectations." (*Ps.* 118:116; 119:116, Vulg.). Then let all the community thrice respond adding the *Gloria Patri*. Then let that novice brother cast himself down at the feet of all so that they may pray for him. From that day forth, let him be considered as one of the community.

If he has any property, let him first either grant it to the poor or bestow it on the monastery by a solemn donation, reserving nothing for himself; indeed, he should understand that from that day forward he will no longer have power even over his own body. For that reason, he should be divested at first opportunity of the garments with which he is clothed, and be vested in the garb of the monastery. Let this be done in the oratory. But let the clothes of which he was divested be laid by in the storeroom to be kept, that, if on the devil's prompting he should ever consent to leave the monastery (which God forbid) he be then stripped of his monastic habit and cast out. But let him not receive the document of his profession which the Abbot received from the altar, but let it be preserved in the monastery.

CHAPTER FIFTY-NINE
On the Children of the Noble and of the Poor Who Are Offered

IF IT HAPPEN that a nobleman wishes to offer his son to God in the monastery and the boy is of tender age, let his parents execute the written promise which we have mentioned above. Let them wrap that document and the boy's hand with the oblation of bread and wine in the altar cloth and in this manner offer him.

As to their property, let the parents bind themselves under oath in the same document promising that they will never give him anything themselves, nor through an intermediary agent, nor in any way whatever, nor establish the means for his owning anything. Now if they do not wish to do this but desire to make an offering to the monastery as alms for their own benefit, let them make a donation to the monastery of whatever goods they wish, reserving for themselves the income of it, if they so desire. And let everything be so strictly construed that the young man suffer from no ambiguity, which might deceive and ruin him (which God forbid)—we have learned by experience that this can happen.

Let those who are poor act in like manner. But as to those who have nothing at all, let them simply make their promise, and with the oblation offer their son in the presence of witnesses.

CHAPTER SIXTY

On Priests Who May Wish to Live in the Monastery

IF ONE of the priestly order ask to be received into the monastery, let consent not be granted too quickly; still, if he urgently persists in his request, let him know that he must keep the whole discipline of the Rule, and that nothing will be relaxed in his favor, that it may be as it is written: "Friend, whereunto art thou come?" (*Matt.* 26:25).

It may be granted him, however, to stand next after the Abbot and to give the blessing or offer the solemn prayers, but only if the Abbot orders him to do so; otherwise, let him not presume to do anything of the sort, knowing that he is under the discipline of the Rule. Rather he really ought to give examples of humility to all. And if there is a question of an appointment in the monastery, or any other matter, let him be ranked by the time of his entry into the monastery, and not out of respect for the priesthood.

But if one of the clerical order, moved by the same desire, wishes to join the monastery, let him too have a middling place, provided he promises to keep the Rule and personal stability.

CHAPTER SIXTY-ONE

How Pilgrim Monks Are to Be Received

IF A MONK on pilgrimage arrives from a distant lands and desires to live in the monastery as a guest, and he is content with the customs he finds there and does not trouble the monastery with unnecessary demands, but is content with what he finds, let him be received for as long a time as he desires. A situation may arise in which that visiting monk, with humility and charity, censures or reasonably critiques something. The Abbot should consider the matter carefully, especially, since the Lord may have sent him for that very purpose.

If later on this monk desires to promise his stability let his wish not be denied, especially since his manner of life will have been reviewed during his stay as a guest. If during the time that he was a guest he was found to be demanding or morally disordered, not only must he not associate with the monastic body but he should even be politely told to leave, lest others be infected by his wretched character. But if he is not the sort that deserves to be cast forth, he should not only be admitted to join the community, if he should seek it, but he should even be urged to remain, that others may be taught by his example. For in every land we serve the same Lord and fight under the same King.

If the Abbot should recognize the visiting monk to be such a man he may also place him in a somewhat higher rank. The Abbot may, in fact, place not only a monk, but also those of the aforementioned grades of priests and clerics in a higher position than according to their date of entry—if he observes their lives to be such as to deserve it. But let the Abbot take care never to admit a monk of any other known monastery to residence, without the consent of his Abbot or commendatory letters, because it is written: "What thou wilt not have done to thyself, do not to another." (*Tob.* 4:16).

CHAPTER SIXTY-TWO
On the Priests of the Monastery

IF THE Abbot desires to have a priest or a deacon ordained for his monastery, let him select from among his monks one who is worthy to discharge the priestly Office.

The one ordained should be on his guard against arrogance and pride, and should not attempt to do anything except what is commanded him by the Abbot, knowing that he is now all the more subject to the discipline of the Rule. The priesthood should not provide him with an occasion to forget the obedience and discipline of the Rule, rather it should inspire him to advance more and more towards the Lord.

Let him, however, always keep the place which he was given when he entered the monastery, except when performing his duties at the altar, unless the choice of the community and the wish of the Abbot have promoted him in acknowledgment of the merit of his life. Let him know, however, that he must observe the established rule of the Deans and the Priors.

Should he presume to do otherwise, let him be judged not as a priest, but as a rebel; and if after frequent warnings he does not amend, the Bishop should even be brought in, as a witness. If even then he does not amend his ways and his guilt is clearly shown, let him be cast forth from the monastery, provided his obstinacy is such that he will neither submit nor obey the Rule.

CHAPTER SIXTY-THREE
On the Order in the Monastery

LET ALL keep their order in the monastery as follows, as determined by the time of their conversion and the merit of their life, or as the Abbot will arrange. Let the Abbot not disturb the flock committed to him, nor should he dispose of anything unjustly by an arbitrary use of his powers; but let him always bear in mind that he will have to give an account to God of all his judgments and works. Therefore, the brethren should approach for the kiss of peace or for Communion, intone the psalms, or stand in choir according to that order which the Abbot has established, or which the brethren hold. In no place whatever should age determine the order or be a disadvantage, for Samuel and Daniel when mere boys judged the priests. (Cf. *1 Sam.* 3; *Dan.* 13:44–62). Therefore, apart from those whom, as we have said, the Abbot from higher motives has advanced, or, for certain reasons, has demoted, let all the rest take their place according to the date of their conversion: thus, for instance, let him who came into the monastery at the second hour of the day, know that he is younger than he who came at the first hour, whatever his age or dignity may be. Children are to be kept under discipline at all times and by everyone. Let the younger honor their elders, therefore, and the older love the younger.

In addressing each other no one should call another by his simple name; but let the older call the younger, *fraters*—brothers; let the younger, however, call their elders, *nonni*—fathers, which communicates the reverence due to one's father. As the Abbot is believed to hold the place of Christ, let him be called Lord and Abbot; this is not because he has made claim to the title, but out of honor and love for Christ. Let him think on this and so show himself to be worthy of such an honor.

Wherever, then, the brethren meet each other, let the younger ask a blessing from the elder; and when the elder pass by, let the younger rise and give him place to sit; and let the younger not presume to sit down with him unless his elder bid him to do so, that it may be done as it is written: "In honor preempting one another." (*Rom.* 12:10).

Children and young men should take their proper places in the oratory and at table with all due discipline; moreover, outdoors, or wherever they may be, let them be kept under close observance and discipline until they reach the age of understanding.

CHAPTER SIXTY-FOUR
On the Installation of the Abbot

IN THE installation of an Abbot let this principle always be observed: that he be placed in the position whom the whole community, in the fear of God, chose. Even part—regardless of how small—may successfully do so, when done with sounder judgment.

But let him who is to be selected be chosen for the merit of his life and his mastery of wisdom, though he be the last in the community.

If even the whole community should by mutual consent select a man who agrees to connive at their evil ways (banish the thought) and these offenses should somehow come to the knowledge of the Bishop in whose diocese the place is found, or if news should come to neighboring Abbots (or nearby Christian people), let them not permit the intrigue of the wicked to succeed, but let them appoint a worthy steward over the house of God, knowing that they shall receive a bountiful reward for this action, if they do it with a pure intention and godly zeal; whereas, on the other hand, they commit a sin if they neglect it.

But when the Abbot hath been installed let him bear in mind how great a burden he has taken and to whom he must give an account of his stewardship. (Cf. *Luke* 16:2). Let him realize that it befits him more to provide than preside. He must, therefore, be versed in the divine law, that he may know whence "to bring forth new things and old." (*Matt.* 13:52). Let him be chaste, sober, and merciful, and let him always exalt "mercy above judgment" (*Jas.* 2:13), that he also may obtain mercy.

Let him hate vice, but love the brethren. And even in his corrections, he should with prudence and not go to extremes, lest, while trying too vehemently to scrape away the rust, he break the vessel. Let him always keep his own frailty in mind, and remember that "the bruised reed must not be broken." (*Is.* 42:3). By this we are not saying that he should allow vices to take root, but that he should uproot them with prudence and charity, in the manner he determines best for each one, as we have already said; and let him strive to be loved rather than feared.

Let him not be restless or over-anxious, exacting, or headstrong, nor jealous or overly suspicious, because then he will never have rest. In all his commands, whether they refer to things spiritual or temporal, he should be deliberative and considerate. Let him be discerning and moderate in the tasks which he imposes, recalling the discretion of holy Jacob who says: "If I should cause my flocks to be overdriven, they would all die in one day." (*Gen.* 33:13). Adopting this and other maxims about discretion—which is the mother of all virtues—let him so temper everything that the strong may still have something to desire and the weak nothing to demoralize them. Above all, let him take heed the present Rule in every detail, so that after he has served well, he may hear from the Lord what the good servant heard who gave his fellow-servants grain in due season: "Amen, I say to you," He says, "he shall set him over all his goods." (*Matt.* 24:47).

CHAPTER SIXTY-FIVE
On the Prior of the Monastery

IT OFTEN happens that grave scandals arise in monasteries through the installation of the Prior; since there are some who, puffed up with the wicked spirit of pride and thinking themselves to be second Abbots, take for themselves usurped power. As a result they foster scandals and cause dissension in the community. This is especially the case in those places where the Prior has been appointed by the same Bishop or the same Abbots who appointed his Abbot. The absurdity of this custom is easily observed because, from the very beginning of his installation, he is spurred to pride when his thoughts suggest to him that now he is exempt from the authority of the Abbot, because "thou too hast been installed by the same power by whom the Abbot was installed." From this material arise envy, discord, slander, quarrels, jealousy, and disorders. While the Abbot and the Prior are thus at odds with each other, it must follow that their souls are endangered by this discord and that those who are under them, as long as they favor one party over another, rush to their ruin. The blame for this evil rests on the heads of those who were the authors of such disorders.

We foresee, therefore, that for the preservation of peace and charity it is best that the governance of the monastery should depend on the will of the Abbot. When at all possible, the affairs of the monastery (as we have explained before) should be overseen by deans, as the Abbot shall dispose, so that, the same Office being shared by many, no one will become proud.

If, however, the needs of the place require it, or the community reasonably and with humility makes a request—and the Abbot shall deem it useful—the Abbot himself should appoint as whomever he wish as Prior, but he should do so after the counsel of the God-fearing brethren. Let the Prior reverently undertake what his Abbot has enjoined on him, doing nothing against the will or the direction of the Abbot; for the higher he is placed above others, the more careful ought he to be in obeying the precepts of the Rule.

If the Prior be found disorderly or blinded by vainglory, or has been proved to be a scoffer of the Holy Rule, let him be admonished up to the fourth time. If he does not amend, the correction of the regular discipline should be applied to him. But if he does not amend even after that, let him be deposed from the Office of priorship, and another who is worthy be appointed in his stead. Afterward, if he is not quiet and obedient in the community, let him also be expelled from the monastery. Still, let the Abbot reflect that he must give an account to God for all his decisions, lest perhaps the flame of envy or jealousy should consume his soul.

CHAPTER SIXTY-SIX
On the Porter of the Monastery

LET A wise old man be placed at the gate of the monastery, one versed in how to listen and give an reply, and whose mature age does not permit him to wander about.

The porter should have his cell near the gate so that those come will always find someone on hand who will respond to their requests. As soon as anyone knocks or a poor person calls out, let him answer, "Deo gratias," or invoke a blessing; and with gentleness born from the fear of God let him return his reply speedily in the fervor of charity.

If the porter should need an assistant, let him have a younger brother.

If it is possible the monastery should be so constructed that all the necessaries—such as water, the mill, the garden, the bakery—are enclosed, and the various arts may be plied inside of the monastery. In that way, there will be no need for the monks to go about outside, because this would have no advantage to their souls. Furthermore, we desire that this Rule be read in the community quite often so that none of the brethren can excuse himself on grounds of ignorance.

CHAPTER SIXTY-SEVEN
On the Brethren Who Are Sent on a Journey

LET THE brethren who are to be sent on a journey commend themselves to the prayers of all the brethren and of the Abbot. And after the last prayer in the Work of God, let a commemoration always be made for the absent brethren.

On the day that the brethren return from the journey, let them lie prostrate on the floor of the oratory at all the Canonical Hours, when the Work of God is finished, and beg the prayers of all on account of their failings, for they may have been caught off guard by the sight of evil or the sound of frivolous speech while on their journey.

And no one should presume to tell others what he has seen or heard outside of the monastery; for manifold difficulties arise from it. But if anyone presumes to do so, let him undergo the punishment of the Rule. The same applies to anyone who presumes to go beyond the enclosure of the monastery, or anywhere else, or to do anything, however little, without the order of the Abbot.

CHAPTER SIXTY-EIGHT
If a Brother Is Commanded to
Do Impossible Things

IF IT should happen that any difficult or impossible task is placed upon a brother, he should nevertheless accept the order of the one who commands with all meekness and obedience. If, however, he sees that the weight of the task is altogether beyond the measure of his strength, let him patiently and at the right moment share with his superior the reasons why. He should do this without any display of pride, or stubbornness, or conceit. After this explanation, however, if the superior still considers his orders appropriate, let the junior monk be convinced that this is in his best interest; and let him obey from love, relying on the help of God.

CHAPTER SIXTY-NINE
That in the Monastery No One
Presume to Defend Another

CARE must be taken that on no occasion one monk presume to defend another in the monastery, or to act as if he were his patron protector, even in cases where they may be closely related by ties of blood. No such presumption should be undertaken by the monks ever, because such conduct can give rise to very grave scandal. If anyone should overstep this rule, let him be rather severely punished.

CHAPTER SEVENTY
That No One Presume to Strike Another

LET EVERY occasion for presumption be avoided in the monastery. We decree that no one be permitted to excommunicate or to strike one of his brothers, unless the Abbot has given him the authority.

But let those who transgress be taken to task in the presence of all, that the others may fear. (Cf. *1 Tim.* 5:20).

Children under the age of sixteen should remain under the careful watch and discipline of all; this endeavor too must be done with moderation and understanding. For if anyone should presume, without the Abbot's instructions, to chastise young adults or to vex the children with a fiery display of temper, that monk should subject to the discipline of the Rule; because it is written: "What thou dost not wish to be done to thee, do thou not to another." (*Tob.* 4:16).

CHAPTER SEVENTY-ONE
That the Brethren Be Obedient to One Another

NOT only must the brethren render the good gift of obedience to the Abbot, but they must also obey one another, knowing that they shall go to God by this path of obedience. Hence, all younger brothers must obey their elder brothers with complete charity and zeal. The only exception springs from a command of the Abbot or one of the officers established by him (no personal command can contravene this). But if anyone is found to be obstinate, let him be corrected.

And if a brother be corrected in any way by the Abbot or by any of his superiors for even a slight reason, or even if he just barely perceive that the temper of any of his Superiors is ruffled or excited against him in the least, let him without delay cast himself down on the ground at his feet making satisfaction, until the agitation is healed by a blessing. If anyone refuse to do this, either he should undergo corporal punishment, or, if he should remains obstinate, let him be expelled from the monastery.

CHAPTER SEVENTY-TWO
On the Virtuous Zeal Which the Monks Ought to Have

JUST as there is a bitter and evil zeal which separates us from God and leads to hell, so there is a virtuous zeal which separates us from vice and leads to God and life everlasting.

Let the monks, therefore, practice this zeal with a most ardent love: namely, that they outdo one another in showing honor. (Cf. *Rom.* 12:10). Let them bear one another's infirmities, whether of body or of character, with the utmost patience; let them vie with one another in obedience. Let no one pursue what he deems advantageous to himself, but rather to another. Let them practice fraternal charity with a self-giving love.

Let them fear God. And let them love their Abbot with sincere and humble affection; let them prefer nothing whatsoever to Christ—and may He lead us all together to life everlasting.

CHAPTER SEVENTY-THREE
That the Whole Observance of Justice Is Not Laid Down in this Rule

NOW, we have set down this Rule so that, by observing it in monasteries, we may show that we have acquired at least some measure of moral integrity and the beginnings of the monastic life.

On the other hand, for someone who is rushing toward the perfection of the monastic life, there are the teachings of the holy Fathers, the observance of which carries a man to the heights of perfection. For what page or what utterance of the divinely inspired books of the Old and the New Testament is not a most exact guide for human life? Or, what book of the holy Catholic Fathers does not echo with directions to our Creator by a straight path? So, too, the *Conferences* of the Fathers, and their *Institutes* and their *Lives*, and the *Rule* of our holy

Father, Basil—what are these for monks striving to live well and under obedience but the tools of the virtues? But for us lazy monks—leading poor lives marked by neglect—they provoke the blush of shame.

Therefore, whoever you are, hastening to your heavenly fatherland, with the help of Christ fulfill this little Rule that I have set down for beginners; and then with God's help, upon those high peaks of doctrine and virtue which we have recounted above, you will at last arrive. Amen.

THE TWELVE DEGREES
OF HUMILITY
AND PRIDE

———————•———————

By Saint Bernard of Clairvaux

PREFACE TO THE
TWELVE DEGREES OF
HUMILITY AND PRIDE

LIGHT IN THE VALLEY—
FROM LAW TO DESIRE

By William Edmund Fahey, Ph.D.

———————————•———————————

THE Roman mind of St. Benedict would have understood Leo XIII's re-organization (and rejuvenation) of the Benedictines in the nineteenth century. Finally recovering from the devastation of the Enlightenment and its Revolutions, the Catholic Church entered into a period of re-organization. Through the Papal brief *Summum Semper*, Leo brought together the scattered remnants of the Benedictine houses and—in an authoritative act—fashioned them into a single confederation or "order" under one Abbot Primate. Today, we bring to monasticism a largely nineteenth-century notion of a single, centralized order of Benedictine monks. Yet monasticism is again showing its diversity of forms and the Benedictines themselves have long been progressing back towards a decentralized model. There are currently twenty loosely affiliated congregations of Benedictines, seven of which date from after *Summer Semper*.

For all his *Romanitas*, St. Benedict did not intend a monolithic idea of an "order." His conception of monasticism was an attempt to understand how the Christian life could be lived purely and effectively. The confederation of monasteries that sprung out of his Rule was not a blueprint for a homogenized corporation. As the last chapter of the Rule makes clear, his directives were for beginners and envisioned modification and flexibility—much like the norms of classical Roman law and rule, in fact. By the tenth century, the various monastic communities in Western Europe had largely adopted the Rule of St. Benedict, while adapting it to local conditions and preserving, at least in part, ideas, customs, and rules taken from other authors. The Rule was successful in providing the essential architectural structure, but never envisioned uniformity, only unity of principles.

With its success came a diffusion of the vision and spirit of the Rule, as is often the case with organic and institutional growth: the further monasticism spread over geography and time, the less the fervor of the founding generation remained. Yet monastic literature and the Rule itself contained the principles of western monasticism's own reform, and its elasticity was limited, of course, by the Gospel and the life of grace. By the tenth century the spirit of development and renewal awoke in Europe, taking a northern and southern form.

In southern Europe, the desire for austerity was voiced anew by St. Romuald and St. Peter Damian. The anchoritic or hermitical fervor limited by St. Benedict rose up again to call Italian monasticism away from its distractions and, in some monasteries, its decadence. At the beginning of the eleventh century in the mountain valley of the Apennines near Arezzo, the Camoldoli movement began, harkening back to the most primitive roots of monasticism; and the solitude that was largely an interior solitude amongst Benedictines became once again a structural solitude. Men were not to be alone and apart for God while still amongst men, rather they were to be alone and apart physically. The Camodolese monks organized themselves over whole sections of mountain valleys in a form similar to eastern monasticism.

In northern Europe, the desire for austerity had resulted in a massive internal reform of Benedictines, first initiated by St. Benedict of Aniane

(747–821), and then a century later by William Duke of Aquitaine's successful foundation of an abbey at Cluny in 910. The initial Cluniac reform was spurred on by a scholarly reawakening and a heightened sense of the world's fragility and the ultimate judgment of God.

Cluniac monasticism vigorously cultivated the private and corporate prayer life of its members. Corporate solitude was to be protected not only by the physical cloister, but by the aural cloister of near continual chant and vocal prayer. Under the dynamic direction of St. Hugh and with strong papal backing, Cluny, positioned in the very heart of France, became a vehicle for the far-reaching reinvention of monasticism and inspired two centuries of splendor in the liturgical arts and church architecture. In one of the most beautiful paradoxes in European history, a zeal for absolute concentration on the soul and a life of endless praise in the face of the end times led to one of the greatest bursts in material creativity and enrichment in Church history.

In response to the Cluniac development and the arguable departure from primitive Benedictine observance, a group of men originally associated with the monastery at Molesme, turned away for the marshy thickets of Cîteaux, twenty miles south of Dijon. On Palm Sunday in the year 1098, a monk named Robert (1028–1111) and a small group of disciples left their larger community to live as the early Christians, understanding the Rule of St. Benedict as providing them a "formula of perfect penance" (*formula perfectae penitentiae*). A vision of this new life would soon be set out in the *Exordium Parvum*, one of the founding documents of a new kind of monastery. The members of the new association were to be poor men living with and contemplating a poor Christ, as they would say. Their common life, according to the Rule of St. Benedict, was to lead them back to a strict simplicity in all things exterior and interior. The perceived lavishness of the Cluniac-inspired Benedictines would be utterly rejected. Among the early founders was the English lawyer, St. Stephen Harding, whose hand was decisive in the *Exordium* and other early documents. These men were to be the Cistercians—the name originating from the simple place name for their new community: *Cistercium* in Latin (the site of modern Cîteaux), an abbreviation of *cis tertium* [*lapidem miliarum*] or "nearby the third milestone." How appropriate that men questing for simplicity would take their name from nothing more than a wayside road marker.

Behind this somewhat romantic narrative about the origins of this new branch of the Benedictine family was the common reforming spirit of the age. St. Robert of Molesme was seventy years-old in 1098. He had held a variety of positions within various monastic communities and clearly was restless in his pursuit of simplicity. At least three times prior to the attempt at Cîteaux, St. Robert had led groups of men into the wilds of France to establish hermitages. Molesme, which he would dramatically depart from and denounce, was initially his own attempt at a reformed Benedictine community. His early work had been fruitful; many were attracted to his austere zeal. St. Bruno, for example, who would eventually go on to found the most successful of the hermitical forms of western monasticism—the Carthusians—studied at Molesme under St. Robert in the 1070s. But ultimately St. Robert desired a more perfect form to structure his imitation and service of Christ. In his last attempt, he leaned heavily on St. Stephen Harding, a man marked by a deep understanding of the scholarship and legal reforms that were emerging throughout western Christendom.

For the new community at Cîteaux, law would take an almost mystical meaning. Law—the law of Benedict through his Rule and the laws or customs of the new Cistercian norms—was the means by which the Holy Spirit communicated His love. Obedience to the Rule of Benedict and the Cistercian documents led one to see the spiritual rectitude and purity that could be found in the selfless observations of rules in their integrity. Prayer life was simplified and the concept of pursuing an "ordered life," an *Ordo*, came to the fore. The "order" of Cistercian life re-emphasized things found in the Rule of St. Benedict—silence, mortification, manual labor—but recovered the centrality of charity as the objective. Observance of the law was not impersonal obedience, but the complete alignment of the monk's heart to the heart of Christ and to the will of the Father. In so doing, he would become a vessel of grace and love, untainted or diluted by the material riches or worldly apostolates (such as education, ornate liturgical craftsmanship, or diplomacy) that were increasingly becoming the expertise of the Cluniac Benedictines. It was into this setting, in the year 1113, under St. Stephen Harding as the third abbot of Cîteaux that a young Burgundian noble then named Bernard of Fontaines arrived with thirty companions, seeking Christ according to the principles of the new monastery.

The impossibility of adequately sketching the life St. Bernard of Clairvaux can be understood in Thomas Merton's remark that "Bernard contained the whole twelfth century in himself." Born for knighthood and adventure, St. Bernard (1090–1153) displayed his remarkable character most magnificently in his youthful rejection of either the straightforward pursuit of military and political prowess as a feudal lord or the apparently obvious route towards authority by way of the Cluniac monasticism. An inner impulse drove Bernard toward the austere vision of a kingly power which demanded displays of love and loyalty in the miry woods of Cîteaux. Yet in choosing the harder path of nascent Cistercian monasticism, Bernard would discover that all the functions of a feudal lord or powerful Churchman were not removed from his life, but only purified and multiplied under the laws of charity and the *ordo* of the Cistercian life which he would do much to shape and develop. St. Bernard would have a life filled with drama: interventions (political and ecclesial), public preaching, the reform of the papacy, the countering of grave theological and moral errors, and the organization of Christendom's greatest military endeavor—the Crusades—as well as its most best-known military order—the Templars. Finally, St. Bernard would oversee the reform or foundation of more than sixty monasteries; he stands as one of the most charismatic leaders in history.

The work which follows this introduction—*De Gradibus Superbiae et Humilitatis* (or *The Degrees of Humility and Pride*) was composed before Bernard of Fontaines was transformed by trial, conflict, and ardent fidelity into St. Bernard of Clairvaux, the "Doctor Mellifluus" of the Church. This was Bernard's first work. He had recently been sent by Stephen Harding along with a small group of followers to found a monastery in a marshy valley of Champagne, a site Bernard would name Clairvaux—"the clear valley"—testifying both to Bernard's humor and his faith-filled vision of what would rise up there. Despite a future punctuated by travel, he would remain the Abbot of Clairvaux until his death thirty seven years later. But 1115, the year of this work's appearance, witnessed little that could hint at future renown.

The life of the white-robed monks at Clarivaux was precarious, the health of their ascetic young abbot marked by illness, and the most basic material security of the establishment was a decade away. Those who know the restrained architecture that the Cistericians would later create or who envision something like that which inspired the "serene and blessed mood" which fell upon Wordsworth while walking near Tintern Abbey, must put aside such thoughts. The ideas fashioned to give monasticism its most mystical form were shaped under conditions on which men murmured for lack of food and the author spent many months in and out of the makeshift infirmary. Yet this is precisely what allowed the passionate heart of Bernard to develop the essential teaching of the Cistercians: that all the mortification and order of the monastic life was but preparation for the mercy and rapture of God's love.

For Bernard, men would ascend or descend, and they needed formal guidance on how to steady their souls, but the goal of monasticism was *an experience* of God's love beyond mere knowledge. The rules of Benedict were to keep the monk humble in their observation *and* in their breach, for God's intervening mercy would move the monk from the austere bruising of justice back towards the soul's ascent. Humility was the ladder to climb or fall, but even in falling, the ladder would remain for all who accepted the monastic life—not as a set of Pharisaical "rules," but as a path through one's own frailty and ever towards Christ. The Rule of Benedict was designed to strengthen the soul not only by successful ascent through the virtues, but through the hard yet necessary revelation of our vices. Only what was purified could be united to God. Bernard's early meditation marked a profoundly psychological turn into Catholic spirituality and the beginning of a sensual language that could strike some as distant from the spare *Romanitas* of St. Benedict. Yet these men are of a piece: without Benedict the lawgiver, Bernard the mystic would have no sturdy frame for his ardent contemplative journey. In the seventh chapter of Benedict's Rule, St. Bernard found the means for exploring the soul and working with God to return it to its Source, as a spouse gives her body to her true love. Readers of the *Ladder* should read and re-read that chapter as they move through this text.

Readers should note also the essential structure of the treatise: there are two basic parts, an exploration of the relationship between humility and truth, followed by a detailed analysis of the degrees or steps of pride and humility. The steps upon which Bernard focuses his attention are largely the precipitous steps taken in pride—steps that move one away from God—yet in honestly recognizing them for what they are, the Christian recognizes that an ascent can again begin in truth and through grace and mercy.

In the opening exposition on humility and truth, St. Bernard explains that our knowledge of the truth begins in humility and only with humility: we must understand ourselves as we really are. This perception of truth is then sharpened when we see others as ourselves—that is, as mortal men, limited and marred by sin and, like us, in need of mercy. The process by which we call for mercy on behalf of others and show mercy to others leads to the third stage of truth, the clear perception of what is true through contemplation of God. This contemplation is only possible because the heart has been utterly cleansed by grace, cleansed precisely because we have shown and, therefore, participated in God's mercy. While parts of this analysis can be found in both Christian and pagan authors, Bernard gives this exploration of the truth a Trinitarian dimension, pointing to the progressive aspect of mystical union. Christ the Son teaches us through our intellect first the purpose of humility. This stage is chiefly directed towards the self.

The Holy Spirit enables man to love in charity, act with justice and show mercy through his will and actions. This stage is chiefly directed towards neighbors. God the Father leads the thoughtful and merciful man—like St. Paul—into the rapture of true Wisdom. The second half of the treatise carefully portrays the descending grades of the spiritual life with a delightful, humorous, and painfully accurate depiction of human self-deception and frailty.

This treatise, penned by the man whom the seventeenth-century Benedictine scholar Jean Mabillon called the "last of the fathers," displays the florid, patch-work style of the Patristic age, where a host of Church Fathers reinforce the principles of Scriptures and find themselves occasionally supported by unlikely pagan poets. The text is highly rhetorical. St. Bernard aims at the kind of delight alluded to in the words of the prophet Jeremiah: "Thou hast seduced me, Lord, and I let myself be seduced." (*Jer.* 20:7—*Seduxisti me, Domine, et seductus sum*). A principle of Cistercian spiritual writing from Bernard on is the movement of the person from carnal desire to spiritual desire. The language of love and desire and, indeed, the whole range of secular literature remain in place, but purified gently and progressively so that the soul does not cease to desire, but desires all the more its truest object: God.

Further Reading

The two best introductions to the early legislation and literature of the Cistercians may be found in:

> *The Cistercian World: Monastic Writings of the Twelfth Century,*
> trans. and ed. P. Matarasso (London: Penguin Books, 1993).
> Contains selections from the found documents of Cîteaux,
> Bernard of Clairvaux, William of St. Thierry, Guerric of Igny,
> Aelfred of Rievaulx, and others.

The Great Beginning of Cîteaux: A Narrative of the Beginning of the Cistercian Order—The Exordium Magnum *of Conrad of Eberbach*, trans. Benedicta Ward and P. Savage; ed. R. Elder (Kalamazoo, MI: Cistercian Publications, 2012).

General Studies

Stephen Tobin, *The Cistercians: Monks and Monasteries of Europe* (Woodstock and New York: The Overlook Press, 1995). Tobin's work is replete with excellent photographs and embeds the Cistercians in the social and political culture of medieval Europe.

J. B. Dalgairns, *Life of St. Stephen Harding, Abbot of Citeaux and Founder of the Cistercian Order*, ed. John Henry Newman, with notes by Herbert Thurston, S.J. (New York: Benzinger Brothers, 1898). Dalgairns was one of Newman's most committed students at Oxford and joined Newman in the founding of the English Oratorians. At Newman's suggestion he worked steadily with a company of scholars on the history of early English saints. This particular work provides important perspective for understanding the Cistercians and their significant English influence.

Louis Bouyer, *The Cistercian Heritage*, trans. E.A. Livingstone (Westminster, MD: The Newman Press, 1958). The second and third chapters of this work focus on St. Bernard. Bouyer finally synthesizes the work of earlier generations with his own insights on Bernard. The book as a whole remains the best theological introduction to the Cistercian contribution.

L. J. Lekai, *The Cistercians: Ideal and Reality* (Kent, OH: Kent State University Press, 1977).

St. Bernard: his life and his impact on Catholic Spirituality

Cuthbert Butler, *Western Mysticism* (London: Constable, 1922).

G. R. Evans, *Bernard of Clairvaux* (Oxford: Oxford University Press, 2000).

Etienne Gilson, *The Mystical Theology of St. Bernard*, trans. A. H. C. Dowens (New York: Sheed and Ward, 1939). Gilson deftly applies a synthetic approach to St. Bernard's thought. On the one hand, the book is helpful for creating a structural unity to the varying creativity found in Bernard's writings. On the other hand, the coherence is at times more Gilson's than Bernard's— who like any prolific thinker develops his views from work to work and even within a single work, sometimes to an exasperating degree. Readers should not expect from St. Bernard himself the same kind of coherence that Gilson discloses.

Jean Leclercq, O.S.B., *Bernard of Clairvaux and the Cistercian Spirit*, trans. C. Lavoie (Kalamazoo, MI: Cistercian Publications, 1976). Dom Leclercq is perhaps the most thoughtful of Bernard's Benedictine students; his *Bernard of Clairvaux* is a delightfully written meditation.

Ailbe Luddy, *The Life and Teachings of St. Bernard* (Dublin: Gill, 1927).

Thomas Merton, O.S.C.O., *The Last of the Fathers: Saint Bernard of Clairvaux and the Encyclical Letter*, Doctor Mellifluus (New York: Harcourt Brace Jovanovich, 1954). Merton's own introduction carefully glosses and contextualizes the more visionary and general pronouncements of Pope Pius XII's encyclical.

Basil Pennington, O.C.S.O., "Introduction" in Bernard of Clairvaux, *The Steps of Humility and Pride*, trans. M. Ambrose Conway, O.C.S.O (Kalamazoo, MI: Cistercian Publications, 1989), pp. 1–24. This is the most careful analysis of Bernard's treatise in English.

John R. Sommerfeldt, The *Spiritual Teaching of Saint Bernard of Clairvaux* (Kalamazoo, MI: Cistercian Publications, 1991).

AUTHOR'S CORRECTION

———•———

IN ORDER to strengthen and support a certain opinion expressed in this little book I quoted the passage in the Gospel (*Mark* 13:32) in which Our Lord states that He was unaware of the date of the final Judgment. To this I inadvertently added a word which, as I have since discovered, does not occur in the Gospel. For the text has simply "*neither the Son knoweth*," whereas I, thinking rather of the sense than of the wording, and with no intention to mislead, by mistake wrote: "*The Son of Man Himself knoweth not.*" (*Mark* 13:32) On this I based the whole of the subsequent argument, in which I attempted to prove the truth of my assertion by means of an inaccurate quotation. I did not discover my mistake until long after the publication of the pamphlet, and when a number of copies had been made. It is impossible to correct a mis-statement in a book which has had a wide circulation, so I have thought it incumbent on me to resort to the only possible remedy—an admission that I was wrong. And in another passage I have expressed a definite opinion about the Seraphim which I never heard, and have nowhere read. Here also my readers may well consider that it would have been more reasonable on my part to have said "I suppose," as I had certainly no desire to offer more than a conjecture on a matter which I was unable to prove from Scripture. It is also possible that the title chosen *Concerning the Degrees of Humility* may incur censure—but this will come only from those who overlook or misunderstand the meaning of that title—an explanation of which I have been careful to give in the conclusion of the tract.

—Saint Bernard

AUTHOR'S PREFACE

———•———

YOU have asked me, brother Godfrey, to expand and put in writing the substance of the addresses *On the Degrees of Humility* which I had delivered to the brethren. I admit that, anxious as I was to give to this request of yours the serious answer that it deserved, I was doubtful whether I could comply with it. For with the evangelist's warning in my mind, I did not venture to begin the work, until I had sat down and calculated whether my resources were sufficient for its completion. Then, when love had cast out the fear that I had entertained of ridicule for failure to complete my work, it was replaced by misgiving of a different kind; for I was apprehensive of greater danger from the credit that might attend success than of the disgrace that might attach to failure. So I found myself, as it were, at the parting of the ways indicated respectively by affection and by fear; and I was long in doubt as to which was the safer choice. For I was afraid that if I said anything worth saying about humility, I might myself be found wanting in that virtue, whereas if, on grounds of modesty, I refused to speak, I might fail in usefulness. And I saw that, though neither of these courses is free from peril, I should be obliged to take one or the other. So I have thought it better to give you the benefit of anything that I can say, than to seek personal safety in the harbour of silence. And I earnestly trust that, if I am fortunate enough to say anything which commends itself to you, I may have in your prayers a safeguard against pride, whereas if—as is more likely—I produce nothing worthy of your attention, there will be no possible cause for conceit.

—Saint Bernard

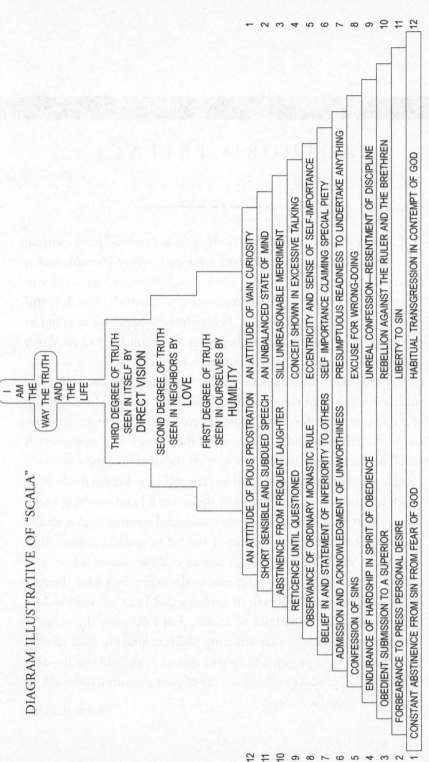

DIAGRAM ILLUSTRATIVE OF "SCALA"

I AM THE WAY THE TRUTH AND THE LIFE

THIRD DEGREE OF TRUTH
SEEN IN ITSELF BY
DIRECT VISION

SECOND DEGREE OF TRUTH
SEEN IN NEIGHBORS BY
LOVE

FIRST DEGREE OF TRUTH
SEEN IN OURSELVES BY
HUMILITY

12	AN ATTITUDE OF PIOUS PROSTRATION	AN ATTITUDE OF VAIN CURIOSITY	1
11	SHORT SENSIBLE AND SUBDUED SPEECH	AN UNBALANCED STATE OF MIND	2
10	ABSTINENCE FROM FREQUENT LAUGHTER	SILL UNREASONABLE MERRIMENT	3
9	RETICENCE UNTIL QUESTIONED	CONCEIT SHOWN IN EXCESSIVE TALKING	4
8	OBSERVANCE OF ORDINARY MONASTIC RULE	ECCENTRICITY AND SENSE OF SELF-IMPORTANCE	5
7	BELIEF IN AND STATEMENT OF INFERIORITY TO OTHERS	SELF IMPORTANCE CLAIMING SPECIAL PIETY	6
6	ADMISSION AND ACKNOWLEDGMENT OF UNWORTHINESS	PRESUMPTUOUS READINESS TO UNDERTAKE ANYTHING	7
5	CONFESSION OF SINS	EXCUSE FOR WRONG-DOING	8
4	ENDURANCE OF HARDSHIP IN SPIRIT OF OBEDIENCE	UNREAL CONFESSION—RESENTMENT OF DISCIPLINE	9
3	OBEDIENT SUBMISSION TO A SUPERIOR	REBELLION AGAINST THE RULER AND THE BRETHREN	10
2	FORBEARANCE TO PRESS PERSONAL DESIRE	LIBERTY TO SIN	11
1	CONSTANT ABSTINENCE FROM SIN FROM FEAR OF GOD	HABITUAL TRANSGRESSION IN CONTEMPT OF GOD	12

The first two stages of the ascent must be made before admission to the monastery.

The last two of the descent can be made only after departure or expulsion therefrom.

SUMMARY

---•---

THE TWELVE DEGREES OF HUMILITY

The heads of the following book.[1]

XII. A permanent attitude of bodily, and spiritual prostration.

XI. The speech of a monk should be short, sensible and in a subdued tone.

X. Abstinence from frequent and light laughter.

IX. Reticence, until asked for his opinion.

---

1. These twelve degrees of humility are taken from the seventh chapter of the Rule of St. Benedict, the title of which is *Concerning Humility*. Its second paragraph runs thus: "Brethren, if we wish to arrive at the highest point of humility and speedily to reach that heavenly exaltation to which we can only ascend by the humility of this present life, we must by our ever-ascending actions erect such a ladder as that which Jacob beheld in his dream by which the Angels appeared to him descending and ascending. This descent and ascent signifieth nothing else than that we descend by self-exaltation and ascend by humility. And the ladder thus erected is our life in the world which if the heart be humbled, is lifted up by the Lord to heaven. The sides of the same ladder we understand to be our body and soul, in which our divine vocation hath placed various degrees of humility or discipline which we must ascend." (*Rule of St. Benedict.* Eng. Trans. by D. Oswald Hunter Blair, p. 43.)

This *scala* or "ladder" as constructed by St. Bernard, exhibits the plan and purpose of the treatise. The chart appended is an attempt to show how, in his opinion, the degrees of humility and of pride correspond to and counterbalance each other.

VIII. Observance of the general rule of the monastery.

VII. Belief in and declaration of one's inferiority to others.

VI. Admission and acknowledgment of one's own unworthiness and uselessness.

V. Confession of sins.

IV. Patient endurance of hardship and severity in a spirit of obedience.

III. Obedient submission to superiors.

II. Forbearance to press personal desire.

I. Constant abstinence from sin for fear of God.

These degrees of humility are set out in an ascending scale. The first two stages must be passed outside the monastic cloister. He who has so risen may thus in the third degree, make his submission to his superior.

THE TWELVE DEGREES OF PRIDE
TAKEN DOWNWARDS

I. Curiosity, when a man allows his sight and other senses to stray after things which do not concern him.

II. An unbalanced state of mind, showing itself in talk unseasonably joyous and sad.

III. Silly merriment, exhibited in too frequent laughter.

IV. Conceit, expressed in much talking.

V. Eccentricity—attaching exaggerated importance to one's own conduct.

VI. Self-assertion—holding oneself to be more pious than others.

VII. Presumption—readiness to undertake anything.

VIII. Defence of wrong-doing.

IX. Unreal confession—detected when severe penance
is imposed.

X. Rebellion against the rules and the brethren.

XI. Liberty to sin.

XII. Habitual transgression.

The two last named downward steps cannot be taken inside the cloister. The first six denote disregard for the brethren, the four following disrespect for authority, the two that remain contempt for God.

PART ONE

The Twelve Degrees of Humility

———•———

CHAPTER ONE
The search for Truth—Christ the goal and the road

I PROPOSE to speak of the degrees of humility, as St. Benedict sets them before us, as not only to be enumerated but to be attained. And I will first indicate, to the best of my ability, the goal that may be reached by their means, so that when you have heard the result of its attainment, the toil involved in the ascent may be less severely felt. So let our Lord set before us the difficulties that we shall encounter, and the reward that we shall receive for our toilsome journey.

I *am*, saith He, *The Way and the Truth and the Life. (John* 14:6). He calls humility "the way" because it leads to the truth. In the former lies the labour, in the latter is the reward. But, you may ask, how am I to know that He was here speaking of humility, since He says without further explanation, *I am the Way?* Listen to His more explicit statement, *Learn of me because I am meek and humble of heart. (Matt.* 11:29). In this He exhibits Himself as a type of humility, a model of meekness. If you imitate Him, you are not walking in darkness, but you will have the light of life. What is the light of life, unless it be the truth, which lightens every man that comes into the world, and shows us wherein true life consists? For this reason, to those words of His *I am the Way and the Truth*, He added *and the Life*, as though He meant to say, I am the way because I lead to the truth, I am the truth because I promise life, I am myself the life which I give. *For this*, saith He, *is life eternal, that they may know thee the true God, and Jesus Christ whom thou hast sent*. (*John* 17:3). But admitting this, you may still say, I recognize humility as the way; I long for truth as the reward; but what if the toil of the journey be so great that I am unable to reach the desired goal? To this He replies, *I am the life*, that is the provision for the journey by which you will be supported on the way. So He exclaims to the wanderers and to those who do not know the road, *I am the way*, to the doubters and disbelievers, *I am the truth*, to those who have begun the ascent and are getting tired, *I am the life*.

I think that it has been made sufficiently clear by the passage quoted from the Gospel that the reward of humility is the apprehension of the truth. And take another passage, *I praise thee, Father of heaven and earth, because thou hast hidden these things* (that undoubtedly means "secret truths") *from the wise and prudent* (that is from the proud) *and hast revealed them unto babes* (that is to the humble). (*Matt.* 11:25).

This affords further evidence that the truth which is withheld from the proud, is disclosed to the humble. And the following may be taken as the definition of humility. It is the virtue which enables a man to see himself in his true colours and thereby to discover his worthlessness. And this is the characteristic virtue of those *who are disposed in their hearts to ascend by steps* from virtue to virtue, until they reach the summit of humility; where, standing on Sion as on a watch-tower, they may survey the truth. For, saith the Psalmist, *the law-giver shall give a blessing*. He then who gave the law will also provide the blessing—that is to say, he who has prescribed humility will conduct us to the truth. And who is this lawgiver but the kind and righteous Lord who has given a law to those who fail in the way? And surely those who have forsaken the truth have failed on the way. But are they on that account forsaken by the kind Lord? Nay, but it is for these very persons that the kind and righteous Lord prescribes the path of humility, by their return to which they may discover the truth. He allows them an opportunity of regaining salvation because He is kind, yet not without the discipline of law because He is righteous. In His kindness He will not permit their ruin, in His righteousness He cannot omit their punishment.

CHAPTER TWO

The ladder of humility, foreshadowed by that which Jacob saw in his vision. The refreshment provided by Christ—humility, love, and contemplation—of which love is the central course, as on Solomon's table.

ST. BENEDICT enumerates twelve degrees in this law by which the return to truth is made; so that as access to Christ is gained when the Ten Commandments and the two-fold circumcision—which together make up the number of twelve—have been passed, truth may likewise be attained by passing through these twelve degrees. And what can be the significance of the fact that the Lord appeared leaning over that ladder which was shown to Jacob as a symbol of humility, but that the recognition of truth begins when the height of humility is reached? For then the Lord, whose eyes, as He is the embodiment of truth, could neither deceive nor be deceived, was looking down from the top of that ladder over the sons of men—to discover whether there is anyone who understands or seeks after God. And does He not seem to you to cry aloud from on high and to say to those who seek Him (for He knows who are His) *Come over to me ye who desire me, and be filled with fruits* (*Ecclus.* 24:26), and also, *Come unto me ye who labour and are burdened and I will refresh you?* (*Matt.* 11:28). But what refreshments is this that Truth promises to those who attempt and gives to those who attain? Is it perchance love? Then this it is at which, as St. Benedict says, the monk who has passed through all the degrees of humility will ere long arrive. Truly love is delightful and pleasant food, supplying, as it does,

191

rest to the weary, strength to the weak, and joy to the sorrowful. It in fact renders the yoke of truth easy and its burden light.

Love is good food, which, as the central dish on Solomon's dinner table, by the aroma of various virtues as by the fragrance of different condiments, refreshes those who are hungry and delights those who give the refreshment. For on it are set out peace, patience, kindness, forbearance, *joy in the Holy Ghost* (*Rom.* 14:17); and if there are any other products of truth or of wisdom, they too are there. Humility also has her dishes on the same tray, namely, the bread of affliction and the wine of remorse. These are the things which Truth offers in the first place to beginners, for to them it is said, *Rise after ye have sat down, ye who eat the bread of sorrow.* There also contemplation has its solid food, made of the fat essence of the corn, and the wine that maketh glad the heart of man. To this food Truth invites those who have accomplished their course, saying: *Eat, my friends, and drink and be inebriated, my dearly-beloved. The midst,* saith he, *he covered with love, for the daughters of Jerusalem* (*Cant* 3:10)—that is to say, for the sake of the immature souls which, while they are as yet unable to receive solid food, must meanwhile be fed with the milk of love instead of with bread, and with oil instead of with wine. And love is rightly called the central course, because beginners are unable, through their timidity, to take advantage of its sweetness, while to those who have arrived at maturity it is an insufficient substitute for the deeper delight of full vision. The first still require to be cleansed, by a very bitter dose of fear, from the pestilent poison of fleshly lust, and have not yet discovered the sweetness of milk. The latter have already turned away from milk and are revelling in the delight derived from their entrance into glory. Those only in the middle—who are on the journey—have found some delicious little morsels of love, with which, owing to their weak digestion, they so far have to be content.

So the first course is humility, purifying by its bitterness, the second is love, comforting by its sweetness, the third is full vision, secure in its strength. *Alas for me, Lord God of righteousness—how long wilt thou be angry against the prayer of thy servant, how long wilt thou feed me with the bread of tears and give me tears for my drink?* (Ps. 70:5; 69:5, Vulg.). Who will call me even so far as to that delightful company of love, where the righteous feast in the sight of God, and revel in the fulness of their joy; where I need no longer speak in the bitterness of my heart, but may say to God "condemn me not," if while I feast on the unleavened bread of sincerity and of truth, I sing joyously in the paths of the Lord, for great is the glory of the Lord? Yet good also is the path of humility, for by it truth is sought, love is reached, and a share of the fruits of wisdom is obtained. As in a way Christ is the end of the law, so is He the perfection of humility, and the final apprehension of truth. Christ when He came brought grace. Truth gives grace to those to whom it has become known. But as it is by the humble that it is known, it is to them that it gives grace.

CHAPTER THREE

The process by which the road of humility leads to the attainment of Truth. The three degrees of Truth. The teaching of Christ about these. Discussion of the difficulty involved in the statement that He learned compassion through suffering.

I HAVE stated, as well as I can do so, the blessings to be gained by passing upwards through the degrees of humility. I will now, to the best of my ability, explain the process by which these lead to the promised prize—the attainment of truth. But as the recognition of truth is gradual, I will, if I can do so, indicate its three degrees, in order to make it more clear to which of these the twelfth degree of humility leads.

We seek for truth in ourselves, in our neighbours, and in its essential nature. We find it first in ourselves by severe self scrutiny, then in our neighbours by compassionate indulgence, and, finally, in its essential nature by that direct vision which belongs to the pure in heart. Observe both the number and the sequence. To begin with, let Him who is the Truth teach you that you must search for truth in those around you before you look for it in its intrinsic purity. You will afterwards learn why you must search for it in yourself before you do so in your neighbours. Thus in the enumeration of the Beatitudes in His Sermon He placed "the merciful" before "the pure in heart." For the merciful quickly discover truth in their neighbours when they extend their sympathy to them, and so kindly identify themselves with them that they feel their good and evil characteristics as if they were their own. They are weak with those that are weak, with those who are offended they burn. They have made it their habit to *rejoice* with *them that rejoice and weep with them that weep. (Rom.* 12:15). When their spiritual vision has been made clear and acute by this brotherly love, they delight to gaze on truth for its own sake, and in their affection for it they are indulgent towards errors which are not their own. But how can those who, so far from thus associating themselves with their brethren, insult them in their sorrow and deride them in their joy, possibly discern truth in their neighbours, seeing that they cannot enter into the feelings of others about things of which they have no personal experience? Well, indeed, does the common saying fit them "a healthy man has no idea of the feelings of one who is ill, nor does a well-fed man realize what a hungry man suffers." A sick man feels for the sick and a hungry man for the hungry, with familiarity the greater as his own condition approaches theirs. For as pure truth can be discerned only by one whose heart is pure, so can the sorrow of a brother be most truly felt by one whose heart is sad. But if your heart is to be saddened by the sorrows of others, you must recognize your own evil state, which you may see reproduced in your neighbour, and may thus know how to help him. And in this you have the example of our Saviour, who was willing to suffer that He might know how to sympathize, to accept sorrow that He might thus learn to pity. For, as it is written of Him, *He learned obedience by the Things which He suffered,* so may He have suffered that He might learn compassion. This, however, does not mean that He, whose compassion was eternal in its origin and its duration, had not hitherto known pity, but that what He knew in His nature in an eternal, He learned by experience in a temporal, sphere.

But you may find it difficult to accept my statement that Christ who is the Divine wisdom "learned compassion," as though it were possible for Him through whom all things were made, ever to have been ignorant of anything; especially in view of the fact that the passage from the Epistle to the Hebrews which I have adduced in support of my argument, may be understood in a different sense, which would not involve us in this difficulty. For, on this interpretation, the words "*He learned*" would refer, not to His own Person, but to His body which is the Church. In that case the meaning of the sentence, *And He learned obedience by the things that He suffered* would *be that He learned obedience* in His body through what He personally suffered. For what was the meaning of that death, that cross, those insults, spittings and stripes, all of which Christ who is our head endured, unless that they afford to us who are His body, convincing evidence of His Obedience? *For Christ,* saith Paul, became *obedient to his Father, even unto death. (Phil* 2:8). And what was the need for such obedience? Let the Apostle Peter give the answer: *Christ suffered for us leaving to you an example that you should follow his steps* (*1 Pet.* 2:21), that is that you shall imitate His obedience. So from His sufferings we learn how much we, who are mere men, must be prepared to endure for the sake of obedience, in the exercise of which He, who is also God, did not hesitate to die. And this, you may say, is the sense in which it is not unreasonable to allege that Christ learned obedience or compassion, or anything else during His earthly life, although you at the same time believe that it was not possible for Him to acquire while on earth any knowledge which He did not previously possess in His divine Person. Thus He might Himself both learn and teach pity and obedience, since the head and the body is one Christ.

I do not deny that this verse may reasonably be thus understood. But the former interpretation seems to be supported by another passage in the same Epistle, in which it is said *For nowhere doth he take hold of the angels, but of the seed of Abraham he taketh hold, wherefore it behoved him in all things to be like unto his brethren, that he might become merciful. (Heb.* 2:16). I think that these words have so close a reference to His Person, that they cannot be altogether applicable to His body. It is at any rate said of the word of God that He "took," that is He incorporated into His own personality, not "angels" but "the seed of Abraham." For the passage reads not "the word was made an angel" but *the Word was made flesh (John* 1:14), and that from the flesh of Abraham, in accordance with the promise made to him. *Whereupon,* that is by reason of this assumption of the seed, *he ought in all things to be like unto his brethren,* that is to say, it was right and necessary that He should be, as we are, susceptible to suffering and should share with us every kind of misfortune with the exception of sin. If you ask "Wherefore this necessity?" the answer is *that He may become merciful.* And, you may say, why may not this be properly understood as referring to His body? But listen to the words which so closely follow these. *For in that wherein he himself hath suffered and been tempted; he is able to succour them also that are tempted. (Heb.* 2:18). And for these words I can see no better meaning than that He was pleased thus to suffer and to be tempted and to associate Himself with all human misery except sin—which is what being "like unto his brethren in all things" means, in order that He might learn by personal experience to pity and to feel for those who similarly suffer and are tempted. I do not say that this experience added to His knowledge, but that it brought Him closer to us, so that the weak sons of Adam whom He has not disdained to make His own and to call His brethren, need not hesitate to bring their infirmities to Him, who, recognizing what He has Himself endured, as God is able and as their neighbour is desirous to provide the remedy. For this reason Isaiah calls Him a man *of sorrows and acquainted with infirmity (Is.* 43:3), and the Apostle says, *We have not a High Priest who cannot have compassion on our infirmities. (Heb.* 4:15). And to show how He can have such compassion the writer adds, *but one tempted in all things like as we are, without sin.* For surely the blessed God, while in that form in which He thought it not robbery to be equal with God, was beyond doubt incapable of suffering before He had emptied Himself; and taken the form of a slave; and as He had no experience of sorrow or of subjection, He had no opportunity of practicing either compassion or obedience. He had indeed a natural but not an experimental knowledge of these. Yet as He not only laid aside His own dignity, but was made a little lower than the angels, who by favour not by nature are incapable of suffering, He took a form in which it was possible for Him to suffer and to submit, which, as has been stated, He could not have done in that form which was His own. Thus by suffering He learned compassion and by subjection obedience. This experience, however, led, as I have pointed out, to an increase, not of Wisdom on His part, but of confidence on ours, since by the knowledge thus painfully acquired He from whom we had been so widely separated was brought nearer to us. For when would we dare to approach Him while He was incapable of suffering? But now the Apostle advises and exhorts us *to go with confidence to the throne of grace* (*Heb.* 4:16) whereon is He whom we surely recognize as the one of whom it is elsewhere written that *He hath borne our infirmities and carried our sorrows* (*Is.* 43:4), and of whose power to sympathize with us in what He has himself endured we can entertain no doubt.

So there appears to be no contradiction on the one hand, in saying that, as there is nothing of which Christ was ever unaware, His knowledge could have no commencement, and, on the other hand, in maintaining that while in His Divine nature, He knew compassion from all eternity; in another capacity He learned it under bodily and temporal conditions. And note the similar language which our Lord used when in reply to a question from His disciples. He pleaded ignorance of the date of the Last Day. For how could He in whom *are hid all the treasures of wisdom and knowledge* (*Col.* 2:3) be unaware of that day? How could He, for whom ignorance of any sort was clearly impossible, say that He did not know? Could He possibly desire to conceal by a subterfuge, information which He could not profitably disclose? God forbid the thought! For neither could He who is Wisdom be unaware of anything, nor could He who is Truth be capable of falsehood. But in His desire to discourage the useless curiosity of the disciples, He pleaded ignorance of the matter about which they asked Him—not indeed without qualification but in a way in which He could truthfully disclaim such knowledge. For although by His Divine insight—ranging over all things past, present and future, He had that day clearly before Him, it was still true that He was unaware of it by the exercise of any bodily sense. Had it been otherwise He would already have slain Antichrist with the breath of His mouth, would have heard with His bodily ears the shout of the archangel and the sound of the trumpet at whose call the dead are to rise, and would have surveyed with His bodily eyes the sheep and the goats who are then to be separated from each other.

But with the intention of making it clear that it was only in the sphere of that intelligence which He possessed in His human capacity that he asserted His ignorance of that day, He was careful in His answer not to say "I do not know" but "The Son of Man himself doth not know." Now what is this title of "Son of Man" but the one which He assumed on taking on Himself our nature? By its use here, He means it to be understood that when He says that He is ignorant of anything, He is speaking not as God, but as man. When on the other hand He refers to His own Godhead, He usually says not "the Son" or "the Son of Man" but "I" or "We"—as in the passage *verily verily I say unto you, before Abraham was made, I am. (John* 8:58). He there speaks of Himself as "I" not as the "Son of Man." There can be no doubt that He then referred to that existence which was His before Abraham, and which never had a beginning—not to what He became after the time of Abraham and by descent from him. And when He elsewhere asks His disciples what men think of Him, He says *Whom do men say* not "that I am" but that *the Son of Man is? (Matt.* 16:13, 16). But when He afterwards asks the same disciples what they themselves felt about Him, He says, *But whom do you say* not "that the Son of Man is," but *that I am?* So when He asks the opinion of worldly persons about His bodily nature He uses the term "Son of Man," but when He questions His spiritual followers about His Godhead, He significantly says not "the Son of Man" but "me." And that Peter understood what He meant by putting the question in this form is apparent from his reply, for he says *Thou art*, not "Jesus the son of a Virgin," but *Christ the Son of God.* Had he made the former reply he would have said what is no less true. But shrewdly gathering from the wording of the question the meaning of Him who put it, he gave a suitable and sufficient answer by saying, *Thou art Christ the Son of God.*

Now from this you may see that Christ has two natures, albeit in one Person, one in which He has always existed, the other in which He had a beginning, and that while in that nature which is eternal He always knew everything, in that which is temporal He found out many things in the course of time. Why then do you find it difficult to admit that as there was a time when His bodily existence began, so may His knowledge of the ills of the flesh—at all events that sort of knowledge which bodily weakness conveys—have had a beginning? Our first parents would no doubt have been better and wiser had they not possessed knowledge of this sort, since they could acquire it only through folly and misfortune. But God, their Creator, seeking what had been lost, in His mercy followed up His own handiwork. He Himself mercifully descended to the level from which they had miserably fallen, and was willing Himself to endure what they deservedly suffered through their disobedience to Him—and this not from a curiosity like theirs, but from marvelous love, His purpose being not to remain in misery with the unfortunate, but to become merciful and so to deliver them from their misery. When I say that he became merciful I refer not to that compassion which had been His in His eternal condition of bliss, but to that which He acquired through the medium of misfortune, while He bore our nature. Moreover, He completed in the latter the work of love which He had commenced in the former state. He could undoubtedly have made it complete in the former alone, but without the latter it would not have been effectual for us. Both forms were essential, but the latter more closely concerns ourselves. How indescribable is the method of His goodness. Could we ever have understood that marvellous mercy unless previous suffering had given it shape? Could we have discerned His sympathy, of which we had no knowledge, if He had had no previous suffering and had remained insusceptible to pain? Yet had He not possessed that compassion which knows no misfortune, He would never have attained that whose mother is misfortune. If He had not attained this He could not have drawn it to Himself. If He had not so drawn it, He could not have brought it out. And whence did He bring it out if not *from the pit of misery and mire of dregs?* (*Ps.* 40:2; 39:3, Vulg.). Yet He did not abandon that earlier compassion, but added to it the later. He did not alter, He augmented it, as it is written, *Men and beasts thou wilt preserve, O God, O how hast thou multiplied thy mercy, O God.* (*Ps.* 36:6, 7; 35:7, 8, Vulg.).

CHAPTER FOUR

The first degree of Truth—self-scrutiny—
reveals to us our own evil case.

BUT let us resume the thread of our argument. If then He in whose nature there was no sadness, made Himself sad in order that He might have personal experience of something of the existence of which He was already aware, how much more is it your duty, I will not say to alter, but to recognize your condition, which is indeed a pitiable one—and thus to learn compassion of which you could otherwise have no knowledge? For it may well happen that by dwelling on the shortcomings of your neighbour without sufficient attention to your own, you may be moved not to pity but to anger—not to assist but to condemn, and so to destroy in a spirit of wrath, rather than to restore in a spirit of meekness. *Ye who are spiritual,* saith the Apostle, *instruct such an one in the spirit of meekness.* The counsel—aye, the command—of the

Apostle is that you should aid your ailing brother in the same kindly spirit in which you would wish to be helped when you are ailing. And to show how it is possible to be forbearing towards a wrong-doer, he says, *considering thyself lest thou also be tempted.* And please to note how well the disciple of Truth follows the sequence of the Master. In the Beatitudes, to which I have already referred, the "merciful" are named before the "pure in heart," as are the "meek" before the "merciful." And the Apostle when he exhorted those who were spiritual to restore such as were carnal, added *in the spirit of meekness.* For the reformation of the brethren is the mark of the merciful, and a spirit of meekness that of the humble. He says in effect that no one who is not himself meek can be reckoned among the merciful. Note that the Apostle here clearly asserts exactly what I said just now that I would establish, viz., that truth must be sought in ourselves before we can look for it in others, for he says *consider thyself*—by which he means, think how easily you may be tempted—how liable you are to sin—so that by self-scrutiny you may be made humble and may thus come to the aid of others in a spirit of meekness. If, however, you heed not the warning of the Apostle, tremble before the rebuke of the Master. *Thou hypocrite, cast out first the beam out of thine own eye and thus shalt thou see to cast out the mote out of thy brother's eye. (Matt.* 7:5). Pride in the mind is like a thick heavy beam in the eye, whose excessive size is due not to health but to vanity, to swelling rather than to strength. It so darkens the mental vision as to hide the truth. If then it has taken hold of your mind, you will be unable to see yourself as you really are, or to appreciate either your actual or possible condition, but you will fancy that you are or will become just what you would like to be. For what is pride if not—as a certain holy man defines it "appreciation of one's own goodness." If this be so, we may say, on the other hand, that humility is the disparagement of our own goodness. For love and hatred alike ignore the verdict of truth. Would you like to hear what that verdict is? *As I hear so I judge (John* 5:30), not as "I hate" or "I love" nor as "I fear." There is the judgment of hate, such as that which said *We have a law and according to our law he ought to die.*

(*John* 19:7). And there is the judgment of fear like that one *If we let him alone so the Romans will come and take away our place and nation.* (*John* 11:48). But there is a judgment of love, as that of David on the son who would have slain his father, *Spare the boy Absalom.* And I know that it is a rule of human law, which is binding alike in ecclesiastical and in civil actions, that personal friends of the litigants shall not be allowed to take part in the proceedings lest through their affection for their friends they may be misled or may mislead others. And if affection for a friend leads you to extenuate or even to conceal his guilt, how much more will self-esteem preclude an unfavourable verdict upon yourself? So the man who is really anxious to discover the truth about himself must remove the beam of pride which prevents him from seeing the light, and must propose in his heart to ascend by steps by which he may scrutinize his inmost self, and from the twelfth degree of humility may pass on to the first degree of truth. But when a man has found truth in himself—or rather has found himself in truth—so that he can say, *I have believed and therefore have I spoken, but I have been humbled exceedingly,* he may rise to a high spiritual level in order that truth may be held up, and may say in his ecstasy, *Every man is a liar.* Do you not suppose that this was the trend of David's thought? Do not you think that the prophet felt as did the Lord, as did the Apostles, and as we do who come after them and share their feelings? *I believed,* says this man, in Truth who says, *He that followeth me walketh not in darkness.* (*John* 8:12). I therefore showed my faith by following, and expressed it by confessing. And by confessing what? The truth—which I discovered through faith. But afterwards I believed unto righteousness and made confession unto salvation. *I was humbled exceedingly* (*Ps.* 116:10; 115:10, Vulg.), that is entirely. He appears to mean by this—since I was not ashamed of the fact that the truth which I discerned in myself bore witness against me, I carried humility to its utmost extent. For this word "exceedingly" may mean "completely," as in the passage, *He shall delight exceedingly in his commandments.* (*Ps.* 112:1; 111:1, Vulg.). But someone may urge that "exceedingly" is here used for "in a high degree," not for "completely"

202

and that the commentators seem to uphold this interpretation. Even if this be so, there is nothing inconsistent with the meaning of the Prophet, which we may take as being to this effect:

> While I was still unaware of the truth, I did indeed suppose myself to be something—whereas I was nothing. But when I afterwards believed in Christ and therefore tried to imitate His humility, I recognized the truth. It was indeed uplifted in me by my confession, but I was *exceedingly humbled*, that is, was greatly depreciated in my own estimation as a result of my self-scrutiny.

CHAPTER FIVE

The second degree of Truth—wherein consciousness of our own shortcomings makes us merciful to those of other people.

THUS in this, the first degree of Truth, the Prophet is so humbled that he says in another Psalm, *In thy truth thou hast humbled me.*(*Ps.* 119:75; 118:75, Vulg.). He may then reasonably conclude that the wretched condition in which he finds himself to be, is that of mankind in general. And as he thus passes into the second degree, he may say in his ecstasy, *Every man is a liar.* (*Ps.* 116:11; 115:11 Vulg.). And in what does this ecstasy consist? Is it not without doubt due to the fact that in his detachment from himself and attachment to truth, he pronounced his own condemnation? So in that ecstatic condition he may say, not in anger or insult—but with pity and regret, *Every man is a liar.* And why is every man a liar? Every man is weak, every man is poor and powerless, since none can save himself or anyone else. In much the same sense is it said, *Vain is the horse for safety* (*Ps.* 33:17; 32:17 Vulg.), not because the horse deceives anyone but because the rider deceives himself if he relies on the horse's strength. So every man is said to be false, that is, fragile and fickle, because no one can hold out any assurance of safety to himself or to others, and anyone who puts his trust in man is more likely to receive condemnation. Thus the humble Prophet, proceeding under the guidance of Truth, observes in other people what he mourns in himself; where he finds knowledge he will also find sorrow, and so may say broadly but truly, *Every man is a liar.* Now note how widely different was the tone of that haughty Pharisee. What was the purport of his ill-considered utterance? *God, I give thee thanks that I am not as the rest of men. (Luke* 18:11). While he is strangely satisfied with himself, he is offensively rude to others. David takes quite another line. He says *Every man is a liar.* He will make no exceptions which might be misleading, for he knows that *all have sinned and all do need the glory of God. (Rom.* 3:23). The Pharisee, while condemning others claims exemption for himself alone. The Prophet does not exempt himself from the general guilt, lest he be excluded from mercy. The Pharisee stifles mercy by his disclaimer of guilt. The Prophet asserts, of himself as of every one, *Every man is false.* The Pharisee endorses this of all except himself, when he says, *I am not as the rest of men.* And he returns thanks not that he is good, but that he stands alone—not so much for his own merits as for the ill which he sees in others. He has not yet cast out the beam out of his own eye, but he reckons up the motes in the eyes of his brethren—for he adds, *unjust, extortioners.* I think that this diversion from the subject may not have been without its value, if it has enabled you to appreciate the difference between these two utterances.

Let us now return to the main subject. If truth thus compels men to look into themselves and so to learn their own worthlessness, it follows as an inevitable consequence that all those things which have hitherto given them pleasure—yea, even their own selves—should become distasteful to them. For as they sit in judgment upon themselves, they cannot fail to see themselves in a light in which they are ashamed to be seen even by their own eyes. Their present condition displeases them and they long to be what they are not—a result which they distrust their power to achieve. Yet they find their consolation in the fact that their judgment of themselves has been stern and severe;

and they hope that their love of truth and their hunger and thirst after righteousness—even to the point of self-contempt—will enable them to exact a strict satisfaction for the past and to effect a real amendment in the future. But when they perceive their incapacity for any adequate and extensive reform, and realize that when they have done all that is commanded they must still call themselves unprofitable servants, they fly from justice to mercy. And that they may obtain this they follow the advice given by Truth, *Blessed are the merciful, for they shall obtain mercy. (Matt.* 5:7). This then is the second degree of truth, the one in which men look for it in their neighbours—when from the realization of their own shortcomings they discover those of other people and learn from their own painful experience to sympathize with those who suffer.

CHAPTER SIX

The third degree of Truth—the clearing of the spiritual
sight, so that it may gaze on holy and heavenly things.

IF THEREFORE men practice perseverance in the three matters that have been mentioned—*viz.*, the sorrow of repentance, the longing for righteousness, and works of mercy, they clear their spiritual sight of the three hindrances which either through ignorance, infirmity or disposition they have encountered, and may thus pass on to that direct vision in which the third degree of truth consists. These are the ways that seem good to men—at all events to those *who are glad when they have done evil and rejoice in most wicked things*, and who attempt to cover their sins with the cloak of ignorance or of weakness. But vainly do they whose ignorance or weakness is wilful put forward either of these pleas as an excuse for indulgence in sin. Do you suppose that the first man could successfully plead infirmity of the flesh on the ground that he sinned, not of his own accord, but at the instigation of his wife? Or were the men who stoned the first martyr, and had themselves stopped their ears, excusable on the plea of ignorance?

Some people think that they have a natural antipathy to truth, and an inclination to and affection for sin, and that they are overcome by weakness and ignorance. Let such persons turn inclination into aversion, affection into distaste; let them conquer the weakness of the flesh by righteous energy, and dispel ignorance by better education. For if they disregard truth now, when it is needy, naked and weak, they may recognize it to their shame too late, when, coming with full authority and power, it overawes and rebukes them. They will then tremble as they return the vain reply, *When did we see thee in need, and did not minister to thee?* Surely the Lord whom they now disregard when He seeks sympathy *shall be known when he executeth judgments.* (*Ps.* 9:16; 9:17, Vulg.). Finally *they look on him whom they pierced (John* 19:37)— as shall also the covetous on him whom they despised. Thus by the tears of penitence, by the pursuit of righteousness and by persistence in works of mercy, is the spiritual sight cleared from all stain, whether due to weakness, ignorance or disposition. And to it truth promises to reveal itself in its purity. *Blessed are the clean of heart, for they shall see God.* (*Matt.* 5:8). There are then three kinds of degrees of truth; we rise to the first by humble effort, to the second by loving sympathy, to the third by enraptured vision. In the first truth is revealed in severity, in the second in pity, in the third in purity. Reason, by which we analyze ourselves, guides us to the first, feeling which enables us to pity others conducts us to the second; purity by which we are raised to the level of the unseen, carries us up to the third.

CHAPTER SEVEN

The work of the Persons of the Holy Trinity in leading men through the three degrees of Truth.

HERE I seem to discern a certain marvelous and individual operation of each Person of the Trinity—if indeed it is possible for the limited intelligence of man to conceive a difference such as cannot

be expressed in words between persons who co-operate. On this sup-
position, the first degree appears to be due to the action of the Son, the
second to that of the Holy Spirit, and the third to that of the Father.
Would you wish to hear about the work of the Son? *If*, saith He, *I, your
Lord and Master, have washed your feet, how much more ought ye to wash
one another's feet.* The Master of truth thus presented to His disciples a
pattern of humility, that they might therein discern the first degree of
truth. Mark also the work of the Holy Spirit, *Love is poured forth in our
hearts by the Holy Ghost which is given to us. (Rom.* 5:8). Love is indeed
the gift of the Holy Spirit, and this makes it possible for those who,
under the instruction of the Son, have by humility already attained the
first degree of truth, under the guidance of the Holy Spirit to reach the
second by sympathy with their neighbours. Hear also what is said about
the Father. *Blessed art thou Simon Bar Jona, because flesh and blood hath
not revealed it to thee, but my father who is in heaven. (Matt.* 16:17).
And there is another passage, *The father shall make thy truth known to
the children. (Is.* 38:19). And yet again, *I thank thee, Father, because thou
hast hid these things from the wise and hast revealed them to little ones.*
(Matt. 30:25). You see then how the Father at last receives into glory
those to whom the Son first taught humility by precept and by practice,
and on whom the Holy Spirit then shed love. The Son receives them
as learners, the Comforter encourages them as friends, the Father raises
them as sons. For this reason the title of "The truth" is rightly given,
not only to the Son, but also to the Father and to the Holy Ghost.
From this it follows that one and the same truth—preserving the characteristics of each of the Persons—performs this threefold work in the
three degrees. In the first one it gives instruction as does a master; in
the second it affords counsel as does a friend or a brother; in the third
it provides a bond of union as does a father to his sons.

Thus the Son of God—that is to say the word and wisdom of the
Father—first found that intellectual faculty of yours which is called
reason, fettered by the flesh, a captive to sin, blinded by ignorance,
and surrendered to things external. In His mercy He took it up, by His

power He raised it, by His wisdom He taught it, drew it to Himself, and in a marvelous manner made it His representative. He then caused it so to sit in judgment upon itself that, with due reverence to the Word with whom it was associated, it might act as its own accuser, witness and judge, and honestly pronounce condemnation on itself. It is from this first alliance between the Word and reason that humility has its origin. We then come to the second faculty, which is called will, and which was contaminated by the poison of the flesh, though this has already been in a measure counteracted by reason. This the Holy Spirit honours with a visit, administers to it a gentle purgative, imparts to it a genial warmth, and thus renders it compassionate; in such a way that after the fashion of a skin which is stretched by the application of an ointment, so the will that has been treated with the heavenly ointment may be so expanded as to become friendly to those that were its enemies. And this second alliance between the spirit of God and the will of man produces love. The Father finally takes the two faculties—reason and will—the one taught by the Word and sprinkled with the hyssop of humility, the other inspired by the spirit of truth and influenced by the fire of love, and unites them into a perfect soul, from which humility has removed all wrinkles and in which love has left no stain. In it will resists not reason. Nor does reason trifle with truth, for the Father unites it to Himself as His glorious bride, in such a way that reason may not be allowed to think of itself, nor will of its neighbour, but the entire delight of that blessed soul will be to say, *The king has taken me into his chamber.* It was fitting, that that soul should first learn in the school of humility under the tuition of the Son, to enter into herself—in accordance with the warning given. *If thou knowest not thyself, go forth and feed thy kids.* (*Cant.* 1:7) Thus did she become fit to be brought from the school of humility under the guidance of the Holy Spirit through affection into the store rooms of love—by which undoubtedly is meant the hearts of her neighbours. Thence, seated on flowers and surrounded by friends, that is, by good habits and holy virtues, she may at last gain entrance to the chamber of the King, for whose love she longs. There, when silence has been made in heaven for a space, it may be of half an hour, she rests calmly in those dear embraces—herself asleep, but her heart on the watch how she may in the present range over those regions of hidden truth—on whose memory she will feast as soon as she returns to herself—there she sees things invisible and hears things unutterable, of which it is not lawful for man to speak. These are the things that surpass all that knowledge which night showeth to night. Yet day unto day throws out language, and the wise are allowed to speak wisdom, and to compare spiritual things with spiritual.

CHAPTER EIGHT

The same sequence is seen in the "rapture"
of St. Paul to the third heaven.

DO YOU suppose that St. Paul had not undergone the same gradual process when, as he has told us, he was "caught up" to the third heaven? But why was he "caught up" instead of being "led up"? The reason surely was that if so great an Apostle says that he was "caught up" to a place whither no teaching nor leading could bring him, I, who am certainly a lesser man than Paul, may not venture to think that I can reach the third heaven by any strength or effort of my own; so may I neither trust to strength nor shrink from exertion. For a man who is taught or led is obliged, from the fact that he follows his teacher or leader, to use some effort. He at all events does enough in assisting his removal to the place or condition at which he aims to enable him to say, *Not I but the grace of God with me.* (*1 Cor.* 15:10). But the man who is carried away, not by his own action, but by that of others, and without even knowing his destination, cannot take the credit or any part of it to himself, since he accomplishes nothing either alone or with assistance. The Apostle might possibly have been directed or assisted to the first or to the middle heaven—to reach the third one he had to be caught up. For the Son is said to have come down for the purpose of helping men to rise to the first, and the Holy Spirit to have been sent to lead them to the second heaven. But the Father, though He always co-operates with the Son and the Holy Spirit, is never said to have come down from heaven, or to have been sent to the earth. It is true that *the earth is full of the mercy of the Lord* (*Ps.* 33:5; 32:5, Vulg.), and that *heaven and earth are full of thy glory*, and much to the same effect. And of the Son I read, *when the fulness of the time came, God sent his Son* (*Gal.* 4:4), and the Son Himself says of Himself, *The Spirit of the Lord hath sent me.* And through the same Prophet He says, *Now the Lord hath sent me and his Spirit.* (*Is.* 38:16). And of the Holy Spirit I read, *The Paraclete, the Holy Ghost, whom the Lord will send in my name* (*John* 14:26), and, *when I have been taken up, I will send him unto you* with undoubted reference to the Holy Spirit. But though there is no region in which the Father does not exist, I find no mention of His own Person anywhere but in heaven, as in the Gospel, *my father who is in heaven* (*Matt.* 16:17), and in the prayer, *Our Father who art in heaven.* (*Matt.* 6:9). From this I unhesitatingly conclude that as the Father did not come down, the Apostle could not go up to the third heaven in order to see Him, though he recalls that he was "caught up" thither. Moreover, *No man hath ascended into heaven, but he that descended from heaven.* (*John* 3:13). And lest you should suppose that the reference here is to the first or second heaven, David tells you, *His going out is from the end of heaven.* (*Ps.* 19:6; 18:7, Vulg.). And to this He was not suddenly caught up, or secretly conveyed, but, as is stated, *in their sight* (*Acts* 1:9) (that is in that of the Apostles) *he was raised up.* It was not with Him, as with Elias who had one witness, or with Paul who could have none, to attest his statement, and who could hardly do so himself, for he admits I know *not, God knoweth.* (*2 Cor.* 12:2). But as the Almighty, He descended and ascended as He pleased, and chose at His discretion, the place, the time, the day and the hour, as well as the onlookers whom He thought worthy to be the witnesses of so great a spectacle, and *while they looked on he was raised up.* Elias and Paul were caught up; Enoch was translated; our Saviour is said to have been taken up, that is to have gone up by Himself, without help from anyone. He depended neither, on conveyance by a chariot, or assistance by an angel, but on His own power. *A cloud received him out of their sight.* (*Acts* 1:9). And what was the purpose of this cloud? Was it to help Him in weakness, to stimulate Him in slackness, or to sustain Him when in danger of falling? Such ideas are inconceivable. That cloud received Him out of the bodily sight of His disciples who, though they had known Him as Christ in the flesh, did not as yet know Him to be more than man. So those whom the Son calls through humility to the first heaven, the Spirit brings together by love in the second, and the Father raises by direct vision to the third. In the first they are humbled by the truth and say, *In thy truth thou hast humbled me.* (*Ps.* 119:75; 118:75, Vulg.). In the second they rejoice together with truth and sing, *Behold how good and how pleasant it is for brethren to dwell together in unity* (*Ps.* 133:1; 132:1, Vulg.)—as also it is written concerning love. *It rejoiceth with the truth.* (*1 Cor.* 13:6). In the third heaven they are carried up to the recesses of truth and say, *My secret to myself, my secret to myself.* (*Is.* 24:16, Vulg. And Sept. and A.V. Marg.)

CHAPTER NINE
*The writer sighs regretfully over his own
shortcomings in the search for Truth.*

BUT how can a poor creature like myself ramble on about the two higher heavens in a way more suggestive of the outpouring of words than of spiritual activity, seeing that it is as much as I can do to crawl on my hands and feet under the lower one? Yet I have already, with the help of Him who calls me, set up for myself a ladder to that higher level. I am moving in the direction *wherein I may show to myself the salvation of God.* Now I look upwards to the Lord who is leaning over me, now I spring forward at the call of truth. He has called me and I have answered Him, *to the work of thine hands thou shalt reach out thy right hand. (Job* 14:15, Vulg, not A.V.). Thou, Lord, dost indeed number my steps, but I, slow climber and tired traveler, am looking for a resting place by the way. Woe is unto me if the darkness gets hold of me, or if my flight be in the winter or on the sabbath day, yet, though now is the acceptable time, and now is the day of salvation, I delay to set forth towards the light. Why do I thus hold back? Pray for me, son, brother, friend, fellow-traveller with me in the Lord—if such there be. Pray to the Almighty that He will strengthen my feeble foot, yet in such a way that the *foot of pride may not come to me. (Ps.* 36:11; 35:12, Vulg.). For though my foot is feeble and unable to attain to the truth, it is more reliable than one which, when it has reached it, cannot stand therein, as you have it in the Psalm, *they are cast out, and could not stand. (Ps.* 36:12; 35:13, Vulg.).

So much for the proud. But what about their chief? What about him who is called *king over all the children of pride? (Job* 31:25). He, said the Master, *stood not in the truth (John* 13:44), and elsewhere, *I saw Satan falling from heaven. (Luke* 10:18). Why did he thus fall, unless on account of pride? Woe be to me if he who *knoweth the high afar off (Ps.* 137:6), should see me also indulging in pride, and should launch at me the terrible sentence, *Thou wast indeed the son of the most high,* but *as a man thou shalt die, and thou shalt fall like one of the princes. (Ps.* 82:6, 7; 81:6, Vulg.). Who would not quail before this voice of thunder? O how much better it was for Jacob that the sinew of his thigh shrank at the touch of the angel than that it should swell, weaken and perish at that of the messenger of pride. Would that an angel would touch my sinew and make it shrink, so that I, who in my own strength cannot but fail, may from my weakness begin to make progress. I surely read, *The weakness of God is stronger than men. (1 Cor.* 1:25). So also did the Apostle, when he complained of the sinew which an angel, not of God but of Satan, was buffeting, receive the reply, *My grace is sufficient for thee, for virtue is made perfect in infirmity.* What is this virtue? Let the Apostle himself give the answer, *Gladly therefore will I glory in mine infirmity, that the virtue of Christ may dwell in me.* But you may, perhaps, not quite understand to what virtue he particularly alludes, since Christ possesses all the virtues. But though He has them all, there is one which He pre-eminently possesses and specially commends to us in His own Person, namely, humility, for He says, *Learn of me because I am meek and humble of heart.* (*Matt.* 11:29).

Gladly therefore will I glory in mine infirmity, in the shrinking of my sinew, that thy virtue—which is humility—may be made perfect in me. For thy grace is sufficient for me, when my strength has failed. I will then by thy favour put my foot firmly down, and though through its weakness I must move slowly, I will mount safely by the ladder of humility until, by keeping to the truth, I reach the broad expanse of love. Then will I sing with a gesture of thanks, the words *Thou hast set my feet in a spacious place.* (*Ps.* 31:8; 30:9, Vulg.). Thus by close and careful following of the narrow way, by slow and sure ascent of the steep staircase, with steady but painful progress, I limp along until by some marvelous method, the goal is approached, But *Woe is me* that my *sojourn is prolonged. Who will give me wings like a dove* (*Ps.* 55:6; 54:7, Vulg.), wherewith I may fly more quickly to the truth, and so may rest in love? Since these are wanting, lead me, Lord, in thy way and I will walk in thy truth, and the truth shall set me free. Woe unto me that I ever came down thence. For had I not foolishly and madly begun this descent, I should not have had this long and laborious climb. But why do I speak of a "descent" when I might more accurately call it a "fall"— unless indeed because, as no one comes at once to the top but all have to go up gradually, so no one becomes at once utterly bad but goes gradually downhill. Otherwise how could the saying stand, *The wicked man is proud all the days of his life.* There are, in fact, roads which seem good to men, which yet lead to destruction.

There is then an upward as well as a downward road—a road to good and a road to evil. Avoid the evil and choose the good. If you cannot do this by yourself, pray with the prophet and in his words: *Remove from me the way of iniquity* (*Ps.* 119:29; 118:29, Vulg.), and how shall this be? He adds, *Out of thy law have mercy on me.* This means by the law which thou didst give to those who fainted by the way—that is to those who departed from the truth. And of these I, who have indeed fallen from the truth, am one. But does not a man who has fallen use every effort to rise again? For this reason *I have chosen the way of truth* (*Ps.* 119:30; 118:30, Vulg.), by which I may rise through humility to the place from which I fell through pride. I will rise, say I, and I will sing, *It is good for me, Lord, that thou hast humbled me; the law of thy mouth is good to me, above thousands of gold and silver.* (*Ps.* 119:71, 72; 118:71, 72, Vulg.). David seems to have set before you two roads, which, however, you know to be one—identical yet different—and called by different names—either that of *wickedness* for those who go down, or that of *truth* for those who go up. For you go up to a throne by the same steps by which you come down, you use the same road for approaching or withdrawing from a town, and the same door for entering or leaving a house. In like manner the angels appeared to Jacob as ascending and descending on the same ladder. What do these comparisons suggest? Surely that if you wish to return to the truth, you need not look for a new and unknown road, but for the one by which you know that you came down, so that you may follow your own footsteps, and may humbly rise through the same degrees through which you fell in your pride. That which was the twelfth degree of pride in your fall will be the first degree of humility in your ascent, the eleventh will correspond to the second, the tenth to the third, the ninth to the fourth, the eighth to the fifth, the seventh to the sixth, the sixth to the seventh, the fifth to the eighth, the fourth to the ninth, the third to the tenth, the second to the eleventh and the first to the twelfth. And when you have discovered and really recognized these degrees of pride in yourself, you will have no difficulty in looking for the path of humility.

PART TWO

The Twelve Degrees of Pride

———————•———————

CHAPTER TEN
The first degree—Curiosity.
(The opposite of modesty—especially of the eyes.)

THE first degree of pride is curiosity. This you may detect by the following signs. Look at that monk, whom you have hitherto supposed to be a sensible man. He has now taken to staring about him, whether he is standing up, walking about or sitting down. He thrusts his head forward, and pricks up his ears. From his outward movements you can clearly see the inward change that he has undergone. For it is the froward man who *winketh with the eye, presseth with the foot, and speaketh with the finger* (*Prov.* 6:12), and from the unusual movements of his body is seen to have lately contracted disease of the soul—the careless sluggishness of which in self-examination makes it inquisitive about others. So since it takes no heed to itself it is sent out of doors to feed the kids. And as these are the types of sin, I may quite correctly give the title of "kids" to the eyes and the ears, since as death comes into the world through sin, so does sin enter the mind through these apertures. The curious man, therefore, busies himself with feeding them, though he takes no trouble to ascertain the state in which he has left himself. Yet if, O man, you look carefully into yourself, it is indeed a wonder that you can ever look at anything else. You inquisitive fellow, listen to Solomon—you silly fellow, hearken to the wise man, as he says, *With all watchfulness guard thy heart*, in other words, keep all your senses on the watch to protect that which is the source of life. For whither, inquisitive man, will you retire from your own presence—to whom will you in the meantime intrust yourself? How dare you, who have sinned against heaven, lift up your eyes to the sky? Look down to the earth if you want to recognize yourself. It will show you what you are, for *earth thou art, and to earth shalt thou go*. (*Gen.* 3:19, Old Latin).

Now there are two reasons for which you may raise your eyes without being to blame for so doing—one is to seek, the other is to render assistance. David raised his eyes to the mountains for the former, the Lord lifted His over the crowd for the latter purpose. The motive of the one was misfortune; that of the other was mercy, neither was to blame. If you likewise with due regard to place, time and occasion, look up when you or a brother are in distress, I not only do not blame you, I highly commend you. For misfortune allows the one action, mercy approves the other. But in different circumstances I should call you an imitator not of the Prophet nor of the Lord, but of Dina or of Eve, aye, verily, of Satan himself. For Dina when she went out to feed her kids, was snatched away from her father and her maidenhood was taken from her. O Dina, what need was there for thee to look on strange women? Was it necessary—did it serve any useful purpose—or was it done out of mere curiosity? Thy look may have no purpose, but it is not without purpose that men gaze on thee. There is curiosity in thy look, but more in the look that is turned on thee. Who could have supposed that thy curious carelessness or careless curiosity would afterwards prove to be not reckless but ruinous to thee, thy friends and thine enemies?

And thou, O Eve, wast placed in Paradise, that thou mightest work with thine husband and bestow thy care on him; and if thou hadst discharged thy duty, thou wouldst eventually have passed into a better sphere where there would have been no need for thee to be engaged in any work, or to be beset by any care. Leave was given to thee to eat of every tree in Paradise, except that one which is called *the tree of knowledge of good and evil. (Gen.* 2:9). For if the others are good and have a good savour, what need is there to eat of one which also has an evil savour? *Not to be more wise than it behoveth to be wise.* For to know evil is not knowledge but folly. So preserve what is given, await what is promised, avoid what is forbidden, lest thou lose what is allowed. Why lookest thou so eagerly for thy death? Why dost thou so often cast in that direction those wandering eyes of thine? What pleasure hast thou in looking on that which thou mayest not eat? Perchance thou dost reply, "I stretch forth mine eyes not my hand. It is not looking but eating that is forbidden. May I not turn those eyes which God has placed under my control in any direction that I please?" To which the Apostle shall answer, *All things are lawful for me, but all things are not expedient. (1 Cor.* 6:12). Although it may not be in itself a guilty act, it affords an incentive to sin. For if thy mind had not shown insufficient attention to its own condition, it would have had no time for idle curiosity. Although there may be no offence, there is an opportunity as well as a suggestion to offend and a reason for offending. For while thou art thinking of something else, the serpent creeps craftily into thine heart, and addresses thee in an alluring tone. He overcomes thy reason with his enticements, allays thy fear with falsehoods, and tells thee that thou art in no danger of death. He increases thy distress, as he stimulates thine appetite; he sharpens curiosity and strengthens desire. At length he offers what is forbidden and takes away what is allowed. He presents thee with fruit and deprives thee of Paradise. Thou takest poison: thou wilt perish thyself and wilt bring forth children who will perish. Thou hast sacrificed salvation, without losing the power to give birth. We are born, we die and thus we are born only to die, because we are dead before we are born.

And as for thee, "pattern of perfection," thou wast placed not in Paradise, but in Eden the garden of God. What more couldst thou reasonably desire? Filled with wisdom, and exalted in honour, thou shouldst have expected nothing higher and worked for nothing stronger than thyself. Remain where thou art, lest thou fall from thy position, if thou walkest among things that are too great and wonderful for thee. But why dost thou sometimes turn round and look to the north? I see thee, I already detect thee peering too inquisitively into the unknown heights above thee. *I will place*, sayest thou, my *throne towards the north*. The other dwellers in heaven are standing, whilst thou alone dost desire to sit, and dost thereby disturb the harmony of the brethren, the peace of the whole heavenly community, and, so far as it lies in thy power to do so, the tranquility of the Trinity. Does this curiosity carry thee so far, thou wretched being, that with unrivalled presumption thou dost not scruple to give offence to the citizens and to do injury to the king? *Thousands of thousands minister to him and ten times a hundred thousand stand before him*, where no one is allowed to sit, but He alone who *sitteth upon the cherubims* (*Ps.* 80:1; 79:2, Vulg.) and receiveth the ministrations of others. And dost thou—how shall I put it—claiming a wider outlook, a more incisive scrutiny and a freer entrance than that of the others, place a seat for thyself in heaven, that thou mayest be on a level with the Most High? What is thine object—on what dost thou rely? Thou fool, estimate thy powers, think of the result, consider the process. Dost thou presume on the knowledge or on the ignorance— on the willingness or on the reluctance—of the Most High? But how can He whose purpose is all good, and whose knowledge is unlimited, either consent to or be unaware of, thine evil design? Dost thou think that though He undoubtedly knows and disapproves it, He is unable to prevent it? But unless indeed thou art doubtful whether thou art a created being, I cannot suppose that thou canst doubt the omnipotence, omniscience and excellence of thy Creator, seeing that He was able to create thee out of nothing, and, knowing what thou wouldst turn out to be, willed to make thee the powerful being that thou art. When therefore thou thinkest that God will tolerate that of which He disapproves and has the power to prohibit, do I perchance see in thee the completion—aye, and the origin—of that idea which after thee and because of thee is constantly held by those like thee on earth, and which is embodied in the common saying, "An usurper keeps reckless followers? *Is thine eye evil because he is good?*" (*Matt.* 20:15). This wicked presumption of thine on His benevolence has produced in thee an insolent disregard of His knowledge, and a daring defiance of His power. For this, and nothing less than this, thou unholy one, is thy train of thought. This is the wickedness that thou dost devise on thy bed, and sayest "thinkest thou that the Creator will destroy His own work? I am well aware that no thought of mine escapes God, because He is God, nor does any such thought please Him, because He is good. Nor can I escape His hand—if He so wishes—because He is mighty. But need this be a cause of dread to me? For if through His goodness He can have no pleasure in evil done by me—how much less can He derive it from evil action of His own? I should call it evil on my part to wish to oppose His will—and on His part to avenge Himself. He therefore cannot wish to take vengeance for any crime, since He neither will nor can part with His inherent goodness." It is thyself—thou wretch, alone that thou deceivest, not God. Thou deceivest thyself, I repeat, and thy wickedness lies to thyself not to God. Thou dost indeed act deceitfully, but He detects thy motive. Thus thou deceivest thyself not God. And since in return for His great goodness, thou dost contemplate great evil towards Him, thy wickedness naturally leads thee to hate Him. For what can be more unjust than that the Creator should be scorned by thee for the very reason for which He most deserves thy love? What can be more outrageous than that when thou hast no doubt that the power of God shown in thy creation, could be used for thy destruction, thou dost yet rely on His abundant kindness, and that this should lead thee to hope that He will be unwilling to exercise His vindictive power? Wilt thou repay *good with evil* and *love with hatred?* (*Ps.* 109:5; 108:5, Vulg.).

Now I say that this malice is deserving, not of passing indignation but of abiding wrath. For it is thy desire and hope to be on an equality with the most gracious and most high Lord, although that is not His wish. Thou desirest that He shall have always before His eyes the distressing sight of thine unwelcome presence, and thou thinkest that though He is able to cast thee down, He will not do so, but that He will prefer Himself to suffer than to allow thee to perish. It is undoubtedly in His power to overthrow thee, if such be His will—but in thine opinion His kindness will not allow Him to entertain such a wish. If He be such as thou supposest Him to be, it is clear that thy conduct in not loving Him is so much the baser. And if He does allow action to be taken against Himself rather than take action against thee—how great must be thy malice in having no consideration for Him who disregards Himself in sparing thee? But it is inconceivable that He who is perfect can fail to be both kind and just. It is not as though kindness and justice cannot exist together. Kindness is really better when it is just than when it is slack—nay more, kindness without justice is not a virtue. It therefore appears that thou remainest ungrateful for the loving-kindness of God whereby thou wast created without exertion on thy part, but thou fearest not His justice of which thou hast had no experience, and dost therefore audaciously incur guilt for which thou dost falsely promise thyself impunity. Now mark that thou wilt find Him whom thou hast known to be kind, to be also righteous, and thou wilt thyself fall into the ditch which thou hast dug for thy Creator. Thy design seems to be to inflict on Him an injury which He is able to avoid if He wishes to do so—a wish which thou thinkest that He cannot entertain, as He will not be wanting in that kindness which has led Him never within thine experience to punish anybody. The righteous God will most justly retaliate by punishing thee, since He neither can nor ought to allow such a slight on His goodness to remain unpunished. He may, however, so moderate the severity of His sentence that, if thou art willing to return to reason, He will not refuse thee pardon. But such is *thy hardness and impenitent heart* (*Rom.* 2:5), that thou art incapable of such a wish, and therefore canst not escape the penalty.

But now listen to the accusation against thee. *Heaven*, saith He, *is my throne and the earth my footstool.* (*Is.* 66:1). He did not say "east" or "west," or any one region in the heaven, but the whole heaven is my throne. Thou must not therefore seat thyself in a portion of the heaven, since He has chosen the whole of it for Himself. Thou canst not place thyself on earth, for it is His footstool. For the earth is a solid body, on which is seated the Church, founded on a strong rock. What wilt thou do? Driven out of heaven, thou canst not remain on earth. Choose then for thyself a place in the air, not for session but for flight, so that thou, who didst attempt to shatter the security of eternity, shall pay the penalty of thine own unrest. For, whilst thou art driven to and fro between heaven and earth, the Lord is seated on a *throne high and elevated* (*Is.* 6:1) and the whole earth is full of His majesty—so that thou canst find no place except in the air. For the Seraphim with their wings of contemplation fly from the throne to the footstool, and from the footstool to the throne, while with their other wings they cover the head and feet of the Lord. And I think that they are purposely so placed that, as the access to Paradise was barred against sinful men by the Cherubim, so also shall a limit be set to thy curiosity by the Seraphim. The result will be that thou wilt no longer, with more impudence than prudence, investigate the secrets of heaven, nor wilt thou discover the mysteries of the Church on earth, but shalt find a home only in the hearts of the proud, who neither deign to live on earth like other men, nor fly like the angels to heaven. But although His head is hidden from thee in heaven and His feet on earth, thou mayest as it were be allowed to see—and to envy—some part of what lies between, whilst thou art suspended in the air, and dost behold the angels descending and ascending past thee, though thou art altogether ignorant of what they hear in heaven or tell on earth.

O Lucifer, thou who didst rise in the morning, surely a bearer no longer of light, but of night—aye, even of death—thy proper course was from the east to the south, and dost thou invert the order and perversely tend towards the north? In proportion to thy haste to rise is the rapidity of thy decline and fall. Yet, thou curious one, I should wish to investigate more closely the object of thy curiosity. *I will place*, sayest thou, *my throne towards the north.* And as thou art a spirit, I think that neither "north" nor "throne" is to be understood in a local or literal sense. For I suppose that by "the north" is meant evil men, and by "my throne" thy control over them. For in the foreknowledge of God, thou hast from thy chosen proximity to Him, a clearer insight into the future than had others; and as these were neither enlightened by any ray of wisdom, nor warmed by the love of the spirit, thou didst find in them as it were thine opportunity. Thus didst thou establish thy rule over them, so that thou mightest pour into them some of thy clever cunning, and influence them with thy wicked warmth; so that as the Most High controlled all the sons of obedience by His wisdom and His goodness, thou mightest govern these by thy cunning wickedness and wicked cunning, and in this respect thou mightest resemble Him. But I am surprised that, since in God's foreknowledge thou didst foresee thy rule, thou didst not in like manner foresee thy ruin. For if thou didst foresee it, what madness it was to be so wickedly eager for dominion as to prefer rule and wretchedness to submission and happiness. Or was it not better for thee to be a partner in those regions of light than ruler of those dark places? But it is more likely that thou didst not look forward—either for the reason which I gave above—that in thy reliance on the kindness of God thou didst say in thine heart, *He will not require it* (*Ps.* 10:13), and didst therefore wickedly offend Him, or because when thou didst see thy rule, the beam of pride at once rose up in thine eye—which through its interference was unable to discern its danger.

In like manner Joseph did not foresee his sale though he had foreseen his promotion—and this although the sale was to precede the promotion. I should not from this conclude that the great patriarch was guilty of pride, but that his experience proves that those who possess the spirit of prophecy must not be supposed to have foreseen nothing because they did not foresee everything. Someone may, perhaps, maintain that the fact that this youth recorded his dreams—of whose symbolic significance he was at the time unaware—was a mark of self-sufficiency. I still think that this should be ascribed to their symbolic character or to his boyish innocence, rather than to conceit. And if there were such conceit, he was able to atone for it by his subsequent painful experiences. For revelations of a character pleasing to themselves are sometimes made to certain persons, and though such knowledge must inevitably engender conceit in the human mind, the prediction may nevertheless be fulfilled—albeit in such a way that the vanity which has caused even a slight delight in the importance of the revelation shall not be unpunished. For a physician uses not only ointment but fire and iron, with which he cuts out or cauterizes everything which is useless for the treatment of the wound, so that there may be no obstacle to the remedial working of the ointment. In like manner does God as the physician of souls, prescribe and administer to a soul of such a disposition, temptations and troubles in order that, chastened and humbled, it may turn joy into sorrow, and think the revelation a delusion. The result is that vanity disappears, though the truth of the revelation is not impaired. Thus Paul's tendency to self-exaltation is checked by his thorn in the flesh, while he is himself uplifted by repeated revelations. Thus want of faith in Zacharias is punished by loss of speech, yet the declaration of the angel that the truth would be made clear during his lifetime is unaltered. Thus again, *by honour and dishonor* (*2 Cor.* 6:8) do the saints make progress, though among the special gifts which each receives, they are only too well aware of the existence in them of that vanity which is common to mankind; so that while they know themselves to be the possessors of supernatural favour, they may ever remember whom they truly are.

But what about revelations to mere curiosity? I took the opportunity of dealing with these in a digression, when I tried to show that the wicked angel before his fall was allowed to foresee that dominion which he afterwards acquired over wicked men, but not to anticipate his own condemnation. That is a matter about which questions of small moment may be raised which it is easier to ask than to answer, and of which the sum and substance is but this—that he fell from the truth because his idle speculation led him to unlawful desire and thus to presumptuous aspiration.

Curiosity therefore rightly claims the first place among the degrees of pride, and is thus revealed as the beginning of all sin. But unless this is suppressed very speedily it will soon develop into a careless frame of mind which constitutes the second degree.

CHAPTER ELEVEN
The second degree—Levity of mind.
(The opposite of the eleventh degree of humility—
short and sensible speech in a subdued tone.)

FOR the monk who is careless about himself and unduly inquisitive about other people, looks up to some as his betters and looks down upon others as his inferiors—in some he sees cause for envy, while others are the objects of his scorn. It thus happens that his mind, enervated by his habit of staring about him, is oppressed by no anxiety on its own account, now through pride soars to the heights and then sinks through envy to the depths. He shows at one moment a sulky acquiescence in his own wickedness, at another a childish delight in his excellence. In the former he exhibits his weakness, in the latter his vanity, in both his pride; for it is love of his own excellence that gives him distress when others surpass him, and joy when he surpasses them. This unbalanced disposition shows itself in speech sometimes brief and bitter, sometimes full and feeble, alternately jocose and doleful, and always silly. Compare if you please these two earliest degrees of pride with the two highest degrees of humility, and see if the last one of these latter does not repress curiosity, and the one before it levity. You will find the same contrast if the other degrees are similarly compared. But now let us go on to the study of the third degree—without, however, falling into it.

CHAPTER TWELVE

The third degree—Unseasonable merriment.
(The opposite of the tenth degree of humility—
refraining from frequent and light laughter.)

IT IS characteristic of the proud that they always look out for plea
sure and shun sadness, in accordance with the saying: *The heart of
fools is where there is mirth. (Eccles.* 7:5; 7:4, A.V.). So it is that the monk
who has already descended two degrees of pride and through inquisitiveness has arrived at levity, when he sees the joy for which he is always
on the lookout constantly interrupted by the distress which he feels at
the sight of good in others, chafes under the sense of humiliation and
takes refuge in a suggestion of unreal comfort. Henceforth he restrains
his inquisitiveness on that side on which his own worthlessness and his
neighbour's excellence are shown to him, and turns his whole attention
to the other side. He may thus mark only too carefully those things in
which he seems to be the better man, and may hide those in which others surpass him, and so may put away all thought of sorrow and remain
always merry. It thus happens that silly merriment soon gains sole pos-
session of the man whom joy and sorrow alternately claim.

I set this before you as the third degree of pride; now note the
marks by which you may detect it, either in yourself or in anyone else.
You seldom or never hear a man of this kind groan, or see him shed
tears. You will think, if you consider, that his faults are either forgotten or forgiven. His gestures are those of a buffoon, his look that of
a coxcomb, his step that of a dandy. He is always making jokes, and
never loses a chance of laughing. He cuts out of his mind all discredit-
able and therefore distressing recollections, and concentrates his mental
vision on his real or pretended merits. As he thinks of nothing but
what is pleasant without considering whether it is lawful, he can neither restrain laughter nor hide his unseasonable merriment. A bladder
swells when it is full of wind, but if a small hole is pricked in it and it is
squeezed, it creaks as it collapses, and the air does not rush out at once,

but is gradually expelled and gives out frequent intermittent sounds. In like manner when a monk has filled his mind with vapid and vulgar thoughts, the flood of folly which cannot, owing to the rule of silence, find full and free vent, is thrown out from his narrow jaws in guffaws of laughter. He constantly hides his face as if ashamed, compresses his lips, and clenches his teeth. He laughs loudly without meaning to do so, and even against his will. And when he has stopped his mouth with his fists he is frequently heard to sneeze.

CHAPTER THIRTHEEN
The fourth degree—Boastfulness.
(The opposite of the ninth degree of humility,
reticence until questioned.)

BUT when vanity increases, and the bladder begins to be inflated, it becomes necessary to loosen the belt and allow a larger outlet for the air, otherwise the bladder will burst. So the monk who is unable to discharge his superabundant store of unseemly merriment by laughter or by gesture, breaks forth with the words of Elihu, *My belly is as new wine which wanteth vent, which bursteth the new vessels. (Job* 32:19). He must speak out or break down. *For he is full of matter to speak of, and the spirit of his bowels constraineth him. (Ibid.,* 5:18). He hungers and thirsts for hearers, at whom he may throw his banalities, to whom he may pour out his feelings, and let them know what a fine fellow he is. But when he has found his opportunity of speaking—if the conversation turns on literary matters, old and new points are brought forward; he airs his ideas in loud and lofty tone. He interrupts his questioner and answers before he is asked. He himself puts the question and gives the answer, nor does he even allow the person to whom he is talking to finish his remarks. When the striking of the silence gong puts a stop to conversation, he complains that a full hour is not a sufficient allowance, and asks for indulgence that he may go on with his gossip after the time for it is over—not to add to the knowledge of any one else, but to boast of his own. He has the power but not the purpose of giving useful information. His care is not to teach you or to learn from you things which he does not know, but that the extent of his learning may be made known. If the subject under discussion is religion, he is forward with his vision and his dreams. He upholds fasting, prescribes vigils, and maintains the paramount importance of prayer. He enlarges at great length but with excessive conceit on patience, humility and all the virtues in turn, with the intention that you on hearing him should say, *Out of the abundance of the heart the mouth speaketh (Matt.* 12:34, 35), *and that a good man out of his good treasure bringing forth good things.* If the talk turns on light subjects he becomes more loquacious, because he is on more familiar ground. If you hear the torrent of his conceit you may say that his mouth is a fount of such buffoonery as to move even strict and sober monks to light laughter. To put it shortly, mark his swagger in his chatter. In this you have the name and description of the fourth degree of pride. Remember the description and avoid the reality. With this warning, go on to the fifth degree which I call eccentricity.

CHAPTER FOURTEEN
The fifth degree—Eccentricity.
(The opposite of the eighth degree of humility,
observance of the general rule of the monastery.)

A MAN who prides himself on being better than his fellow-men thinks it a disgrace if he does not do something more than they do, whereby his superiority may be apparent. Therefore the general rule of the monastery and the example of its senior members are not enough for him. Yet his anxiety is not to be, but to be seen to be better than they. His effort is not to lead a better life but visibly to surpass others, so that he may be able to say, *I am not as the rest of men. (Luke* 18:11). He takes more credit to himself for having once gone without a meal while others were having theirs, than he does in having shared in a fast of seven days. One little private prayer of his own seems to him more commendable than the recitation of all the Psalms set for an entire night. At mealtime he has a habit of casting his eyes all round the tables, and if he sees anyone eating less than himself, he is annoyed at being outdone. He begins severely to cut down the amount of food which he had hitherto recognized as his necessary ration, because he is more afraid of loss of credit than of the pangs of hunger. If he catches sight of anyone more shrunken and sallow than himself, he cannot rest under what he considers to be a disgrace. And, since he cannot see his own face and the aspect under which he presents himself to onlookers, he examines his hands and arms which he can see, beats his breast, taps his shoulders and loins, and from the more or less attenuated condition of his limbs forms an opinion as to the paleness or colour of his face. But while active in all his private devotions, he is indolent in public worship. He keeps vigil while in bed, and goes to sleep in his stall. He sleeps all night while others are chanting the early Psalms. When the vigil is over, and the other monks are resting in the cloister, he alone lingers in the oratory. He coughs and spits, and the ears of those sitting outside are filled with the sighs and groans from his corner. By his silly and singular action he has established a high reputation with his more simple brethren, who quite approve what they see of his doings, though they do not detect their motive, and, by the commendation which they bestow on him, they aid and abet the wretched man's mistake.

CHAPTER FIFTEEN
Sixth degree—Conceit.
(The opposite of the seventh degree of humility—belief
and acknowledgment of one's inferiority to others.)

H E BELIEVES what he hears, praises his own action, and pays no attention to the motive. He welcomes a favourable opinion and forgets its purpose. And he who in everything else puts more trust in himself than in other men, attaches more weight to the opinions of others about him than to his own. So not only does he think that he exhibits superior religion on account of his verbal profession or special display of piety, but in his inmost heart he considers himself more holy than anyone else. And if he knows that he is praised for anything, he ascribes it, not to the ignorance or the kindliness of the person who commends him, but, with much conceit, to his own deserts. So after eccentricity, conceit has made good its claim to be the sixth degree. After it, audacity shows itself—and in it the seventh degree consists.

CHAPTER SIXTEEN
Seventh degree—Audacity.
(The opposite of the sixth degree of humility—
acknowledgment of oneself as unworthy and useless.)

FOR if a man thinks himself superior to others, is it likely that he will not push himself in front of them? He is the first to take his seat at meetings, the first to intervene in debate. He comes forward without invitation, and with no introduction but his own; he re-opens questions that have been settled, and goes again over work that has been done. He considers that nothing that he has not himself designed and carried out, has been properly organized or satisfactorily executed. He criticizes those who sit in judgment, and tells them what their decisions should be. If, when the time comes for the appointment of a Prior, he is not promoted to the office, he is certain that his Abbot is either jealous or mistaken. But if some less important duty is assigned to him, he is displeased and contemptuous, for, as he feels himself qualified for greater work, he thinks that he ought not to be employed in smaller matters. But it is inconceivable that a man who, with more rashness than readiness, is very anxious to undertake all sorts of work, should not sometimes make mistakes. And it is the duty of the Abbot to reprove such an one for his error. But how will he confess his fault, if he neither thinks himself, nor will allow others to think him, worthy of censure? Therefore when his fault is pointed out to him, it is not removed but grows worse. So if, when he is reproved, you see him incline his heart to wicked words, you may know that he has sunk to the eighth degree, which is called defense of wrong-doing.

CHAPTER SEVENTEEN

The eighth degree—Defense of wrong-doing.
(The opposite of the fifth degree of humility—a humble and
straightforward disclosure of sins and evil thoughts.)

THERE are many ways in which defense is made for sin. A man either says "I did it not" or "I no doubt did it, but I acted rightly in so doing," or "I may have acted wrongly but not to a serious extent," or, "If I was seriously wrong, I had no bad intention." If, however, he, like Adam and Eve, is proved to be guilty, he attempts to excuse himself on the ground that he was tempted by someone else. But if a man unblushingly defends even open sins, will he ever humbly disclose to the Abbot the hidden evil thoughts which come into his mind?

CHAPTER EIGHTEEN

The ninth degree—Dishonest confession.
(The opposite of the fourth degree of humility, willing
endurance of hardship as a matter of obedience.)

BUT although defenses of this kind are considered so wrong that they are called by the Prophet *evil words* (*Ps.* 141:4; 140:4, Vulg.), a false and perverse confession is much more dangerous than ever a brazen and stubborn defense. For there are some who, when they are reproved for rather conspicuous offences, and know that no excuse which they may offer will be accepted, have recourse to a more cunning form of defense—they reply by a deceitful confession. *For there is*, as it is written, *one that humbleth himself wickedly and his interior is full of deceit.* The countenance is downcast—the body is prostrate. They exact from themselves, if they are able to do so, some tears. They interrupt their speech by sighs and intersperse their words with groans. A man of this description not only offers no excuse for the offences with which he is charged, but himself even exaggerates his guilt. He does this that you, when you hear him make a further accusation against himself of some impossible or inconceivable crime, may be disposed to disbelieve even that of which you thought him guilty—and thus, from the fact that he makes a confession which you fully believe to be false, some doubt may be thrown on that which you held to be almost certain. And when these men make a statement the acceptance of which they do not desire, by their confession they excuse, and by their disclosures they conceal, their fault. Their confession sounds praiseworthy in the mouth, but wickedness is hidden in the heart; so that he who hears may think that the confession is made with more humility than accuracy, and may apply to them that Scriptural saying, *The righteous man at the beginning of his speech is his own accuser.* For in the sight of men they would rather be thought wanting in truthfulness than in humility—while in the sight of God they are lacking in both. But if their guilt is so clear that by no subterfuge can it be entirely concealed, they nevertheless adopt the tone, though not the spirit of repentance, and by this means remove the mark, though not the reality of their guilt, as they make up for ignoring an open offence by the credit of a public confession.

A fine sort of humility is this, in which pride seeks to array itself, that it may not lose caste! But this double-dealing is soon detected by the Abbot, unless he is to some extent imposed upon by this haughty humility, and thus induced to pass over the fault or postpone the penalty. *The furnace trieth the potter's vessels (Ecclus.* 27:6), and distress reveals the real penitent. For the man who is truly penitent does not shrink from the trouble of repentance. Whatever is prescribed to him on account of the fault which he detests, he accepts with submissive and silent acquiescence. And if through this very obedience unexpected hardships arise, and he thereby sustains injuries that were not intended, he does not give up, so that he may show that he has his place in the fourth degree of humility. But he whose confession is unreal, when he is confronted with a slight rebuke, or trifling penalty, is unable either to feign humility or to conceal his dissimulation. He murmurs, gnashes his teeth and loses his temper, and it becomes clear that, so far from standing in the fourth degree of humility, he has fallen into the ninth degree of pride, which from the above description of it, may well be called sham confession. How great, think you, must be the proud man's consternation when his deceit is detected, his pardon forfeited, and his fault not condoned? He is at last found out and condemned by all—and the general indignation is all the greater when men see how erroneous was their former judgment of him. It is then the duty of the Abbot to be less ready to pardon him, because the forgiveness of one would be an offence to all.

CHAPTER NINETEEN
The tenth degree—Rebellion.
(The opposite of the third degree of humility—
obedient submission to superiors.)

UNLESS by a merciful intervention of Providence this man quietly accepts the unanimous verdict—a thing which it is very difficult for such persons to do—he soon becomes shameless and defiant, and more hopelessly degenerate, and sinks through rebellion into the tenth degree, so that he who had hitherto by his conceit treated his brethren with veiled discourtesy, now by his disobedience shows open contempt for authority. For it should be observed that all the degrees—which I have divided into twelve—may be arranged in three groups; in the first six there is disrespect to the brethren, in the four that follow defiance of authority, while the last two show complete contempt for God. And it should also be noted that, just as the first two degrees in the ascending scale of humility must be attained before entering the community so the last downward steps in pride, which are their counterpart, cannot be taken whilst in it. That the first two degrees must be previously passed, the language of the Rule makes clear. For it says that "The third degree is that anyone for love of God should submit with entire obedience to his superior." (*Rule*, cap. 7). Therefore if this submission, which beyond doubt is made when the novice enters the convent, is assigned to the third degree, the necessary presumption is that the two preceding degrees have been passed. Therefore when a monk scorns alike the harmony of the brethren and the decision of his ruler, what more can he do in the monastery except cause scandal?

CHAPTER TWENTY
Eleventh degree—Freedom to sin.
(The opposite of the second degree of humility—
forbearance to press personal desire.)

SO AFTER the tenth degree—which has been described as "rebellion"—the man is at once caught in the eleventh. He then enters those paths which are attractive to men, at the end of which (unless God shall perchance have interposed some barrier for his protection) he will be plunged into the nethermost hell—that is into contempt of God.

For *the wicked man when he is come into the depth of evils, contemneth.* (*Prov.* 28:3, Old Latin). The eleventh degree may be called freedom to sin, since in it a monk, who sees that he has now neither a ruler to fear nor brethren to respect, can safely and freely give full play to his own desires, which shame as well as fear prevented him from doing while in the monastery. But although he no longer dreads his brethren or his Abbot, he has not yet lost all awe of God. Reason, some faint echo of which still remains, places this check upon his inclination, and it is not without some hesitation that he enters on his sinful course, and, like a man who is trying to ford a stream, steps rather than runs into the torrent of vice.

CHAPTER TWENTY-ONE
Twelfth degree—Habitual sin.
(The opposite of the first degree of humility—constant
abstinence from sin for fear of God.)

B UT when, by the awful judgment of God, his first offences have
been unpunished, the pleasure that he has derived from them
is freely repeated, and its repetition engrosses him. Lust is quickened,
reason lulled, and habit becomes bondage. The wretched man is drawn
into the abyss of evil, made prisoner to the despotic rule of vice, and
so overwhelmed by the whirlpool of his carnal desires that he forgets
alike his own reason and the fear of God, and says madly in his heart,
There is no God, He now, without scruple, puts pleasure in the place
of law, his mind, his hands and his feet are no longer forbidden to
consider, execute and pursue courses that are unlawful; but whatever
comes to his heart, his mouth or his hand, he designs, discusses and
carries out, with evil intent, idle utterance, and sinful action. Just as a
righteous man, when he has risen through all the degrees, is able by his
habitual goodness to run eagerly and easily to life; so does the wicked
man, who has gone down through the same degrees, in consequence of
his evil practice emancipated from the rule of reason and unrestrained
by the bridle of fear, hasten undaunted to his death. There are some in
the middle who are wearied and worried—who, alternately tortured by
the fear of hell, and hindered by longstanding habit, find the descent
or ascent hard work. The first one and the last one alone move quickly
and without hindrance. The latter hastens to death—the former to
life—the one more speedily, the other with greater care. Love makes
the one eager, lust renders the other inert. The affection of the one, the
indifference of the other make both insensible to toil. So in the one perfect love, in the other consummate wickedness drives out fear. Loyalty
gives confidence to the one; blindness does the same for the other. So
the twelfth degree may be called the habit of sinning, because in it the
fear of God is lost, and its place is taken by scorn.

CHAPTER TWENTY-TWO
*To what extent may prayer be offered for the
incorrigible, and spiritually dead?*

FOR *such an one,* says John the Apostle, *I do not say that any one shall pray.* But sayest thou, O Apostle, that no one may hope? Surely he who loves that man may groan. He ventures not to pray, he need not forbear to weep. What is this that I say—that perchance there remains the resource of hope, where prayer has no place? Take an instance of one who believes and hopes, yet does not pray. *Lord,* she says, *if thou hadst been here, my brother had not died. (John* 11:21). What mighty faith to believe that by His presence the Lord could have prevented death. But what comes next? It is inconceivable that she should doubt that He whom she believed could have kept him alive, was unable to raise him from the dead. *But now,* says she, *I know that whatsoever thou wilt ask of God, God will give it thee. (John* 11:22). Then when He asks where they had laid him, she replies, *Come and see. (John* 11:34). Why dost thou stop there? O Martha, thou dost afford to us ample evidence of thy faith; but, as it is so great, why dost thou hesitate? *Come,* sayest thou, *and see.* Why, if thou art not without hope, dost not thou go further and say, "and raise him up"? If, on the other hand, thou art in despair, why givest thou the Master unreasonable trouble? Is it perchance that faith sometimes obtains that for which we dare not pray? Then as He approaches the corpse thou dost object to His coming near, and sayest, *Lord, by this time he stinketh, for he hath been dead four days.* Was this said in despair, or in pretence? In somewhat the same sense the Lord Himself after His Resurrection *made as though he would go further (Luke* 24:28), while His intention was to remain with the disciples. O ye holy women, intimate friends of Christ, if ye love your brother why do ye not appeal to the compassion of Him of whose power and pity ye cannot entertain a doubt? Their answer is, "We pray all the better for not uttering a prayer, we trust the more completely for concealing our confidence. We show our faith and suppress our feelings. He who has no need of any information Himself knows what we desire. We indeed know that He can do all things; but a miracle so great, so unprecedented, though it is within His power, far surpasses anything that in our insignificance we deserve. It is enough for us to have afforded scope for his power and an opportunity for His pity and we prefer patiently to await His will than daringly to demand that which it may not be His pleasure to give. And finally our modesty may perhaps obtain for us something more than we deserve."

And I observe that Peter wept after his serious fall, but I do not hear that he prayed. Yet I have no doubt about his pardon.

Learn further from the Mother of the Lord how to have full faith in the marvelous and in the fullness of faith to preserve modesty. Learn to adorn faith with modesty and to avoid presumption. *They have no wine* (*John* 2:3), says she. With what brevity, with what reverence she made a suggestion on a matter in which she felt a kindly anxiety. And that you may learn in similar circumstances rather to heave a sympathetic sigh than to venture to make a direct request, she concealed her eager earnestness under a shade of shyness, and modestly refrained from expressing the confidence she felt in prayer. She did not come boldly forward with a clear request, and say straight out before every one "I appeal to thee, my son: the wine has run short, the guests are annoyed, the bridegroom is dismayed—show what thou canst do." But although as her breast was burning with these and many other thoughts, she might have expressed her feelings warmly, yet the devout Mother quietly approached her mighty Son, not to test His power but to discover His will. *They have no wine*, says she. How could she better have combined modesty and confidence? There was no lack of faith in her devotedness, of seriousness in her voice, or of earnestness in her desire. She, however, though she was His Mother, waived the claims of kinship, and did not venture to ask for a miraculous supply of wine. With what face, then, can I, a common slave, to whom it is a high honour to be in the service at once of the Son and of the Mother, presume to ask for the life of one who has been dead for four days?

It is also recorded in the Gospel that two blind men had sight given or restored to them—one the sight which he had lost, the other that which he had never possessed—for one had become blind, the other had been so born. But the one who had lost his sight earned marvelous mercy by piteous and persistent prayer, while the one who was born blind received from his divine enlightener a yet more merciful and more marvelous benefit without any previous petition from himself. To him it was afterwards said, *Thy faith hath made thee whole. (Luke* 28:42). I also read of the raising of two persons who had lately died—and of a third one who had been dead for four days; but only the one who was still lying in her father's house was thus raised at his prayer—the other two were restored by a great and unexpected manifestation of mercy.

So if, in like manner, it should happen (which may God avert) that any one of our brethren should meet not bodily but spiritual death; as long as he shall be with us, I, sinner that I am, will persistently assail the Saviour with my prayers and with those of the brethren. If he revives, we shall have gained our brother; but if we do not deserve to be heeded and the time comes when he cannot endure those who are alive, or be endured by them, but must be carried out for burial, I go on faithfully with my mourning, though I cannot pray with so much confidence. I dare not say openly, "Lord raise up our dead brother," but with anxious heart and inward trembling I cease not to cry out. If by any chance at all the Lord shall listen to the desire of the poor, his ear will heed the readiness of their hearts. And there is that saying, *Wilt thou show wonders to the dead? or shall physicians raise to life and give praise to thee? (Ps.* 88:10; 878:11, Vulg.) and concerning him who has been dead four days. *Shall anyone in the sepulcher declare thy mercy; and thy truth in destruction? (Ps.* 88:10; 87:12, Vulg.). Meanwhile it is possible that the Saviour may be pleased to meet us unforeseen and unexpectedly, and moved by the tears, not by the prayers of the bearers, to restore the dead man to those who live, or actually to recall from among the dead one who is already buried. But I should describe as dead the man who by excusing his sins, has already come down to the eighth degree. For *praise perisheth from the dead as from one who does not exist.* But after the tenth degree, which is third from the eighth, he is already being carried out into liberty to sin, when he is expelled from the monastic community. But after he has passed the fourth degree he is rightly said to be "four days dead," and when he falls into the fifth degree of habitual sin he is already buried. But God forbid that we should cease to pray in our hearts for such even as these—though we do not venture to do so openly, as Paul also mourned for those whom he knew to have died impenitent. For although they shut themselves out from our united prayers, they cannot altogether do so from their effects. They should nevertheless realize the great danger which those incur whom the Church, which prays confidently for Jews, heretics and heathen, dares not to mention in her worship. For when on Good Friday prayer is expressly offered for certain wicked persons, no mention is made of those who are excommunicated.

You may perhaps say, brother Godfrey, that in thus describing the degrees of pride instead of those of humility, I seem to have gone beyond your request and my own tardy promise. To which my answer is that I was unable to teach anything but what I had learned. I did not think it seemly on my part to speak of an ascent, since I am aware that my own movements have been in a downward rather than in an upward direction. Blessed Benedict may set before you the degrees of humility, for he has previously set his own heart upon them. I have nothing to put before you, unless it be my own downward course. Yet if that is carefully examined, the way to go up may haply be found therein. For if as you are going towards Rome, a man who is coming thence meets you, and you ask him the way, how can he better tell you than by pointing out the route that he has followed? In naming the castles, villages, cities, rivers and mountains which he has passed, he records his own journey and foretells yours, so that as you go on you may recognize the places that he has passed. In like manner in this downward course of mine you may possibly discover the upward steps, and as you ascend, may you study them to more purpose in your own heart than in my book.

ACKNOWLEDGMENTS

THE editor is indebted to Lesly Bratt and Christian Tappe, whose patience and deft editorial guidance ensured a successful conclusion to this project. I am appreciative of the encouragement given by my colleagues Christopher Blum and Denis Kitzinger of Thomas More College, and am especially blessed by assistance from my old comrade-in-arms, Edward Strickland who took time from his busy schedule at Christendom College to scrutinize my rendering of Saint Benedict's Latin. Any errors that remain are due solely to the translator's obstinacy. Finally, every good marriage is so because of a *mulier fortis*; my work here has been sustained and enriched by the erudition, careful reading, and excellent cooking of my wife Amy Elizabeth Fahey.